D1733010

Pathways to Individuality

Pathways to Individuality

Evolution and Development of Personality Traits

Arnold H. Buss

American Psychological Association • Washington, DC

Published by
American Psychological Association
750 First Street, NE
Washington, DC 20002
www.apa.org

To order
APA Order Department
P.O. Box 92984
Washington, DC 20090-2984
Tel: (800) 374-2721; Direct: (202) 336-5510
Fax: (202) 336-5502; TDD/TTY: (202) 336-6123
Online: www.apa.org/pubs/books
E-mail: order@apa.org

In the U.K., Europe, Africa, and the Middle East, copies may be ordered from
American Psychological Association
3 Henrietta Street
Covent Garden, London
WC2E 8LU England

Typeset in Goudy by Circle Graphics, Inc., Columbia, MD

Printer: Maple-Vail Book Manufacturing Group, York, PA
Cover Designer: Mercury Publishing Services, Rockville, MD

The opinions and statements published are the responsibility of the authors, and such opinions and statements do not necessarily represent the policies of the American Psychological Association.

Library of Congress Cataloging-in-Publication Data

Buss, Arnold H., 1924-
  Pathways to individuality : evolution and development of personality traits / Arnold H. Buss. — 1st ed.
       p. cm.
  Includes bibliographical references and index.
  ISBN-13: 978-1-4338-1031-2
  ISBN-10: 1-4338-1031-X
  1. Personality. 2. Individuality. 3. Evolutionary psychology. I. Title.
  BF698.B876 2011
  155.2—dc22
                                        2011014850

British Library Cataloguing-in-Publication Data

A CIP record is available from the British Library.

Printed in the United States of America
First Edition

DOI: 10.1037/13087-000

For Ella

CONTENTS

Pathways to Individuality

INTRODUCTION

This book is about the development of personality from an evolutionary perspective. The focus is mainly on personality traits, so let me start by discussing basic issues involving traits.

TWO DISCIPLINES

More than a half century ago, "The Two Disciplines of Scientific Psychology" (Cronbach, 1957) distinguished between the perspective of experimental psychologists and that of personality psychologists. Experimental psychologists seek laws of behavior that apply to everyone, and differences among subjects typically contribute to the error term. Personality psychologists seek information about how people differ across at least some situations. This division among psychologists resonated enough for a later optimistic article by Vale and Vale (1969), a pessimistic article by Fiske (1979), and an optimistic article by Kenrick and Funder (1988). The split between the two kinds of psychologists was in the methods used, the questions asked, and, inevitably, the empirical answers.

The split was widened by the assertion that behavior is strongly affected by manipulations but only weakly by traits (Mischel, 1968). This view confirmed the already-held belief, especially by experimental social psychologists of the time, that their manipulations were so powerful, they could ignore personality traits.

The challenge was taken up by Funder and Ozer (1983), who analyzed the findings from three widely used experimental paradigms in social psychology at the time: forced compliance, bystander intervention, and obedience. When tests of significance were converted to correlations, they ranged from .36 to .43, approximately the range found in many studies of personality traits:

> The effects on behavior of several of the most prominent situational factors in social psychology seem to average slightly less than .40. Moreover, because in most social psychological experiments only two or three levels of situational independent variables are studied, and because these levels are deliberately chosen to be quite different from each other, situational linear effects such as calculated here quite possibly *over*estimate the true state of affairs. (Funder & Ozer, 1983, p. 110)

This demonstration that personality traits had at least as much impact on behavior as experimental manipulations seemed to answer the challenge of whether personality traits were important (Epstein & O'Brien, 1985).

These 20th-century facts, however, did not eliminate the debate, for it is still with us in the 21st century. As a group of evolutionary psychologists wrote,

> Specific situations are inherent to the study of personality because individuals *cannot* exhibit rigid global dispositions if they are to outcompete conspecifics by better solving situationalized adaptive problems. Instead, individuals must exhibit flexible behavior that solves adaptive problems presented by each specific situation. (Figuerredo et al., 2011, p. 228)

To cite a specific example, in the study of leadership in organizations, one side views situations as paramount, with little room for personality traits (Andersen, 2006), whereas the other side sees a prominent role for personality traits (Hogan & Kaiser, 2005), and Fleeson (2004) splits the difference.

My position is clear:

> What distinguishes personality from other specialties are the individual differences called personality traits. In the absence of traits, personality would be Balkanized among the areas that contribute to knowledge about personality: clinical, developmental, experimental, and social psychology, to name a few. . . . However, if there is to be a distinct field of study called personality, its central and defining feature must be traits. (A. H. Buss, 1989, p. 1387)

AGGREGATION

It must be admitted that in some research, the correlation between personality traits and behavior is low, a major reason being that single acts may be unstable and unreliable. The solution is to aggregate, as in a study by Gormly and Champagne (1974). Knowledgeable peers rated the subjects for energetic behavior, and the subjects performed laboratory tasks requiring a quick tempo. The median correlation between peer ratings and performance on each task was .20, but when the task performances were averaged, the mean correlated .78 with peer ratings. These findings were supplemented in a study of energetic acts on campus or in class, for example, walking speed, rate of climbing stairs, rates of head movement, and adjustments in posture (McGowan & Gormly, 1976). The correlations between each specific behavior and peer ratings ranged from .20 to .60, but the average of specific behaviors correlated .70 with peer ratings. Similar findings emerged from studies that aggregated over time (Moskowitz & Schwarz, 1982), mood (Diener & Larson, 1984), and situations (Magnusson & Hefler, 1969).

Long before psychologists started to aggregate, it was happening in baseball. The momentary determinants of whether a batter gets a hit at one at bat are these: early or late in the game, playing at home or away, a night game or a day game, a right-handed pitcher or a left-hander, whether a sacrifice bunt is needed, and whether the batter is fatigued. The enduring determinant is, of course, talent, but for any single at bat, its impact is overwhelmed by transient determinants. Over the course of a season of 500 at bats, these transient determinants cancel out, and now talent is revealed, such that a team with many .300 hitters plays in the World Series, whereas a team of mainly .250 hitters watches it on television. By analogy, personality psychologists typically study a season, not an at bat.

However, for Walter Mischel, the leading critic of personality traits, and his colleagues, aggregation misses the essence of personality because it overlooks individual patterning of behavioral organization. The patterning refers to how a particular person construes situations and behaves in them. That this is the idiographic approach to personality, as opposed to studying how people differ from each other, and was expertly detailed in "Intraindividual Stability in the Organization and Patterning of Behavior: Incorporating Psychological Situations Into the Idiographic Analysis of Behavior" (Shoda, Mischel, & Wright, 1994). There is an echo here of the writings of a long-standing critic of the individual differences approach to personality, who prefers the term *idiothetic* to *idiographic* (Lamiell, 1981, 1997). In contrast, the *nomothetic* approach to personality seeks similarities among behaviors in a cohort of individuals in the investigation of traits. Except for the patterning I see in sources of identity (Chapter 7), my approach is necessarily nomothetic.

THE TRAIT DISTRIBUTION

A more serious problem is the moderate middle of trait distributions. An early review of literature on the achievement motive revealed that moderates were more inconsistent in their behavior than extremes (Sorrentino & Short, 1977). Later research on the observability of trait-related behavior found that

> people who are more extreme on a bipolar trait, high or low, are more likely to behave in a trait consistent manner across occasions and situations than those who are moderate on the trait; those extreme people are more likely to be observed by others. (Paunonen, 1989, p. 825)

More recent longitudinal studies of aggression press home the point. Six-year-old boys were followed until they were 17 (Brame, Nagin, & Tremblay, 2001). Although there was little stability for the sample as a whole, boys high in aggression at 6 were likely to be high in it at 17. Similarly, there were relatively stable trajectories for social aggression (nasty gossip, exclusion) from childhood though adolescence for children high or low in aggression but not for moderates (Underwood, Beron, & Rosen, 2009). In a 3-decade longitudinal study, there was little continuity for the entire sample, but Huesmann, Dubow, and Boxer (2009) "found that continuity of aggressiveness is owing to not only the high-aggressive participants staying high but also owing to the low-aggressive participants staying low" (p. 136).

Let me offer an explanation, using the trait of sociability. Those high in sociability are strongly motivated to seek others and become restless when away from others because they miss the stimulation that can come only from other people. There might be a drop in their social motivation, but by definition, it cannot go much higher, so this *ceiling effect* means less variability in their behavior. Those low in sociability, although not hermits, want a minimum of social interaction. Parties, discussion groups, and extended telephone talks are not for them, and being alone is comfortable. Their social motivation might rise, but it cannot go any lower, so this *floor effect* means less variability in their behavior. Those in the middle of the sociability distribution are more socially motivated but well below those who are high in sociability. These middles might drift toward being more sociable or less sociable, and this variability poses a problem for the trait concept.

The lesson here seems clear: The trait concept works best for people who score high or low in trait-related behavior but not as well for moderates. Accordingly, I concentrate on the top and bottom thirds of trait distributions, with an exception to be noted.

PLAN OF THE BOOK

This book consists of four parts. Part I is on theory. Chapter 1 ("Evolution") presents three related evolutionary perspectives: how we are like other animals, how we are a unique species, and trends in the evolutionary line that led to our species. It then offers evidence for a set of personality traits we share with other animals and makes the case for distinguishing between a self we share with other animals and a self that is uniquely human.

Chapter 2 ("Development") offers a theory of personality development that depends on concepts borrowed from biology. One key concept is *differentiation*: an initially broad tendency branches into more specific tendencies during the course of development. The other key concept is *canalization*: an initial tendency becomes more strongly entrenched during the course of development. These processes occur within the context of particular environments.

In discussing person–environment interaction, I emphasize how people in part determine their own environments by choosing to be in certain situations, setting the tone, and reinforcing others. I specify the tilts that help shape personality traits and the resultant cascades, and I outline how the needs of each developmental era are linked to specific personality traits.

In Part II, Chapters 3 and 4 ("Temperament I: Activity and Emotionality" and "Temperament II: Sociability and Impulsiveness," respectively) discuss temperament, which consists of a subset of the personality traits that are part of our evolutionary heritage, have a genetic input, and are present in infancy. I emphasize the differentiation of each temperament trait into subtraits during the course of development.

Chapter 5, "Later Developing Traits," includes the remaining three traits that are part of our evolutionary heritage but that first occur during the preschool period. Again, I emphasize differentiation during the course of development.

Part III, consisting of Chapters 6 and 7 ("Self I: Self-Consciousness" and "Self II: Self-Esteem and Identity," respectively), deals with uniquely human aspects of personality. These include the personality traits of self-esteem and private and public self-consciousness, as well as the components of identity, and the role of culture looms large here (Kitayama et al., 2010). The concepts of differentiation and canalization do not apply and are replaced with concepts appropriate to understanding all self-related behavior, the broadest concept being the personal versus social dichotomy.

In Part IV, the focus is on dimensions of personality. Chapter 8 ("Personality and Abnormality") views abnormal behavior from the perspective of personality—that is, by assuming that certain kinds of abnormal behavior are the extremes of personality trait dimensions. Chapter 9 ("Style") represents an attempt to bring back style as a component of personality: the *how* of behavior in contrast to the *what* of behavior. As such, style is the other face of a number of content traits, but style in and of itself—the way we sit, walk, or laugh—is a basic aspect of our individuality, and I offer a set of psychological dimensions of style.

This book consists mainly of my perspectives on various aspects of personality. For example, I have a particular approach to the role of evolution in personality, to temperament, and to the self. However, other perspectives must be respected, and they are offered in summary form at the end of chapters, starting with Chapter 3. My conceptions and those of others are complementary and therefore offer a more complete understanding of major areas of personality

The book closes with an epilogue, a summing up and integration of what has gone before.

In concluding this introduction, I wish to acknowledge the help I received from Laura Buss and Ira Iscoe and from the staff at American Psychological Association Books: Peter Pavlionis, Elizabeth Budd, Ron Teeter, and Harriet Kaplan.

I

THEORY

1

EVOLUTION

First, a few paragraphs on evolution. This information is surely known to the reader but nevertheless must be the starting point of this chapter.

Darwin's theory of evolution, as modified in the 20th century, is so well buttressed by facts and so well accepted by scientists that there is disagreement only on details. Our lineage can be traced back through more primitive creatures and finally to the chemical molecules that mark the beginning of life. Our DNA overlaps that of other animals and even plants, and the structure of parts of our nervous system date back to primitive vertebrates. We are mammals and must nurture helpless newborns. We are primates, for example, seeing the same colors, sharing some of the same facial expressions, and having fingernails and sensitive finger pads.

Our animal heritage is not only biological but also psychological. Some of our basic behavioral tendencies derive from this legacy, and so do aspects of personality. Our animal heritage is the first of three evolutionary perspectives on human behavior. The second is our distinctiveness as a unique species, and the third consists of trends in the line that led to our species. These perspectives complement each other, offering a broad view of human behavior.

HOW WE ARE LIKE OTHER MAMMALS

Like other mammals, our internal body temperature remains roughly the same whether the climate is hot or cold. Being warm-blooded helps chemical processes occur quickly, which allows an enduring level of activity. We surely have evolved from among the more active mammals, for humans tend to have a relatively high energy level. The mammals with more energy also tend to be somewhat curious. When curiosity is linked to activity, the result is a tendency to be strongly exploratory, and such mammals tend to wander around their territories searching for novel stimuli.

Mammalian mothers carry offspring in the womb and nurture them after birth, the result being a close bond between infant and mother. In many mammalian species, there is a relatively long period of dependence on the mother in a protected environment so that the young can explore, try out new responses, and make mistakes that would otherwise be costly. Such mammals can acquire adaptive responses through early learning, which means that their childhood is a crucial period of life.

There are persistent threats to survival from attacks by other animals, the common adaptation being the flight–fight reflex. The threat may cause fear, an emergency reaction that triggers escape. Alternatively, the threat may cause anger, which triggers an aggressive reaction in the service of getting rid of the threat.

In most mammals, there is gender dimorphism, males being larger and stronger than females. Males are more aggressive and compete for females, who are the ones that typically select the mate. These biological sex differences set the stage for human culture, which widens or narrows the difference between men and women.

In brief, our mammalian heritage consists of several behavioral tendencies. We tend to be *active* animals and are *curious* and strongly *explorative*. There are *mother–infant bonds* and juvenile *play*. We respond to threat with *fear* (escape) or *anger* (aggression). And there are *sex differences*.

HOW WE ARE LIKE SOCIAL MAMMALS

In many mammals, the mother–offspring bond tends to dissipate when the offspring enters the juvenile period. In highly social mammals, this bond continues into adulthood and is part of a strong motive to be with others. The young take their place as members of a group, and the worst punishment is to be expelled from the group. Wolves demonstrate the benefits of this sociality: In the face of danger, the group coheres to better fight off the threat, and there is often a division of labor, with some members hunting and bringing back food and others minding the pups. In this respect, wolves are very much like us, which may be why we treat our dogs (bred from wolves) as members of the family.

Highly social mammals, by definition, live in close proximity, a potentially explosive situation because males tend to fight for access to food and mates. One solution is a dominance hierarchy in which alpha dominates beta, beta dominates delta, and so on. This dominance ladder often gets established during aggressive juvenile play but is not frozen there. As the dominant animal ages—it is typically a male—a younger male gathers strength and challenges him. The younger animal becomes the dominant male or slinks away in defeat. Harmony prevails, demonstrating the adaptive advantage of a dominance hierarchy.

PERSONALITY IN SOCIAL MAMMALS

Do social mammals have individual personalities? Ask the owner of a dog or cat, and you will get a strong affirmative. If dogs and cats have personalities, perhaps other social mammals do as well. Beyond testimony, formal research is necessary, and fortunately, there is research on a wide variety of animals (Gosling, 2001). For example, the traits of sociability, aggression, and exploration have been found in piglets (Forkman, Furuhaug, & Jensen, 1995). Like us, dogs and hyenas are among the animals high in sociality, so it is worth looking into their personality traits, as summarized in Exhibit 1.1.

I have arranged the traits for maximum comparability because slightly different trait names were used in each study. Sociability was reported in all three studies. (It should be noted that Extraversion, reported in one study, incorporates Sociability.) The second line of the exhibit is more difficult to interpret. I suggest that what some observers of animal behavior call *excitability* is another term for *reactivity*, and in the "Big Five" personality classification of supertraits (McCrae & Costa, 1987), it falls under the heading of Neuroticism.

EXHIBIT 1.1
Personality Traits in Hyenas and Dogs

Gosling (1998), hyenas	Gosling, Kwan, and John (2003), dogs	A. C. Jones and Gosling (2005), dogs
Sociability	Extraversion	Sociability
Excitability	Neuroticism	Reactivity
Assertiveness	Agreeableness	Submissiveness
Curiosity	Openness	Activity

In the third line, assertiveness appears to be at the opposite end of the traits of agreeableness and submissiveness. The term *dominance* would seem to cover all three traits.

Curiosity is one facet of the supertrait of Openness (McCrae & Costa, 1987), and I assume that an active animal is likely to be the one to explore and might as easily been called curious. The arrangement of the traits in Exhibit 1.1 attempts to make sense out the variety of trait names. As has been noted by personality psychologists, the same personality trait may be given different names. Notice the two traits on the bottom line. Aggressiveness might be regarded as extreme assertiveness or as the opposite end of the trait of Agreeableness. Fearfulness might be regarded as reactivity or as a major part of the supertrait of Neuroticism. Wherever one places these latter traits, it is clear from Exhibit 1.1 that social mammals have personality traits comparable to those reported in humans.

HOW WE ARE LIKE PRIMATES

As with social mammals, there is often a dominant male: "All other chimpanzees direct submission toward the dominant male. Coalitions, however, remain crucial in regulating the degree of domination by the alpha male . . . who does not ignore his fellow male allies" (Bauer, 1980, p. 109). Longtime observation of chimpanzees led primatologist Frans de Waal to call his book *Chimpanzee Politics* (1982):

> When two apes come to blows or threaten each other a third ape may decide to enter the conflict and side with one of them. The result is a coalition of two against one. In many cases the conflict extends still further, and larger coalitions are formed. Because everything happens so quickly, we might imagine that chimpanzees are carried away by the aggression of others and that they join in blindly. Nothing is further from the truth. Chimpanzees never make an uncalculated move. (de Waal, 1982, p. 42)

de Waal went on to describe two kinds of power. The first is straightforward dominance with an alpha animal at the top. The second is a subtler network of influence comparable to what we see in our own species.

Beyond politics, primates tend to react to one another as individuals. Their social systems are based on

> the membership of individuals as individuals and not just as representatives of a particular age-sex class. In other words, if you see monkey A interacting with monkey B you are not simply seeing an adult male interacting with a juvenile male. Rather you are seeing two individuals with special personalities, special social relations and alliances, and a past history of associations with each other. (Lancaster, 1975, p. 13)

Like other mammals, primates are curious, but their curiosity extends to seeking information for itself, with no extrinsic reward. There is an anecdote about a chimpanzee who was rewarded with banana slices for solving problems. The chimpanzee evidently was not hungry, so he lined up the banana slices as he received them. When the experimenter's supply of bananas ran out, he continued to present problems and received a banana slice back for each problem the chimpanzee solved, until he had every slice back. The problems were intrinsically rewarding for the chimpanzee.

This strong curiosity sometimes combines with an advanced brain to produce innovation. Japanese macaques enjoy eating sweet potatoes but are bothered by all the dirt on the roots. One discovered that washing them got rid of the dirt. She then took the next step by casting wheat in the shallow ocean water. The heavier dirt sank to the bottom, and the clean wheat could be scooped up on the surface. This practice spread rapidly to other members of the troop, reflecting primates' strong ability to imitate.

The ability to imitate, together with an advanced brain, is the source of the great apes'—chimpanzees, gorillas, and orangutans—capability of learning sign language. It started with the training of Washoe, a chimpanzee caught in the wild and taken to the home of two psychologists to be home-reared (Gardner & Gardner, 1969). After 4 years of training in American Sign Language, Washoe developed a vocabulary of 132 signs and offered two-word combinations. Subsequently, chimpanzees could converse with each other without humans being present (Jensvold & Gardner, 2000). Other research extended such signing to the other great apes, and other chimpanzees were taught a language based on lexigrams presented on a computer screen. Their close relatives, the pygmy chimpanzees called bonobos, can identify these lexigrams when they are spoken to in English (Savage-Rumbaugh, McDonald, Sevcik, Hopkins, & Rubert, 1986) and can even initiate a conversation with the lexigrams (Segerdahl, Fields, & Savage-Rumbaugh, 2005). Such learning reveals how close their cognitive abilities are to ours, including their having a sense of self (Gallup et al., 1995).

Let me summarize how primates are like us:

1. They are "politicians," who develop a social organization based not only on rank-order dominance but also on networks of influence.
2. On the basis of experience, they respond to each other as individual personalities.
3. They can closely imitate and innovate.
4. They can acquire a primitive language.
5. They have a primitive sense of self.

In reviewing the cognitions of primates, Tomasello and Call (1997) wrote,

> Some primate skills lie latent, and all that is needed are motive and opportunity. Also, there are latent skills that require specific training to become overt. Part of what goes on is the apes learning to pay close attention to specific things. They may mimic human teachers by teaching themselves, but not in the wild. We do not yet know the limit of their potential. (p. 392)

The lesson here is that whatever innate capabilities these primates are endowed with, an enriched environment brings out the potential that was there all along. This lesson applies not only to cognitive ability but also to personality—and not only to their personality but to ours.

PERSONALITY IN PRIMATES

Although the social behavior of primates has been studied extensively, there is less research on primate personality. It has concentrated on three species: rhesus monkeys, bonobos, and chimpanzees.

In an older study, observations of behavior in rhesus monkeys were coded to increase reliability (Chamove, Eysenck, & Harlow, 1972). A factor analysis yielded three factors: fear, aggressiveness, and sociability. A 4-year study offered three bipolar dimensions: (a) fearful, tense, and subordinate versus aggressive, effective, and confident; (b) slow and equable versus active and excitable; and (c) solitary versus sociable (Stevenson-Hinde, Stillwell-Barnes, & Zung (1980).

This variety of personality descriptions cries out for organization. Accordingly, I have grouped them into two broad categories of bipolar traits. The first group involves social interactions:

- sociable–unsociable
- assertive–timid
- dominant–submissive
- aggressive–even tempered

The second group is broader, involving both social and nonsocial situations:

- active versus lethargic
- fearful versus confident
- emotional versus calm
- rash versus cautious

Examination of these eight bipolar traits reveals that some of them overlap. Such overlap occurs in trait descriptions of human behavior, so it appears to be inevitable. How much overlap is open to debate. Are the distinctions too fine grained, or are they necessary for a full description of personality? I suggest the latter because it offers the advantage of a more detailed picture of personality. These eight traits have been described in humans and appear in most classifications of personality.

One source of information comes from long-term close observation of individual chimpanzees. The pioneer researcher Robert Yerkes wrote,

> Wendy is willful, obstinate, unpredictable, courageous, rash, determined, persistent, unaffectionate. . . . Bill, one of the first chimpanzees I came to know intimately, may be fairly described as her opposite. He was notably good-natured, even-tempered, buoyant, suggestible, and cooperative, friendly and adaptable, dependable, cautious, and for a male, quite timid, conservative, observant, alert, gentle, and affectionate. (Yerkes, 1943, p. 133)

Half a century later, Jane Goodall (1986), having observed chimpanzees in the wild for many years, described several individuals. One she called Evered doggedly pursued dominance and often achieved it. Figan was tense and emotional. Flo's aggressiveness—for a female—often led to dominance. Gigi was shy and unsociable. Hugo attained dominance through leadership rather than aggression.

de Waal (1982) arranged to have captive chimpanzees roam freely in a large fenced-in area. He contrasted the personalities of several individuals. One chimpanzee moved slowly, became fatigued easily, and was generally lethargic. The other was "the moving force behind all developments. His boundless energy and provocative behavior has had the effect of a catalyst" (p. 70). "Luis is more sociable than Yeroen. He has an open and friendly character and sets great store by company" (p. 63). Mama dominated others by the force of her gaze and the respect she demanded of others. Yeroen was staid but sometimes took over Mama's leadership through his guile. These descriptions of individual chimpanzees offer the flavor of their personalities, but there is also systematic research on captive rhesus monkeys that coded information into categories.

This early research and the research that followed were aptly summarized in Gosling's (2001) review. When psychopathy is eliminated as not being a normal personality trait, the following traits emerged from multiple studies: emotionality, fearfulness, confidence, activity, sociability, and aggressiveness. Notice that dominance and rashness, which were on the list of rhesus monkey traits, are not included. When we add these two traits to the rhesus traits, we can see the extensive overlap with the traits found in hyenas and dogs (see Exhibit 1.1).

Subsequent research on dogs yielded the traits of playfulness, sociability, and curiosity–fearfulness (Svartberg, 2005) and the traits of energy, affection, emotional reactivity, and intelligence (Gosling, Kwan, & John, 2003). Studies of primates offered the traits of aggressiveness, curiosity, dominance, gregariousness, impulsiveness, physical activity, and playfulness. Some of these traits with different names obviously are the same trait—gregariousness and sociability, for example. However, this research clearly establishes our animal legacy of personality.

TRENDS

Most trends in personality derive from our advanced cognitions. Having considerable intellectual ability, we move from being playful to being inventive. We do not accept the world the way it is but insist on changing it by cutting down forests and building houses, using fire and making fire, and extracting electricity from fossil fuel.

In the line that led to our species, the ratio of childhood to life span increases dramatically. The lengthening of childhood poses a risk, for the longer the juvenile period, the greater the likelihood that children will not survive to adulthood. Females especially might not survive long enough to bear children and offer the necessary nurturance. If delaying maturity is potentially maladaptive, why is this trend there?

To start answering this question, let me mention another trend: fewer and more malleable innate tendencies. Animals in our line but distant from our species have more fixed action patterns that work in particular environmental niches, but they lack flexibility. Our built-in tendencies are more generalized and more open to change. Robert Ardrey (1961) called *Homo sapiens* a "bad-weather animal," one who could adjust to wildly fluctuating situations.

The other part of the answer is that in the evolutionary line that led to our species, there has been more to learn, more time needed to become acculturated. In broad terms, human culture consists of technology (knives, baskets, computers) and social arrangements (kinship, tribes, nations), so it takes many years to become an adult.

The combination of adaptations—broader and more open programs as well as a longer childhood—has enabled us to occupy environmental niches all over the world. They have enabled us to move from hunter-gathers to farmers to industrial workers and recently to computer users and inhabitants of a virtual world.

When we trace our evolutionary history from distant mammals to our species, there is another trend: from a litter of offspring to a single offspring.

There is more maternal attention and care of each child, and therefore more psychological separation between children of the same family.

The next trend is the surge of cognitions as important determiners of behavior. Mammals distant from us in evolution tend to be creatures of habit and innate tendencies. Our habits and innate tendencies are powerful too but can be over overridden by cognitions—for example, anorexics whose distorted body image overcomes hunger.

The evolution of cognition may be seen in the capability called *theory of mind* (Premack & Woodruff, 1978) in which an animal—in most of the research, a primate—discovers the knowledge or intentions of another animal (Tomasello & Call, 1997). The evidence bearing on this capability has been challenged (Heyes, 1998; Towner, 2010), so it seems prudent to conclude that animals come close to what in our species is a theory of mind but perhaps do not quite achieve it.

These various cognitions are essential to the increasing complexity of social organization, involving a variety of social roles and statuses. The culmination of this trend and the others just mentioned is a larger number of personality traits and therefore greater individuality.

OUR UNIQUE SPECIES

We make rules and observe them. Americans drive on the right side of the street, the British on the left; these rules are arbitrary, as are most rules, but not obeying them is costly. When rules are combined with play, the result is a uniquely human kind of play: games. We develop rules that determine our social interactions—manners, morality, politics—and are tempted to get around them in the interest of selfish gain.

We are as curious as any primate but take the next step by seeking understanding. We ask "why" questions and seek to determine causality. We make attributions to the behavior of others and to our own behavior. We examine the world and imbue it with meaning through science or religion. Our brains tell us of our own mortality but not how to deal with that fact.

We have the advanced cognitive ability that allows us to take the position of another person. This move away from egocentricity to the perspective of another sets the stage of our being the only species with true teachers. Beyond being models that our children imitate, we instruct them while taking into account their immaturity and lack of skills and knowledge.

The ability to take a perspective different from our own enables us to attend to ourselves as social objects. This social awareness combines with the ability to internalize social rules and regulations, the result being our uniquely self-related, public emotion of embarrassment. However, there is a complementary private self-focus: the ability to introspect, knowing there is a psychological world not open to direct observation by others.

As we saw earlier, social animals develop a primitive culture that includes social networks. We have a broader set of kinship relations: not only blood relationships (grandparents, cousins) but also relationships via marriage. Beyond that, each successive generation is taught the myths and lore of the clan or larger social entity. Small wonder that our childhood is so long.

PERSONALITY TRAITS

A major part of this book deals with traits that are part of our primate legacy, with appropriate changes and additions to take account of our uniqueness as a species. These traits have a genetic component, as do most human personality traits (Plomin, Defries, McClearn, & McGuffin, 2001). An evolutionary approach immediately poses the following question: Why are they in the gene pool? There are several possibilities. One is that they are merely genetic noise: traits that are not adaptive but carried along because they are not damaging. Examples are hair color, eye color, and fingerprints.

In a related argument, personality traits that were once important in animal or human evolution may no longer be important. For example, research has shown that dominant males have greater access to food and to females. If females prefer dominant males, in the long run, virtually all males would be high in dominance, wiping out individual differences in the trait. The corollary is that present differences in dominance would be temporary and on the wane. The problem with this null argument is that it focuses on a single trait. It has been established in a wide variety of cultures that women prefer not only men with status but also men who have an exciting personality, for mate preference involves a package of traits (D. M. Buss, 2003).

There is another relevant mating issue. Most people do not get to mate with their ideal and therefore settle for less: "If some women pursue the man with the highest status or greatest resources, then some women would achieve more success by courting males outside the arenas in which competition is keenest" (D. M. Buss, 2008, p. 409). Thus, less preferred traits remain in the gene pool.

Another reason for individual differences remaining in the gene pool is a preference for both ends of a trait dimension. For example, just as some women prefer men high in sensation seeking, other women prefer men low in this trait.

A powerful argument for the continuance of inherited personality traits is *assortative mating* (Thiessen & Gregg, 1980). The literature on who marries whom offers consistent evidence across cultures that we marry those who are somewhat similar to us in personality (McCrae et al., 2008). The inevitable outcome is individual differences in the gene pool, which become especially important in a changing environment. If all members of a species were essentially the same, a sudden change in ecology would wipe out all of them, but in a species with abundant individual differences, some members inevitably live on.

Assortative mating is especially relevant to personality traits, but as for the broader issue of inherited individual differences, a variety of explanations have been suggested, summarized by their adherents in an edited book (D. M. Buss & Hawley, 2011). In addition to theory, one chapter was especially relevant in that it reviewed the adaptiveness of certain personality traits in animals distant with respect to evolution from our species, for example, the conditions under which there is selection for high or low sociability in lizards (Reale & Dingemanse, 2011).

PERSONALITY IN EVOLUTIONARY PERSPECTIVE

Evolutionary Heritage

We are like animals with respect to two sets of personality traits. As the exposition has so far revealed, there is a set of traits observed and reported in animals: emotionality, fear, activity, sociability, aggressiveness, and dominance. The other traits have not been reported in animals but are included here for reasons to be given shortly: anger, shyness, sensation seeking, and impulsiveness.

Anger has been described in detail in animals but falls under the heading of aggression and therefore is not mentioned specifically as anger. The two are, of course, linked, but in our species, anger appears as a trait earlier in life than the trait of aggression, hence the need to distinguish between the emotion (anger) and the instrumental behavior (aggression). If anger is an emotion, is it also a personality trait? Individual differences in proneness to anger have been assessed by two frequently used questionnaires (A. H. Buss & Perry, 1992; Spielberger, 1988).

Shyness actually has been reported in primates as part of a shyness–boldness dimension of behavior (Svartberg, 2005). Sensation seeking is never reported as such, perhaps because the term was not in broad circulation until late 20th century. However, individual differences in curiosity have been reported in the great apes (Uher & Asendorpf, 2008), and this trait falls under the heading of sensation seeking.

Impulsiveness has been noted in several species of animals (Diamond, 1957). Diamond observed that as a species, dogs tend to be impulsive, especially compared with cats who "are less impulsive in their actions, less stimulus bound, seeming to follow their own intent while ignoring distractions that would redirect the activity of a dog" (Diamond, 1957, p. 62). Chimpanzees have been observed to be notoriously impulsive unless they are home-reared by humans, and impulsiveness has been reported in other great apes (Uher & Asendorpf, 2008).

I have organized these traits into two groups based on their occurrence during development: Activity, emotionality, fearfulness, shyness, sociability, and impulsiveness appear during infancy. Sensation seeking, aggression, and dominance appear later in childhood, and anger, although it appears in infancy, is treated with aggression because of its obvious link with it.

I see these traits as part of our evolutionary heritage, and all of them meet three criteria:

1. They have an inherited component analogous to the inheritance of body type. It is the likely default, the tendency most likely to develop but also subject to moderate change.
2. They appear during childhood, specifically by the end of the preschool era, during the first 5 years of life.
3. They also appear in adulthood, the assumption being that there is at least some continuity.

These traits comprise only part of personality but a larger part than the small number implies. As will be seen, each trait is assumed to differentiate into subtraits, thereby enlarging the arena of personality that they cover.

Human Uniqueness

The Self

Our advanced cognitions and culture have given rise to self-related behavior that may be specific to our species, but there is evidence that animals also have a sense of self, starting with the pioneering research of Gordon Gallup Jr. (1970). He placed young, wild-born chimpanzees in a small room that had only a mirror in it. For the first few days, they responded to the mirror image with social behavior, which implies they perceived the image as another animal. Thereafter, they groomed parts of the body they could not otherwise see, picked food from their teeth, blew bubbles, and made faces—behavior that indicates recognition of self.

In a more objective test, older chimpanzees were anesthetized, and red dots were placed above one eyebrow ridge and at the top of the opposite ear of the unconscious animals. After they regained consciousness, the mirror was again introduced. They repeatedly attempted to touch the red dots on their own heads and spent an inordinate amount of time looking at themselves in the mirror.

As Gallup's (1977) summary of his own experiments and later reviews of mirror-image recognition in other animals demonstrated, mirror-image recognition is limited to two of the three great apes: chimpanzees and orangutans (Gallup et al., 1995; Parker, Mitchell, & Boccia, 1994). Later research, however, added the home-reared gorilla Koko (F. Patterson & Gordon, 1993) bottlenose dolphins (Reiss & Marino, 2001), and the Asian elephant (Plotnik, de Waal, & Reiss, 2006), all large-brained, highly social mammals.

We humans are of course capable of mirror-image recognition, but how early in development? Amsterdam (1972) placed a mirror in front of infants and observed their reactions. At 14 months of age, a precocious few admired themselves, a few more at 17 months, and most infants by 24 months. Bertenthal and Fischer (1978) followed up by showing that such recognition of self occurs even earlier. At about 6 months, infants touched a part of themselves while looking at their mirror image. At roughly 10 months, when a toy that can be seen only in a mirror was presented, infants looked at the toy. These experimenters dabbed a rouge dot on 18-month-old infants, who touched their face and mentioned that it seemed different. When 2-year-old children were asked who is in the mirror, they said their name or "me." This and subsequent research established that the norm for full mirror-image recognition is 18 to 24 months.

Another kind of self-awareness occurs in animals. They sense the difference between their body and the environment, between internal stimuli and external stimuli. This basic boundary must be considered an aspect of self.

Birds and prehensile animals also sense the difference between touching themselves and touching something else. In self-stimulation, the animal is both the deliverer and the recipient of the stimuli. Awareness of this double stimulation is the third kind of self-related behavior.

Animals also know to which species they belong, knowledge acquired early in life, for many species, through the mechanism of *imprinting* (Lorenz, 1966). Like mirror-image recognition, this is a primitive kind of identity and therefore falls under the heading of self-related behavior.

So, do animals have the same self as we do? For Gallup (1977), the answer is yes:

> The capacity to correctly infer the identity of the reflection must, therefore, presuppose an already existent identity on the part of the organism making the inference. Without an identity of your own, it would be impossible to recognize yourself. And therein lies the basic difference between monkeys and apes. The monkey's inability to recognize himself may be due to the absence of a sufficiently well-integrated self-concept. (p. 334)

Can we now infer that primates have the same self as ours? Not necessarily:

> Sometimes mirror self-recognition is viewed as indicative of the whole array of the diverse types of self-awareness found in humans—imagining ourselves recognizing others' perspectives on us, and evaluating ourselves according to their perspectives. . . . It is more parsimonious to suggest, however, that the kinesthetic-visual matching likely responsible for MSR [mirror self-recognition] creates a self-representation of a very specific and more limited sort—one that can be used to imagine and recognize ourselves. (Mitchell, 1994, p. 90)

There are other reasons as well to distinguish between a primitive animal self and an advanced human self. When human infants learn to speak, they blurt out all their feelings and emotions, but preschoolers gradually learn to lie and to keep some of their feelings and motives hidden from others. As a result, they become aware of a private self that is not available to anyone else. They can distinguish between the private and the public self and between an inner psychological world and the world of everyday life, that is, a sense of *covertness*.

Human infants and some social animals may swagger around, displaying their obvious self-confidence. This is a precursor of the *self-esteem* that develops only in older children and adults, who have the necessary cognitive ability.

As part of the process of socialization, young children are taught to view themselves as other see them. Building on the cognitive ability underlying the theory of mind, they gradually become aware of themselves as social objects: *public self-awareness*.

By the preschool period, children know about their extended family, their religion, and their nationality, or, in some instance, their tribe. Said another way, they have a *cultural identity*.

So there are four aspects of self-related behavior that are exclusively human. These and the comparable aspects of animal self are summarized in Table 1.1. Notice that human infants have only an animal self. The uniquely human self of older children and adults requires years of cognitive maturation.

TABLE 1.1
Animal Self Versus Human Self

Animal self (observed in human infants)	Human self (observed in older children and adults)
Body boundary	Covertness; private self-awareness
Double stimulation	Self-esteem
Mirror-image recognition	Public self-awareness
Species identity	Cultural identity

Uniquely Human Traits

We engage in self-evaluation, focus on an inner psychological world, and are socialized to become aware of ourselves as social objects. The respective personality traits are self-esteem, private self-consciousness, and public self-consciousness.

Our advanced cognitive ability produced subtraits of the personality traits that are our animal legacy or unique outlets for traits involving motives. For example, we aggress not only physically but also verbally, and we become not only angry but also hostile. Our cultures are advanced enough to provide opportunities to achieve dominance not only through aggression but also through leadership and success in competition. Advanced technology offers options for sensation seeking available only in our species, for example, spectatorship or drugs.

The subtraits and the opportunities to develop them are not there in infancy and must await sufficient maturation. So for both the unique and the animal aspects of personality, we need to know how they develop, starting with the next chapter.

2

DEVELOPMENT

In presenting his model of biological development, Waddington (1957) imagined a ball rolling down an incline. Grooves are present, and the ball goes down one fork or another: "We have to picture the surface as grooved by valleys, each leading to one of the normal end states. The number of separate valleys must increase as we pass down from the initial toward the final condition" (Waddington, 1957, p. 30). This imagery was designed to illustrate the biological process of differentiation, in which a variety of cells develop from a single fertilized cell. As the ball proceeds down the slope, each groove deepens so that the ball stays in the groove rather than moving to another groove; this deepening is called *canalization*. The imagery refers to the conservative tendency of a particular path, once taken, to continue throughout development, changing only in response to strong environmental pressure.

Waddington also dealt with variation within a path, using this imagery: "If canalization is represented as valley in an epigenetic landscape, the noisiness of the system might perhaps be symbolized by the imperfection in the sphericalness of the ball which runs down the valley" (Waddington, 1957, p. 40). Such imperfection presumably refers to individual differences in innate tendencies.

These concepts are relevant to personality development, and as a transition I extend them to a particular behavioral development: handedness. When infants first become capable of handling objects, they use either hand. Within a few months, most infants are picking up objects mainly with the right hand. A minority of infants starts picking up things mainly with their left hand. Clearly, there has been a fork in the road that leads to one hand being used for skilled activities. The original amorphous state of no hand preference differentiates into handedness. There are also individual differences ("noisiness") in the degree of handedness, with most children being extremely right-handed and some children being slightly ambidextrous.

How the hands are used provides an example of how differentiation may occur sequentially. The first differentiation is, of course, handedness. The second involves how objects are manipulated. Infants first grasp objects with a power grip, using all five fingers when they grasp a spoon and use it to bang on a table. As they mature, children develop the precision grip, consisting of the thumb and first two fingers, which is used when they write. Thus, depending on the situation, an adult might use the power grip (hammering) or the precision grip (applying lip stick).

Handedness becomes increasingly ingrained during childhood—through the process of canalization. Canalization typically is linked to crucial periods in development. Thus, if early in childhood right-handedness is somehow forfeited because of body or brain damage, the child can switch to left-handedness and reach adulthood as a normal left-hander; the groove is shallow enough to allow change. However, if the damage occurs in adulthood, it is extremely difficult to become left-handed, and typically there are motor deficits; the groove became deep enough to hinder a changeover.

As these examples illustrate, Waddington's concepts apply to motor behavior and, by extension, to other kinds of behavior—for example, intelligence (Turkheimer & Gottesman, 1991). What follows are extrapolations and necessary additions that go beyond Waddington's (1957) biological model in the service of a developmental theory of personality traits. Thus, the basic assumption of my approach to personality traits is that an initial undifferentiated state diversifies into differentiated states during development

DETERMINANTS OF PERSONALITY TRAITS

Heredity

One determinant of canalization is *heredity* because most personality dispositions are inherited (Plomin, Defries, McClearn, & McGuffin, 2001). To state it simply, such inheritance is not at all like that of eye color, which is unchanging throughout life. Rather, it is analogous to body type, which is inherited but may be altered by diet or exercise. Like body type, inherited personality dispositions tend to place a limit on how much change might occur because of life experiences, and like body type, an inherited personality tendency might be considered the most likely outcome, one that will occur unless there are powerful forces for change.

With respect to personality traits, heredity may be regarded as having us especially prepared to react to life contingencies. If there is a threat, we may exaggerate it, amplifying the reaction to it, or modulate it, reacting more calmly. If there is a reward, we may be delighted or barely pleased. If there is pressure to conform, we may resist or just give in. Heredity is also involved in individual differences in important motives and emotions, both social and nonsocial. These various tendencies may of course be altered by experience, but the initial motive or emotional reaction is attributed to heredity.

ENVIRONMENT AFFECTS PERSON

Some personality tendencies are initiated by strong social pressure, such as the demands of parents and teachers. These demands of agents of *socialization* are likely to be consistent, encouraging children not to stray from a path that leads to the end point: what is regarded as mature, adult behavior. Thus, there may be unremitting pressure for a girl to develop traditionally feminine interests and modes of expression and for a boy to develop traditionally masculine interests.

The personality dispositions may also originate in *life experiences* that vary greatly from one child to the next. To the extent that life experiences are idiosyncratic, science has no obvious way of dealing with them, but some of them are systematic. One is the particular position of a child in a family—say, a girl with an older brother and a younger sister. This permanent familial position affects adult personality (see Sulloway, 1996), suggesting that the impact may well be enduring. Alternatively, having an older sibling may temporarily damp down an inherited tendency, as we shall see in the chapter on dominance.

We gradually become accustomed to each other's habitual ways of behaving and typically are surprised and uncomfortable with marked changes in the behavior of those around us. Without deliberately trying to maintain and solidify the behavioral tendencies of others, we do so by not liking changes in them. Thus, a *stable environment* of social reactions is likely to deepen the groove.

The environment may offer few options, or it may be so suppressive that some built-in personality tendencies are given little opportunity to flourish. Alternatively, the environment may offer *potential paths* that may be followed, ignored, or deliberately avoided. Early in the 20th century, a piano was bought for Ira Gershwin. He was uninterested in the piano, but his younger brother George spent hours playing and grew up to be a major American composer. Ira eventually wrote the lyrics for George's songs.

So the environment is expected to have different effects on children who already vary in their personality traits. Again, consider dominance, specifically a dominant father of two young sons. If one son is submissive, he is likely to become even more submissive. If the other son tends to be dominant, he does not willingly accept being dominated, and because he cannot dominate his father, his only recourse is to become rebellious. Thus, the same environmental input, a dominant father, may have opposite effects on the two sons. The broader point here is that a person may *modify the impact of the environment.*

PERSON AFFECTS ENVIRONMENT

As the last example suggests, we are not merely pawns to be pushed around the chessboard of life: We can also have an impact on the environment. The idea was put forth more than half a century ago by Solomon Diamond (1957), who used the example of an infant's smile. He suggested that smiling elicits parental warmth, which facilitates social development, and he concluded, "Thus dispositions tend to be strengthened in experience (obeying the maxim that "the rich get richer") because they create opportunities for their own reinforcement" (Diamond, 1957, p. 190).

Richard Bell (1968b) is perhaps a better known pioneer of the idea that children are a force in how their parents socialize them, an idea further specified a few years later:

> There is a sense in which a person can make his own environment. He can do this as a *background stimulus object*, setting the tone for social interaction; as an initiator, stimulating others or programming his own environment; or as a *reinforcer*, rewarding or not rewarding the efforts of others. (A. H. Buss & Plomin, 1975, p. 4)

I have elaborated this approach as follows. Consider first *setting the tone* of a social interaction. Extraverts need to interact with others. So if people are in a waiting room, extraverts are likely to strike up a conversation and enliven it with their animation. Introverts tend not to take the first step, and when approached, their response tends to be minimal and less lively. So our initial behavior determines in part how others react to us, these reactions being a major aspect of our social environment. For example, a dominant posture, such as taking up more space, tends to elicit a submissive posture, such as a more constricted space (Tiedens & Fragile, 2003). Thus, we help establish and maintain the very social environment that influences our enduring behavioral tendencies.

To some extent, we are also able to *choose the environments* that affect us (Ickes, Snyder, & Garcia, 1997). We select friends who are compatible with us and likely to give us positive feedback (M. Snyder, Gangestad, & Simpson, 1983). Beyond friendship, "people can choose or create environments in which their proficiencies are crucial and their liabilities are unimportant" (Dunning, 1999, p. 5). Even Walter Mischel, earlier a critic of the concept of personality traits, later wrote that "individuals may select, interpret, respond to, and generate stable social situations and experiences in patterns that are typical of them, ultimately in part shaping their own social environment" (Mischel & Shoda, 1995, pp. 259–260).

Adults can make such choices, but newborn infants cannot. However, as the months and years go by, their repertoire of instrumental behavior broadens, and their intelligence grows. One result is the developmental trend from receiver to determiner of experience. Infants tend to receive the environment adults present to them, accepting or rejecting it, but the direction of effects is largely from environment to person.

Older children can choose their toys, which games they play, and with which children they play. Children opt to play with members of the same sex by at least 3 years of age, and sex segregation increases throughout childhood (Maccoby, 1990). However, even in same-sex play, children can choose their environments. Thus, a boy might seek out other boys for rough and tumble play, or he might opt to play some version of king of the hill in an attempt to establish who is top dog. These choices create environments that are expected to deepen a groove (canalization). Older children have still wider options, as the direction of effects tilts toward "person affects environment." They may also set the tone for an interaction, thereby partly determining their social environment.

The choice might also involve differentiation. When progressing toward adulthood, children may come to a fork in the road when only one path can be taken. In the earlier example of handedness, we saw that the path taken is determined mainly by heredity, but the decision at the fork in the road may be optional—that is, determined by the choice of the individual. As an example, compare two athletic girls of, say, 6 years of age. One decides to become a ballet performer, so her training is directed toward body flexibility, grace of posture, leaping and spinning, and the ability to balance on her toes. The other girl decides to become a tennis player, so her training is directed toward increasing hand–eye coordination, arm strength, and leg speed to move around the court. As the years pass, their neuromuscular development diverges. The ballet dancer becomes more lithe and elegant in her movements, but her dominant arm does not strengthen, nor does she enhance the kind of hand–eye coordination necessary to strike a moving ball. The tennis player becomes more powerful, and her hand–eye coordination greatly improves, but grace and elegance are secondary. They might have started as young children with comparable athletic ability, but by adulthood, their motor skills have differentiated sharply. The differentiation and subsequent canalization derive from a choice each child made, which helped to determine the very environment that would subsequently affect her.

It follows that a person's initial personality dispositions may establish a positive feedback cycle. For example, some children have been observed to be easy to deal with and others, difficult. Easy children get along better with their parents and siblings and so are liked and suffer fewer restrictions and punishments. There is a cycle of sunny disposition, which elicits pleasant reactions from others, which in turn solidifies the sunny disposition. Difficult children, because they fuss and cause trouble, are disliked and suffer more restrictions and punishments. Their intemperate disposition elicits displeasure from others, which in turn maintains their intemperate disposition. Such cycles set up a *cascade* in which a small initial push may eventually lead to a large and stable change in behavior. The small initial push that sets up a cascade may be regarded as a *tilt*.

An important tilt is gender. Behavior genetics research has established some genetic sex differences in personality, and other sex differences may derive from prenatal variables. Both prenatal and postnatal hormones have been found to affect aggression and childhood play (Collaer & Hines, 1995; Pasterski et al., 2005; Sánchez-Martin et al., 2000). Boys choose different toys to play with than girls, and boys' play is spatially broader and considerably more rough-and-tumble (Bjorklund & Pellegrini, 2002, p. 307; Maccoby, 1990). In addition to these biological tendencies, add that in all cultures, boys tend to be segregated from girls and are socialized differently than girls. Thus, gender surely influences the intensity or amplitude of some personality traits—for example, how aggressive the person is—and the differentiation of aggression—for example, physical versus verbal aggression.

A related tilt is physique. We know from research on social animals that body size and strength are important determiners of dominance. No one would be surprised that physique plays a similar role in human dominance. As will be seen, body size also contributes to the differentiation of the trait of activity level.

In researching and theorizing about personality traits, we necessarily deal with one trait at a time, but each of us consists of an assembly of traits. It follows that in determining the development of any particular personality trait, other traits make a contribution. The trait of fearfulness, for example, provides a tilt away from dominance in the direction of submissiveness.

These first three tilts are personal, each an aspect of an individual. The last tilt is the environment that shapes us. The impact of the environment has already been discussed, and it remains to specify the aspects of the environment that affect particular traits, which will be done in subsequent chapters. To fore-shadow a few aspects, consider the categories of location (rural–urban), social class, family (parents, siblings), and the broader issue of whether the general environment is safe or dangerous.

Person–Environment Interaction

The idea of a match between person and environment also goes back several decades (A. H. Buss & Plomin, 1984, p. 60). More recently, the idea was developed further in relation to abilities that are genetically influenced (Dickens & Flynn, 2001). Basketball was used to illustrate the approach. It starts with a son whose (gene-influenced) athletic skills relevant to basketball are better than average. He is interested in basketball, and so is his father (match). So early on and continuing throughout development, the father plays lots of basketball with his son, whose skill continually improves, as does his motivation to play basketball. He is more likely to be chosen to play on better teams and eventually receive better coaching and compete against better play-ers. The assumption here is that genes and environment are often correlated:

> People who are born with a genetic advantage are likely to enjoy an envi-ronmental advantage as a result. . . . The genetic advantage may itself be rather small. However, through the interplay between ability and envi-ronment, the advantage can evolve into something far more potent. So we have found something that acts as a *multiplier*. (Dickens & Flynn, 2001, p. 350)

These authors' focus was on intelligence, but as they suggested, their approach would be relevant for any trait. Indeed, the idea of a multiplier effect on per-sonality traits brings to fruition these concepts: a match between person and environment, tilts, and the canalization of traits. To repeat, small initial indi-vidual differences early in childhood may thus become magnified during the course of development.

Thus, a parent tends to approve and encourage the child's personality dis-positions when they are similar to the parent's. Children are known to imitate the behavior of parents but, with respect to behavior relevant to personality traits, mostly when there is a match, an issue relevant to the role of family envi-ronment in the development of personality.

Parents react differently to their sons and daughters, differently to first-borns than to later-borns, differently to twins than to singletons, so being raised in the same family does not mean having the same environment. A review of research on heredity and family environment concluded that

> when more than one child is studied per family, it is apparent that sib-lings in the same family experience considerably different environments,

in terms of their treatment of each other, in their peer interactions, and perhaps in terms of parental treatment. (Plomin & Daniels, 1987, p. 49)

Paradoxically, behavior genetics research has shown that family environment apparently plays little or no role in the development of personality traits (Plomin, Defries, McClearn, & McGuffin, 2001). The paradox might be resolved with behavior genetics research on the impact of parental environment when there is a match between parent and child.

More generally, what is the role of environment in the person–environment interaction? It offers potential opportunities, paths that may be taken. These may be followed, ignored, or avoided. It may be too impoverished to offer opportunities to make paths available. As a result, potential abilities or personality traits may wither or be stunted. The environment may suppress a predisposition, one outcome being that the trait never develops. Another outcome is only temporary suppression, a latency period after which the trait emerges. Consider a child with the disposition to be dominant. An overbearing parent or older sibling may block this tendency until the child reaches adolescence and can escape the suffocation of a family member.

DEVELOPMENTAL TRENDS

Inhibition

Inhibition starts with control of muscles:

It is difficult to escape the concept of the infant as a qualitatively different organism, operating through large blocks of relatively undifferentiated, mass muscular effort, triggered by a relatively small number of stereotyped stimuli. The progressive increase of upper-echelon control over these cruder, downstream mechanisms effects (largely by inhibition) increasingly precise motor patterns, progressively more appropriate to stimuli. (Scheibel & Scheibel, 1964, p. 513)

The maturation of control over muscles is just one aspect of a more general neural trend for higher centers of the brain to control lower centers through inhibition. Such maturation also marks the beginning of control over a variety of impulses and motives, starting with the need to eliminate and progressing through biological motives (hunger) and various psychological motives. The relevant trait is impulsiveness or, alternatively, individual differences in *effortful control* (Derryberry & Rothbart, 1997), which is discussed near the end of Chapter 4 in this volume.

Inhibitory control is especially relevant for the expression of anger. Infants are allowed their temper tantrums because parents know that infants lack self-control, but as children mature and gradually achieve control over their emotions, rage reactions are expected to diminish in frequency and intensity. Similarly, older children's displays of angry aggression are strongly punished because children are expected to inhibit violent outbursts.

The maturation of inhibitory control, which starts with control of muscles and proceeds developmentally through control over biological and psychological motives, is assumed to be complete by the end of adolescence.

Instrumentality

As children mature, they become more capable. They can wash their hands and eat their food, and later they can prepare simple food or drink. The growth in instrumental behavior continues through adolescence, as more options become available and, as mentioned earlier, there are more choices about the very environment that controls behavior. It follows that the greater instrumentality and choice of options moves them from being pawns to being (in part) masters of their fate. Add inhibitory control, and adolescents are well on the way to autonomy.

Developmental Eras

Following the lead of developmental psychologists, I have outlined four developmental eras. I discuss the needs and challenges in each era as a prelude to suggesting the personality traits relevant to these needs and challenges.

Infancy (0–2 Years)

It takes only a few weeks for infants to reveal their highly social nature by preferring humans to things. Beginning with the 2nd month of life, infants increasingly spend more time looking at humans, seek them more often, appear more satisfied with they are present, and cry more when they leave. Thus, starting in the 2nd month of life, infants become progressively more attached to humans. Not coincidentally, social smiling starts at about the same time. Smiling, a purely social response, has no function other than to indicate friendly intentions to others. During the 1st half-year of life, infants smile not only at their parents but at other humans as well.

Infants want to be held and touched. They like to clutch soft, furry objects, such as stuffed toy animals. This basic tendency of mammalian young may be seen in pet dogs and cats, and it has been demonstrated in primates. Harlow and Harlow (1962) constructed two robot mothers for their infant rhesus monkeys. One offered a nipple that would deliver milk but was made of wire mesh; the other gave no milk but was covered with a soft, furry cloth. When presented with both robot mothers, the monkeys occasionally suckled from the wire mesh robot but spent most of their time clinging to the soft, furry robot. The same tendency may be seen in human infants who clutch soft, cuddly toy animals.

Infants tend to be startled easily because they have not yet habituated to the sights and sounds that are familiar to older children and adults, and infants may become cold, hungry, or ill. Whatever the cause, infants regularly become fussy and need to be calmed. The best way to do this, known to all parents, is to pick them up and cradle them, offering contact comfort, softness, and warmth.

As the months pass, infants start to crawl and eventually to walk, but they still need to feel safe. Parents, especially mothers, remain a safe haven, sheltering them from a threatening world. Gradually, however, young children need not be in physical contact with parents, and being able to keep a parent in sight usually offers enough security. A security blanket, favorite teddy bear, or doll may offer a partial substitute for the security of the physical presence of a parent, a testament to our evolutionary heritage as primates (Harlow & Harlow, 1962).

When infants are secure, they are strongly motivated to explore the environment. Long before they can crawl or walk, infants stare fixedly at novel objects and events or listen carefully to new sounds. Early on, they attempt to insert into the mouth anything they can grasp. Thus, through their various sensory modalities, they are seeking stimulation. Once infants can crawl or walk, they will move toward novel stimuli to investigate them. Turn infants loose in the kitchen, and they will empty every available drawer or cabinet.

Infants need both security and stimulation, but they will seek stimulation only when they are secure. This fact has been demonstrated in monkeys with a robot terry-cloth mother (Harlow & Harlow, 1962). When presented with an unfamiliar toy, the infant monkey clung in terror to the robot mother. Once secure, however, the infant gradually let go of the mother and began to explore the new toy. Similar behavior can be observed in human infants, who will move away from the mother to investigate a new toy so long as the mother is close and can be easily reached (Ainsworth, Blehar, Waters, & Wall, 1978; Grossmnan, Grossman, & Waters, 2005). The infants may occasionally return to the home base of mother just to be reassured by contact. Crying infants tend to ignore the environment, but once offered the security of being held and comforted, they eagerly look around and are ready to explore.

As intensely social animals, human infants are especially interested in social stimuli, particularly novel social stimuli. Strangers fascinate them, but the social novelty may also be threatening. A fairly typical response to strangers in 8-month-old infants is to cling to the mother while staring intently at this intriguing unfamiliar person. Here the need for stimulation is opposed by the need for security. Many children of this age will let a stranger approach and touch them only when in contact with their mothers. Thus, beginning at roughly 8 months of age and continuing for the next year or two, many infants have *stranger anxiety* (to be discussed in the next chapter).

When infants are upset, they cry, and there is perhaps no more aversive sound than that of a howling infant. Parents typically rush to allay the outburst, playing something like "20 Questions" to themselves to discover the course of the discomfort. By 4 to 6 months of age, infants do not merely cry but throw temper tantrums. By the 2nd year of life, most parents start to demand at least some self-control of these tantrums. Progress is at first slow, but this is the start of the long process of control over emotions and motives that characterizes maturity.

Late in the 1st year of life, infants are crawling and exploring the immediate world around them. In the 2nd year of life, they are walking and eventually hopping, skipping, and jumping so much that parents need to allow them room for all that activity.

I have been discussing the average infant, but there are pronounced individual differences, and for each need or development, there is a relevant personality trait:

1. the need for security: emotionality
2. motor development: activity
3. the need to be with others: sociability
4. the need to control outbursts: impulsiveness
5. the need to explore and seek novel stimuli: sensation seeking

Preschool Era (2–5 Years)

During the preschool period, there are more opportunities to expend energy on playgrounds and in simple athletic games such as tag. There are more opportunities to wander into areas beyond the house and the immediate yard. Toward the end of this era, children are taken on trips and do some exploring on their own.

There is considerably more interaction with siblings and peers in the neighborhood or in preschool. Inevitable conflicts occur about the possession of toys and who did what to whom. Fights break out, older siblings tend to boss younger ones, and some peers start to initiate activities and get others to follow them.

Now socialization starts, as parents more strongly emphasize self-control over behavior. There is some resistance to parental demands, part of a developing tendency toward assertiveness. An important part of socialization is teaching children to regard themselves as social objects. By the 4th year of life, children are capable of turning the object of focus on themselves—on their appearance and social behavior. They get laughed at for social mistakes and become embarrassed. When their blunders are more serious and do some damage to objects or to others, they are shamed.

During this era, a sharp distinction is drawn between the sexes, which marks the start of gender identity. Children also learn about their religion and their nationality, also part of identity.

Children start to partake in skilled tasks such as drawing and modeling with clay, and they play simple games. When they win, they comment on how great they are. When they offer drawings, parents respond with praise and display them on the refrigerator door.

Again, the discussion refers to the average child, but there are individual differences, so for each developmental tendency, there is a relevant personality trait or self-related disposition:

1. energy expenditure: activity
2. exploration: sensation seeking
3. conflict: aggressiveness
4. leading or being led: dominance
5. demands of greater self-control: impulsiveness
6. resistance to parental demands: assertiveness
7. socialization in the context of the ability to self-focus: public self-consciousness
8. gender and social distinctions: identity

Elementary School (5–12 Years)

It is no accident that children start school at age 5 years because by this time, most of them have enough self-control to interact in a group without causing undue disruption. Now more serious socialization begins. A survey of files from 50 countries revealed that the 5- to 7-year period is an age of transition (Rogoff, Sellers, Perrota, Fox, & White, 1975). Before this period, children are allowed considerable latitude in their behavior. During it, they are strongly inculcated with the traditions, beliefs, and values of their society and must adhere more strictly to rules, including the rules governing aggression, and must prepare for adulthood by practicing the roles that they will later assume. If previously boys and girls played together easily, now they tend to be separated, and distinct gender roles are emphasized.

The school and after-school environments pose their own problems. In the upper grades, students are expected to focus on their studies and behavior so as not to disturb other students in the classroom. Competition is rife both in the school room and on the athletic field. There is verbal sparring among girls and fighting among boys; bullying starts during this era.

Cognitive maturation continues, and children become capable of introspecting. This ability to focus on the self makes them open to lessons from

socialization agents about greater self-control through verbal self-punishment. There are, of course, individual differences occurring in the context of all these events:

1. separation of the sexes: gender identity
2. adhering to rules and classroom discipline: impulsiveness
3. competition: competitiveness
4. verbal sparring and fighting: aggressiveness
5. introspection: private self-consciousness

Adolescence

Adolescents are confronted with several kinds of novelty. The rapid bodily changes make them self-conscious. Dealing with the opposite sex is daunting enough for many adolescents to render them inhibited, even socially anxious, and dating brings with it the potential for jealousy. Getting even may lead to nasty gossip designed to hurt another person. In high school, some students assemble into cliques that shut out other students, causing resentment. There are also organized clubs that open the door to leadership.

Adolescents strongly desire freedom from continual supervision. This need sets up an inevitable clash between many parents and adolescents. The parents want their adolescents to assume greater responsibility but are reluctant to give them freedom. The adolescents want greater freedom but not added responsibility.

There are personality traits relevant to these developments:

1. bodily changes: self-consciousness
2. dealing with the opposite sex: shyness
3. jealousy, resentment, and getting even: aggressiveness, hostility
4. leadership: dominance
5. desire for autonomy: assertiveness (dominance)

This exposition of the psychological events of the four eras of development is necessarily brief. I examine the details in the chapters that follow.

II

TEMPERAMENT AND OTHER PERSONALITY TRAITS

3

TEMPERAMENT I: ACTIVITY AND EMOTIONALITY

Recall that temperaments are here regarded as inherited personality traits that appear during infancy, roughly the first 2 years of life. Four personality traits meet this definition: emotionality, activity, impulsiveness, and sociability. In discussing them (and, later, other personality traits), I use the device of comparing people high in a trait with those low in the trait.

ACTIVITY

Activity involves expending energy in body movement. Active people tend to move more, hurry more, and keep busier than others; they tend to keep going when others are played out. Vacations are opportunities for mountain climbing, seeing all the sights, and making the most of the limited time available. They have a strong motive to expend energy, which becomes manifest in two ways: (a) When confined to inactivity, they chafe at the enforced idleness, and (b) they are satisfied and relaxed when they are active.

People with low activity have little or no motive to expend energy. They are not in a hurry, have little need to keep busy, and easily deal with enforced idleness. Vacations are times for rest and relaxation.

Most of the research on activity level is found in sports and medical journals, in which the physical activities themselves are described. However, a recent study in a psychology journal estimated activity level from reports of subjects in longitudinal research started 90 years ago (Kern, Reynolds, & Friedman, 2010): "Higher levels of childhood energy and sociability, rated by parents in 1922, predicted higher levels of activity at age 29 for both males and females" (p. 1069). So the trait of activity endures over decades, and sociability is a tilt in the direction of higher activity level. The study also confirmed the everyday observation that men are more active than women.

Differentiation

There are two major ways of expending energy, the basis of differentiation. One is through rapid movement: hurrying up the stairs or dashing for the elevator. The appropriate term for setting a fast pace is *tempo*: walking fast; talking fast; and, in general, wanting to get from here to there quickly.

The other means of expending energy is through behavior of greater amplitude or intensity, that is, *vigor*. Gestures are broader, the stride is longer, and the laugh is heartier. Vigorous people willingly heft a 60-pound backpack to climb thousands of feet. They are in the gym not only for aerobic fitness but also to satisfy the need to expend energy.

Tempo and vigor both involve expending energy, so we expect them to be correlated. My colleague and I (A. H. Buss & Plomin, 1975, Appendix 2) constructed separate questionnaires for each. An example of a tempo item is "My life is fast paced"; an example of a vigor item is "My movements are forceful and emphatic." The correlations were .48 for men and .52 for women. Thus, tempo and vigor are clearly related, but the correlations are moderate enough to continue to separate them

There is a minority of active people who are high in tempo but not vigor, just as there is a minority high in vigor but not tempo. Those at the inactive end of this trait tend to expend little energy so that there is no room for differentiation.

The major objective measure of activity is the *actometer* (Bell, 1968a), a modification of a self-winding watch that records movements of an arm or leg. Actometer readings correlate well with ratings by parents or teachers of level of activity (Eaton & Enns, 1986). Actometers record only the number of movements, which is a measure of tempo, not vigor.

An important tilt in the differentiation of activity is physique, especially in males. Active men with large, well-muscled bodies tend to expend energy through vigorous action, but active men with slim bodies are more likely to be high in tempo. Physique is also involved in a sex difference. Women, who are on average smaller and less well muscled than men, are more likely to expend energy through tempo.

Person and Environment

People high in activity tend to choose exercise that depends on the two differentiates of activity. If vigorous activity is sought, there is weight lifting. If a fast tempo is sought, there are the fast-moving sports of tennis and squash or the rapid pace of Wii video games. People low in activity tend to avoid energetic pursuits and become spectators rather than participants in sports.

The trait of activity also helps set the tone of a social interaction. People who speak rapidly and with expansive gestures can animate a conversation or social gathering. People who speak slowly with few gestures and with long pauses may modify the very environment that affects them. A fast-tempo person who feels slowed down by stately music can replace it with driving rock music; a slow-tempo person might do the opposite. A vigorous person in need of exercise can dissipate energy by doing isometric exercises or by stretching in the absence of any equipment. A low-active person, when walking with others, may be able to slow down the pace of the group merely by lagging behind, forcing the others to stroll.

Then there is the special case of overcoming obstacles in the environment placed there by one's own limitations: the publicized incidents of energetic people disabled by illness or accident. Confined to a wheelchair, they enter marathons, play basketball, or lift weights. They campaign strenuously to obtain ramps, special parking spaces, access to classes and workrooms, and generally insist on changing the physical environment that may limit their movement.

Children at the high extreme of the temperament of activity may have difficulty adjusting to an environment that requires them to sit still, as in a classroom. Clearly, this is a mismatch between person and environment. Some of these children, under the strong motive to move around, may modify the environment, behaving as though the classroom is a playground. They may leave their seats when they are not supposed to, jump up and down, and generally disturb the other children.

Development

Infancy

Babies differ little in activity level until they can move on their own. With the development of creeping, crawling, and eventually walking, marked differences in activity level appear. By the 2nd year of life, highly active infants are wearing out their caregivers. They constantly seem to get into cabinets and drawers, run when other children walk, and keep going when other children are resting. They are likely to play with the toys of their older siblings and get in the way when adults are doing chores.

Infants low in activity are easier on their siblings and parents. They are less likely to jump up from the supper table and more likely to be ready for bed when it's time. Infants' movements still lack the motor coordination they will have later, so tempo and vigor are as yet undifferentiated. Overall activity is relatively easy to assess, and sex differences are already present. A meta-analysis of 45 studies revealed that infant boys are more active than girls by 0.2 standard deviations (D. W. Campbell & Eaton, 1999). Thus, even in infancy, gender slightly tilts activity level somewhat, but so does body fat, which correlates negatively with activity level even when food intake is controlled (Li, O'Connor, Buckley, & Specker, 1995).

Preschool

Active toddlers do not just walk; they skip and slide. They scamper up and down stairs; rush to get to the playground; and in a shopping mall, they hop up and down, dash back and forth, chase one another, and dart into aisles. They are exuberantly full of life; they trot rather than walk, and they bounce up and down. Crowded halls are not the best place for active preschoolers but are fine for low-active preschoolers, who are content to move at a slow pace.

The end of this era marks a developmental trend toward goal-directed behavior and therefore fewer random movements. Actometers revealed that the play of 4 year olds is less active than the play of 3 year olds (Eaton & Enns, 1986), and the energy level of highly active 5 year olds is sometimes too much for parents (D. M. Buss, 1981).

Elementary School

Opportunities for expending energy open up vertically and horizontally. Children now climb trees or scoot to the top of huge water slides, and they play games over broad horizontal expanses, such as soccer. For reasons to be discussed in the Person and Environment section, the disparity between high-active and low-active children widens, and tempo and vigor differentiate.

A sex difference in play is relevant here. Boys are known to use wider play spaces that require more energy, and the play of boys is more vigorous than that of girls. After reviewing 90 studies, Eaton and Enns (1986) concluded that "males were more active than females by roughly one-half of a standard deviation" (p. 24). So the sex difference widens during this era.

Our biological heritage may be relevant here. Primate males are known to be more active than their female counterparts, and energetic play can be increased by prenatal male sex hormones in rhesus monkeys (Goy & McEwen, 1980).

There is a gradual drop in energy level during the school years, as revealed in a study that compared 5- to 9-year-olds and then 8 to 11-year-olds (Kendall & Brophy, 1981). A later longitudinal study confirmed this decrease: "During middle childhood, average ratings of activity level . . . dropped significantly, indicating a shift toward lower activity level with increasing age from 8 to 12 years" (Guerin, Gottfried, Oliver, & Thomas, 2003, p. 238). A study of limb movements (actometer) of subjects ranging in age from infancy to middle age revealed an inverted U shape, with a peak at middle childhood (Eaton, McKeen, & Campbell, 2001).

Older children do not bounce around as much. Their movements are more efficient, expending less energy. Still, highly active children make their own choices in favor of high-energy pursuits, especially in sports such as soccer, football, and basketball. Preparation for these sports and playing them enhance endurance, which opens a wider gap between high-active and low-active children.

Late in this era, physique comes into play. By now, there are marked differences in body fat, with obesity in children becoming a serious problem. An unfortunate cycle is established for fat children who are already low in activity and have available a variety of low-energy pastimes, especially watching television. These "couch potatoes" do not develop their muscles, making it harder for them to engage in strenuous exercise. They become less fit, making it even harder to exercise, and the cycle continues.

Children high in activity are attracted to high-energy sports. By exercising more, they become fitter, making it easier to play high-energy sports, a benign cycle. They are the ones likely to fidget in class at the forced inactivity. Some can control their urge to move around, but as we shall see in Chapter 4, impulsive children cannot.

Adolescence

During adolescence, sports and active games proliferate, and swimming, running, and working with weights become available. Although lifting weights is more popular with young women today than it once was, they are used mainly for toning muscles. Observe what young women and men are doing in a gym. More young women are on the aerobic machines, increasing their cardiac health. More young men are on the weight machines, especially those for arms and torso. These practices reflect a gender tilt: The adolescent surge in testosterone bulks up the torso of male adolescents, increasing the gender gap in vigor but not tempo.

Perspective

The trait of activity has been part of questionnaires for more than a half century, sometimes as part of extraversion and other times as a stand-alone trait, as in the Active and Vigorous scales of Thurstone's (1951) Temperament Schedule (the terms *temperament* and *personality* were interchangeable then). There were even earlier experimental measures of the behavior itself. Tempo was assessed by the rate of clapping, tapping, turning cranks, and sorting cards by Frischeisen-Köhler (1933) and Harrison (1941).

There has been little attention paid to the distinction between tempo and vigor, perhaps for two reasons. One is the self-winding calendar (Schulman & Reisman, 1959) and its successor, the actometer—particularly the actometer for infants and children (Bell, 1968a). The actometer, which measures tempo, not vigor, is widely used to study hyperactivity. Another reason is that self-report questionnaires have come to dominate assessment of personality because of their ease of use and of obtaining enormous subject samples. When a single trait is studied intensively, its subtraits are likely to be noticed—in this instance, tempo and vigor.

EMOTIONALITY

The high end of the trait of emotionality is best described by such adjectives as *upset, keyed up,* and *overwrought.* Emotional people tend to be oversensitive to slights, threats, and perhaps even changes to their usual routine; they are also touchy, easily hurt, and difficult to soothe.

At issue here are the concepts of arousal and reactivity. Emotional people have a low threshold of arousal. They are excitable, responding emotionally to situations that would not bother others, the result being more frequent upsets and frustrations than the average person. The intensity of the reaction is greater, so that what might mildly disturb the average person causes emotional people to be flustered and overwrought. Emotional people are especially sensitive to stress (Strelau, 2001).

People low in emotionality seem to be buffered against the events that would upset others and make them feel uncomfortable. Those low in emotionality tend to be temperate, composed, and perhaps even nonchalant in the face of everyday hassles and frustrations. Like everyone else, they have days when everything seems to go wrong, but their distress is muted. Their threshold for getting upset is relatively high, so they are distressed less frequently.

Differentiation

Emotionality is assumed to differentiate during the first year of life into fear and anger (Bridges, 1932). Fear and anger involve the same physiological arousal as preparation for dealing with threat: the flight–fight reaction. As personality traits, fear and anger correlate .52 for women and .63 for men (A. H. Buss & Plomin, 1984), which may be explained by their common link as differentiates of emotionality.

The correlations are high, but they still leave enough variance for keeping the traits separate, and there are other reasons for the distinction. They differ in their facial and body expressions, the instrumental behavior associated with them, and their linkage to abnormal behavior. It would be difficult to discuss anger without mentioning aggression, so I deal with anger in the chapter on aggression. Fear is discussed immediately after emotionality in this chapter.

Within emotionality there is another kind of differentiation. When upset, does the person helplessly go to pieces or attempt to deal with the situation: mope or cope? In discussing future areas of research on coping, Compas (1987) suggested the need for research on

> the relation between effortful coping responses and more stable, non-volitional factors such as temperament. . . . Research in this area might clarify the ways in which stable features of individuals limit or constrain the type of coping responses they are willing or able to use. (p. 401)

The relevant temperament is emotionality.

Moping raises the issue of cognitions, becoming pessimistic, optimistic, or even neutral about the future. Some pessimists, paradoxically called *defensive pessimists* (Norem, 2001), feel stressed and uncomfortable when confronted with abilities tasks but perform as well as optimists; although uncomfortable, these emotional people cope.

The trait of activity is relevant: High activity tilts toward coping, and low activity tilts toward moping. Gender is another tilt: Girls are allowed to cry and therefore express their distress, whereas boys are taught not to cry because expressing distress is considered unmanly.

Those who do not cope have cognitions that are associated with negative mood. In a study of self-reported mood recorded daily for 7 days, a general factor included these items: depressed, felt hemmed in and constrained, felt pessimistic and cynical, couldn't think clearly, touchy and easily hurt, and lacked confidence in self (A. H. Buss & Plomin, 1975, pp. 204–205). This moodiness factor correlated with emotionality: .29 for men and .42 for women.

Given that emotional people, by definition, tend to become upset more deeply and more frequently, do they express their distress? Some wail and howl, but others bear it stoically, hardly displaying their negative affect.

Person and Environment

The environment, especially during childhood, strongly affects emotionality. It might be tumultuous and unsettling, with one parent missing or neither parent available for soothing. Meals might be haphazard and sleeping patterns irregular. Parents might move often so that children repeatedly must adjust to a new school and a new social environment. Such chronic stressors promote emotionality. Alternatively, there may be stability and regular routines of eating and sleeping, with parents being settled, stable, and available when needed. The relative absence of stressors promotes low emotionality.

We also affect the environment. There are two opposite ways of reacting to a fire. Emotional people get so upset that they lose control, ratcheting up the panic that may occur during a fire. People low in emotionality tend to stay calm and try to steady those around them.

Development

Infancy

Distress is easy to observe as early as the 1st day of life. The infant—say, a boy—crinkles his face, his face reddens, and he breathes in gasps. He is obviously distressed but often can be calmed with milk, warmth, or cuddling. What about individual differences? Two-day-old infants of European American parents were compared with those of Chinese American parents (D. G. Freedman, 1971). European American infants were observed to be more upset than Chinese American infants:

> In an item called *defensive movements*, the tester placed a cloth firmly over the supine baby's face for a few seconds. While the typical European-America infant immediately struggled to remove the cloth, the typical Chinese-American infant lay passively. (D. G. Freedman, 1971, p. 93)

This group difference in emotionality on the 2nd day of life is indirect evidence of an individual difference because the group difference must have arisen from individual differences.

In terms of differentiation, fear has been reported to occur at about age 3 months (Bridges, 1932) on the basis of the infant's crying, tensing, and even kicking. These are signs of distress, however, not necessarily of fear or anger. During the 1st year, the infant will develop the stereotyped facial expressions of fear, part of our primate heritage, but for the first several months of life, these are absent. At about 3 months, infants try to escape from threatening or annoying stimuli. They now have the motor ability to turn their heads and bodies and recoil from the noxious stimulus. This attempted flight response is what distinguishes fear from the more amorphous distress reaction.

Anger appears later during the 1st year of life, when the child has better motor control. Now he pushes or throws away the annoying stimulus, often accompanied by kicking and thrashing around. In fear, the infant shrinks back and tries to avoid the aversive stimulus, whereas in anger he tries to get rid of it. These are the flight–fight reactions to threatening or disturbing events, which are more easily observed as better motor control develops.

More undifferentiated emotionality may be observed when an infant is challenged. The earliest challenge is the discomfort of being hungry, colicky, or cold. Highly emotional infants are prepared by heredity to wail, kick, and thrash about. They set the tone for social interaction by frequent and clamorous demands for attention. The intense reaction makes them hard to soothe, setting up a cycle of a complaining infant, which sooner or later leads to irate parents, who may then magnify the problem by ignoring the infant completely or being oversolicitous, thereby reinforcing the crying. Parents are likely to react at one or the other extreme if they too are highly emotional: a parent–child match in emotionality. One outcome is likely to be an *insecurely attached* infant—in particular, the type called *ambivalent* (Ainsworth, Blehar, Waters, & Wall, 1978). Highly emotional infants tend to become severely upset by strangers, cry excessively, resist separation, and cling to the mother—behaviors that define insecure attachment.

Infants low in emotionality also start off with the challenge of being tired, cold, or hungry, but they are prepared by heredity to react less intensely and less frequently. When they do become upset, their complaints are softer, and they are easily soothed, which sets a more positive tone for social interaction. Parents are rewarded by their ability to care for the infant and so are more likely to offer an appropriate amount of attention and comfort, and this is especially true if the parents match their child in low emotionality. Such infants need less security and can use the mother as a secure base from which to explore the environment, as well as strangers in that environment. They are securely attached.

The next challenges involve giving up the breast or bottle for a cup and achieving regularity in the sleep–awake schedule. Again, highly emotional infants are likely to be upset by such changes in routine, and their overreaction is heightened if there is a parent–child match in high emotionality. However, many parents will act quickly to soothe their crying infants and thereby minimize their distress.

Low-emotional infants easily tolerate changes in feeding and scheduling. By now, their parents have labeled them as easy, just as highly emotional infants have been labeled difficult.

Preschool

After infancy, children need a regular schedule of meals; play; naps; and, for some, going to a preschool educational setting. Some parents cannot provide such stability, and its absence serves to deepen the groove of high emotionality. Even when there is a stable schedule, some changes are inevitable, and they pose a challenge that may especially upset emotional children. Highly emotional children, who are so because of a combination of heredity and prior problems of infancy, are especially disconcerted by abrupt transitions and react to such challenges with tears and moodiness.

A more personal, individual challenge derives from the discrepancy between fast-maturing perception and slow-maturing motor capability. Young children can see what they want to reach for, want to be able to take a toy apart, or want to get the toy to work, but they cannot. The result in highly emotional children tends to be crying and repeated demands for help. Their immaturity poses another problem: forbidden toys, television, outdoor activities, television, or computers, to which their older siblings and parents have access. Highly emotional children tend to whine and complain about these things, to the considerable annoyance of others in the family. In social interaction, they set a tone of turmoil and difficulty, establishing a negative cycle of child to parents to child. Such a cycle is worsened when there is a match between the child's and the parents' high emotionality.

Children low in emotionality are not especially bothered by the various challenges of the preschool period. If there is a match in emotionality—parents being low (and this is likely)—the social environment is likely to be placid. The children easily make the transitions to changes in schedules, remain relatively unruffled when their perceptions outrun their motor abilities, and protest only mildly when their immaturity denies them the perquisites of older children and adults. They seldom cry or whine, which results in their being labeled as easy to get along with. They set a pleasant tone of social interaction, establishing a benign cycle of child to parents and back to child.

Elementary School

Changes in schedule continue to be a problem for school-age children, as they first start going to school and then move into different grades, needing to adjust to different teachers and, for some, a move to a new neighborhood and school. In the face of these challenges, highly emotional children tend to alternate between moping around the house in hurt silence and bitter complaining about their plight.

Many children feel pressured to achieve good grades in school. When highly emotional children receive lower grades than what is expected, they become too upset to study and continue to perform poorly. Most school-age children compete in sports and other games outside of school. When they win, or if they generally win, there is no problem, but when they lose or, worse, if they chronically lose in competitive games, the stress is often so great that they prefer to abandon the games. There is a double problem for emotional children, who not only react immaturely to a loss but lack control while playing the game, which makes losing more probable.

During this era, friendships start assuming importance, especially for girls. Being rejected or neglected is distressing, extremely so for children high in emotionality, who tend to react by crying or lapsing into immature behavior. Emotional children also react poorly to teasing, typically by escaping, crying, and becoming moody. Such reactions initiate further negative treatment from peers, establishing a cycle: rejection or teasing, causing childish behavior, leading to further rejection or teasing.

Children low in emotionality tend to cope with the swirls and eddies of family moves and educational sequences. They are, of course, thrown by poor grades but are more likely either to try harder or to just accept their lot. When competing, they remain calm enough to display what skills they have. If they do lose, it is not devastating. If they are rejected, they usually get over it. If they are teased, they remain composed enough to reply in kind or at least not to regress to childish behavior. As a result, they are likely to maintain friendships because they avoid so many of the negatives that can make others avoid them.

Adolescence

Adolescence is a time of considerable challenge, with marked, overt alterations in the body and more subtle changes in social roles. Sexual impulses surge toward a peak at the same time that parents, especially girls' parents, are pushing for inhibition of these urges. Friendships assume greater importance, and dating begins, both of which make rejection more devastating. Acceptance by peer groups looms large in an adolescent's life, and such groups strongly press for conformity. This pressure brings adolescents into conflict with parents, who typically demand that their children avoid drugs and bizarre clothing and hairstyles. These various challenges serve to maintain an elevated level of emotionality in adolescents already high in this trait. Adolescents have been stereotyped as moody, but this label applies mainly to those high in emotionality.

Those low in emotionality deal with the challenges of body change and social rejection the way they deal with most challenges: with few problems, minimal acquiescence to parental demands, and instrumental behavior that deals with the problems. Other things being equal, these adolescents are not moody.

Perspective

In general parlance, the term *emotional* refers to the intensity of affect, whether positive or negative, but the temperament of emotionality refers only to negative affect. It is linked to a higher order factor from a personality questionnaire, called *negative emotionality* (Tellegen, 1985). Those who score high on this factor describe themselves as "being unpleasurably engaged, stressed and harassed, and prone to experiencing strong negative emotions such as anxiety and anger" (Tellegen et al., 1988). This description sounds like an echo of the temperament of emotionality and its two differentiates, fearfulness and anger.

Negative emotionality has been found to correlate consistently with many of the symptoms of anxiety and depression (Clark, 2007; Watson, Clark, & Carey, 1988). These relationships make sense because anxiety and depression involve negative mood and, by extrapolation, the temperament of emotionality. This chain of reasoning and empirical relationships leads to the conclusion that being extremely high in the temperament of emotionality is likely to be a precursor of mood-related abnormal behavior. Beyond negative emotionality, a factor simply called *emotionality* emerged from a factor analysis of personality adjectives in six European languages and in Korean (Ashton, Lee, Peruginia, et al., 2004).

FEARFULNESS

Fear is part of an ancient adaptation for dealing with threat, an adaptation that in different animals involves freezing, burrowing, running, or flying, all means of escaping threat to life and limb. Several components are involved, starting with the *instrumental* component of withdrawal. However, escape may not be an option because leaving the scene does not solve the problem. For example, a person waiting to hear the results of a test for cancer might pace around the room or engage in other random movements, the spillover of body tension, but there is no escape.

The second component is the *physiological* preparation for dealing with the emergency: the transfer of blood and energy to the massive muscles to be in play. The third component consists of species-wide facial *expressions* and body postures of fear. Some of these we share with primates, and others are uniquely human (Ekman, 2003). There is a fourth component that appears to be unique to our species: We describe as *feelings* the keen awareness of danger, current or future. Such apprehension seems to require the advanced cognitions that occur only in our species.

Differentiation

When people become afraid, all four components might occur, but not necessarily and not in everyone. One component might be most salient, the others being less intense and less important parts of the fear pattern. Some people are more tense or engage in random pacing and self-touching, others have powerful physiological reactions, and still others worry excessively and experience feelings of panic. There are people who are anxious about flying (apprehension) but somehow manage to board the plane and stay on it (instrumental behavior) even though their heart might be racing on takeoff and landing (physiological reaction).

Differentiation of anxiety is relevant to psychotherapy. Hodgson and Rachman (1974) studied clients undergoing psychotherapy to deal with their intense fear of open places. They initially assessed indicators of the cognitive, physiological, and instrumental components of fear: subjective feelings, heart rate increases, and behavioral avoidance. For some clients, called *synchronizers*, the three components were highly similar. For others, called *desynchronizers*, when one measure was elevated, the other two were lower—for example, higher heart rate, but less avoidance and milder feelings of fear. Psychotherapy turned out to be more beneficial for the synchronizers than for the desynchronizers.

Another study of agoraphobics found that the timing of improvement differed for two components (Mavissakalian & Michelson, 1982). The first to improve was instrumental behavior—that is, starting to approach previously feared stimuli. Only later in treatment did the physiological component (heart rate) show similar improvement.

Person and Environment

Environment Affects Person

Everyday situations may bring their fair share of scary events: driving on a slick road, a neighborhood known for its muggings, or a trip to the dentist for a root canal. The threat might be right in the home in the form of bullying by an older sibling, an excessively punitive parent, or even an abusive parent. It might also occur in school, where bullying is common. Alternatively, the threat might come from the verbal and nonverbal relational aggression of peers (Crick, Ostrov, & Werner, 2006); read more on this topic in Chapter 5.

The environment affects fear through several learning mechanisms, starting with *classical conditioning*. When a child has been bitten or even just threatened by a dog, even the sight of one may elicit fear. Exposed to pain in a dentist's office, the associated stimuli of the office or the dentists' chair may elicit fear.

Fear-relevant stimuli such as snakes condition faster than neutral stimuli, presumably part of our evolutionary heritage (Öhman & Mineka, 2001).

Escaping a painful or threatening stimulus reinforces *instrumental conditioning* of subsequent avoidance. As has been demonstrated in traumatic avoidance conditioning in animals and humans, it may require only one trial to produce a lasting avoidance of the stimulus or situation (Solomon & Wynne, 1954). Such avoidance, which prevents extinction of the fear response, is adaptive when there is a serious threat to life and limb, again part of our evolutionary heritage. However, it is not adaptive in most modern, everyday situations, so "once-bitten, twice-shy" children may never discover that the dogs they later encounter will not bite them.

Observational learning is the source of a wide variety of fears. Youngsters, especially, tend to imitate the fears of their parents. Laboratory-raised young monkeys who were not afraid of snakes observed the frightened behavior of adult monkeys who were confronted with a snake, and the young monkeys became scared (Mineka, Davidson, Cook, & Keir, 1984).

Two scary movies produced unrealistic fears in adults. After viewing a woman stabbed to death in a shower in the movie *Psycho*, a number of adults reported avoiding the shower for several months. In the movie *Jaws*, a great white shark devoured several people on a New England beach. Some children subsequently had nightmares about sharks, and that summer so many vacationers avoided New England beaches that the economy of several seaside towns was shattered.

Person Affects Environment

Fearful people tend to interpret relatively safe situations as dangerous, and they exaggerate the intensity of situations when there is only a little risk. In a study group, a worried student may incubate anxiety in the group by reciting the history of bright students who failed the exam. In *setting the tone*, fearful passengers on an airplane may spread panic to others, thereby confirming their own fears. A vicious cycle of exaggerated danger leads to a powerful physiological reaction, which further intensifies the fear into panic, diminishing the ability to cope with the situation.

Fearful people also misinterpret normal bodily reactions as indicating that they are afraid. The experience may escalate into panic, leading to dysfunctional avoidance of everyday situations (Telch, Broulliard, Telch, Agras, & Taylor, 1989; Telch, Jacquin, Smits, & Powers, 2003).

For those low in fear, the danger is realistically appraised or perhaps even minimized because of past experience. The fear reaction is milder, allowing coping mechanisms to operate, which suggests a benign cycle.

When a situation is truly threatening, the trait of fear modifies its impact. In 2009, an airplane from a New York airport lost power just after takeoff, but the low-fear pilot calmly landed it in the nearby Hudson River. On landing, the high-fear passengers became agitated and were ready to stampede, but the low-fear passengers and crew persevered, helped other passengers off the plane, and all were saved.

Development

Infancy

An innate fear reaction in infants is elicited by the flash of lightning, the boom of thunder, and any noise too intense for their delicate ears. A looming figure is frightening, and so is any loss of balance. Fearful infants react more intensely to these stimuli and may become sensitized so that even more moderate stimuli can elicit fear. They are prepared by heredity to acquire conditioned fears with the result that they later have a variety of specific fears.

Infants low in fear gradually habituate to sudden and intense stimuli and tend to remain calm. They are less likely to acquire conditioned fears and therefore have fewer specific fears.

Preschool

Preschool-age children become more aware of adult models who might be imitated. At this stage of development, adult fears are easily transmitted to children, especially those already high in the trait of fearfulness.

The world of the preschool-age child opens to a broader range of stimuli and therefore to more situations that might elicit fear: dogs, snakes, insects, hospitals. Movies and cartoons scare them because they are still slow to realize the unreality of what they are seeing. For the same reason, nightmares are frightening for all preschool children, but the effects linger in fearful children. They are harder to soothe and it takes them longer to understand than less fearful children that the threat is not real.

Elementary School

Fear of the unknown—for example, first attendance at school—becomes important in elementary school children. A small percentage of children, the already fearful ones, develop school phobia. At school there are bullies who instill fear, and fearful children are likely to be the ones who are picked on (Olweus, 1984). Some parents strongly press their children to achieve high grades, which instills fear of failing in children who are already fearful. Cognitive development has proceeded far enough for worry to become a major component in the fear reaction.

Children are also exposed to frightening stimuli beyond those in everyday life. They hear ghost stories and vivid descriptions of hellfire and see violent and horror movies that require no imagination at all.

This era marks the start of a sex difference in fear, specifically in its expression. Girls are allowed to express their fears, but it is unmanly for boys to do so.

Adolescence

There is more social comparison in high school, so pressure to keep grades up increases and test anxiety becomes widespread. Fearful adolescents are especially prone to test anxiety as well as to the social evaluations that occur among acquaintances.

Adolescents are more aware of the physical dangers of being beaten severely or even murdered. It has taken only a few massacres at schools during the past several decades for adolescents to be apprehensive about the potential threat. Girls are appropriately concerned about being raped, widening the sex difference in fear, in both its expression and worry.

Trends

During the course of development there are more threats around and less protection from parents, and therefore the potential for more fear. Countering this trend is the increasing ability to cope with threats and to distinguish realistic threats from unrealistic ones.

The other trend is for an increasing disparity between the sexes in the intensity and frequency of fear. There is no evidence of a sex difference in the preschool era, but there is such evidence, although mixed, in the school era (A. H. Buss, 1988, p. 87). Starting with adolescence and continuing into adulthood, women have more frequent and more intense fears than men.

Perspective

Fearfulness is a personality trait, but a related issue is the origin of particular fears—specifically, which fears are innate. It turns out that no particular fear is innate, but we are especially prepared to acquire fears that may be adaptive (Öhman & Mineka, 2001). It has been suggested that modern fears date back to our evolutionary past, when mammals were starting to evolve but reptiles predominated (Öhman, 1986). It was adaptive then to fear reptiles, and this adaptation presumably continues to the modern era. This adaptation is not an instinctive reflex but a readiness (preparedness) to learn a particular fear as part of a system of defense against predators:

Thus learning is critically involved in selecting which stimuli activate the predatory defense system. But this learning is likely to be biologically primed or constrained in the sense that the responses are much more easily attached to some types of stimuli than to others. (Öhman, 1986, p. 29)

In an experiment mentioned earlier, young, naive, laboratory-reared rhesus monkeys watched their wild-reared parents react with fright to the presence of a snake, and five of the six youngsters likewise immediately became afraid of them (Mineka, Davidson, Cook, & Keir, 1984). In a closely related experiment, seven of 10 youngsters showed evidence of this acquired fear of snakes (Cook, Mineka, Wolkenstein, & Laitsch, 1985). However, four of the 16 monkeys in the two experiments did not develop a fear of snakes, which may be interpreted as their being low in the trait of fearfulness.

No one will attempt to condition a fear in humans, but self-reports of specific fears have been used as evidence for the evolutionary basis of fears that are presumably adaptive. A number of these studies have been summarized by D. M. Buss (2008, pp. 92–98), who views them as strongly confirmatory.

The adaptiveness hypothesis makes sense, but the evidence is not always confirmatory. Consider what happens in certain kinds of classical conditioning: "When the unconditioned stimulus is highly aversive or when a conditioned stimulus without any evolutionary significance is known to be dangerous, the differences between evolutionary primed fears and nonevolutionary fears disappear" (MacDonald & Hershberger, 2005, p. 33). As relevant examples, just one painful episode in a dentist's office is sufficient to condition an enduring fear of dentists, and one bite by a dog is sufficient for some people to fear all dogs. Moreover, the fear of public speaking, which has no evolutionary significance, is the most frequently reported fear. The evolutionary hypothesis does account for the data on fear of snakes and spiders but cannot account for the fears of dentists, dogs, or public speaking.

Next, consider the genetic basis for common fears (Rose, Miller, Pogue-Geile, & Cardwell, 1981). This study of fraternal and identical twins revealed a substantial genetic component for fear of snakes and spiders—consistent with the evolutionary hypothesis—but also for public speaking, and being criticized, which have no evolutionary basis.

SHYNESS

Shyness is a specifically *social fear* that correlates .50 with generalized fear (Cheek & Buss, 1981). Several components are easy to describe when the shyness is intense, which occurs mainly in the presence of strangers.

Components

Observable Behavior

Several studies have surreptitiously observed subjects in a waiting room with another person. Shy subjects talked less and had more touching, and observers rated shy subjects as being more tense, inhibited, and unfriendly (Cheek & Buss, 1981). In a similar experiment, shy subjects were rated higher on a composite of these behaviors: dull facial expression, lip biting or moistening, extraneous hand or foot movements, throat clearing, stammered or quivery speech, and nervous laughter (Bruch, Gorsky, Collins, & Berger, 1989).

Shy people spend less time talking, and they do not initiate conversations. When a reply is called for, it is brief and halting and, more generally, unresponsive. The voice typically is soft, although sometimes it is strained and hoarse. Speech inflections are sparse, and there are few accompanying gestures. If there are gestures, they are likely to be nervous movements such as touching oneself or, at the extreme, tics. Facial expressions are notable by their absence, except possibly for an apologetic half-smile, a tightly clamped jaw, or other signs of tension. Gaze is averted, and sometimes the head is kept down. When shaking hands, there is less eye contact, vigor, and grip strength (Chaplin, Phillips, Brown, Clanton, & Stein, 2000).

There may be behavioral disorganization: stuttering, hesitation, and self-interruptions. Speech may halt in midsentence or trail off into silence. When two shy people meet, there may be long periods of silence as each waits for the other to start talking (Cheek & Buss, 1981). There is more fidgeting and talking to oneself and less reciprocal smiling (Heerey & Kring, 2007).

Shy people often attempt to escape from social situations, especially those with strangers. When a stranger tries to be friendly by making self-disclosures, shy people disclose less in return than unshy people (Meleshko & Alden, 1993). Shy people are likely to be found on the periphery of a conversational group and usually leave parties early.

Their behavior may be preemptive in avoiding parties and dating situations, where people need to maintain conversations. Extremely shy people have been reported to refrain from seeking jobs that require an interview because it would be too painful.

Physiological Reaction

As with any fear, in shyness the sympathetic division of the autonomic nervous system responds with massive preparation for dealing with the threat: increased heart rate, blood pressure, sweating, and rapid breathing.

Cognitions

Research on the cognitions of shy people has been summarized this way (Cheek & Melchior, 1990, p. 68):

1. They perceive that a social interaction will be explicitly evaluative.
2. They expect that their behavior will be inadequate and that they will be evaluated negatively.
3. They hold "irrational beliefs" about how good their social performance should be and how much social approval they should get from others.
4. They think "Who does this situation want me to be?" rather than "How can I be me in this situation?"
5. They adopt a strategy of trying to get along rather than trying to get ahead.
6. They become anxiously self-preoccupied and do not pay enough attention to others.
7. They judge themselves more negatively than others judge them.
8. They blame themselves for social failures and attribute successes to other factors.
9. They accept negative feedback and resist or reject positive feedback.
10. They remember negative self-relevant information and experiences.

Shy people also downgrade their ability to work with others, manage family conflicts, and even voice their own opinions (Caprara, Steca, Cervone, & Artistico, 2003). These thoughts and perceptions help perpetuate a cycle: feeling shy in the presence of unfamiliar people to negative feelings and perceptions about oneself to inhibited social behavior, which in turn leads to more negative cognitions. Peers are likely to exclude shy children (Gazelle & Rudolph, 2004), which reinforces shy children's tendency to withdraw from others, establishing another cycle of shyness.

Differentiation

All the components are present in intensely shy people, but for the majority of moderately shy people, not all components are present. The expressive component, described earlier, predominates for some shy people, but others may remain composed by escaping in their imagination. A dean's wife told me how she dealt with her extreme shyness at parties and other crowded social gatherings by pretending she was off by herself, enjoying a walk through the forest or reading a book of poetry.

Differentiation has relevance for psychotherapy. If the predominant component is the tension of anxiety, relaxation conditioning is appropriate. If the cognitive component predominates, talk therapy designed to produce more realistic social appraisal is appropriate. If the predominant component consists of gaze aversion and other behavioral manifestations of shyness, the client needs training in expressive style.

Person and Environment

Early environment may tilt children in the direction of more shyness or less. If there is little or no exposure to strangers, children never habituate and are likely to become shy around strangers. If there is an abundance of strangers, a variety of nannies, or families having lots of social novelty, the children do habituate and are likely to be unshy. The need for such habituation is especially keen for the children of military personnel, who must repeatedly deal with new schools, neighborhoods, and peers (Sheppard, Malatras, & Israel, 2010).

Two temperaments also tilt toward shyness. One is generalized fear. Temperamentally fearful infants are likely to become insecurely attached, and, by definition, they are afraid of both social and nonsocial objects. Other things being equal, then, temperamental fear is a precursor to shyness.

The rationale for the relevance of temperamental sociability is different (Schmidt & Buss, 2010). Unsociable infants have a relatively weak need to be with others, by definition. Lacking this motive, they are less tolerant of the negatives of social interaction. Strangers arouse less curiosity in them but a full measure of fear. Because others are less socially rewarding, again by definition, young unsociable children are likely to seek immediate escape from social novelty. As a result, they tend not to habituate to strangers, and social novelty continues to be a stimulus for inhibited social behavior.

The interaction between person and environment has already been discussed, although not in this section, so I shall be brief. Social novelty is crucial because in the presence of friends and family, shy people tend to engage in normally expected social behavior. Shy people choose to avoid novel social situations or to try to escape from them. They tend to be unresponsive and even disorganized in such situations, thereby setting the tone for the interaction.

Development

Infancy

Primate infants fear strangers, especially male strangers, and in this respect, human babies are typical primates. Fear of strangers starts in the latter half of the first year of life, as has been documented in an experimental set up called the *strange situation* (Ainsworth et al., 1978). A mother and her infant enter a room with toys the infant might play with. Soon a stranger enters. The infants are wary of the stranger and at first stay close to the mother to calm themselves. Most of them soon relax and resume playing with the toys, but an insecure minority—those high in the trait of shyness—do not relax and continue to display anxiety. Most infants start habituating to strangers in the second year of life, and thereafter fear of unfamiliar others gradually diminishes until it is no longer a concern. The shy children continue to fear strangers (M. T. Greenberg & Marvin, 1982), some of them well into adulthood (Grossman, Grossman, & Waters, 2005).

In a study of fear and wariness, four babies played together over a series of sessions, during which some consistently withdrew and others consistently engaged in the situation, which was interpreted as "some sort of within-baby disposition" (Bronson & Pankey, 1977, p. 1182). (The behavioral disposition is, of course, shyness.) Such behavior in infants predicted how they would interact later at preschool. The shyness of infants has also been studied under the heading of *behavioral inhibition*, but most of that research has been on preschool children.

Preschool

Behavioral inhibition consists of children's shutting down their behavior in the face of uncertainty about how to handle unfamiliar stimuli. Children aged 21 months were exposed to the following situations:

> [an] initial meeting with an unfamiliar examiner, an encounter with an unfamiliar set of toys, a woman model displaying a trio of acts that were difficult to remember, an interaction with another female stranger, exposure to a large, odd-looking robot, and temporary separation from the mother. (Kagan, Reznick, Clarke, Snidman, & Garcia-Coll, 1984, p. 2213)

They were observed again at age 4 years. The formerly inhibited children were more cautious, had more fears, and had a higher heart rate and more heart rate variability than the uninhibited children. These trends continued into the 6th year of life (Kagan, Reznick, & Snidman, 1987).

These researchers and others have equated behavioral inhibition with shyness, but later research showed that they are different (Schmidt & Buss, 2010). Shy children do not have a higher or more variable heart rate (Asendorpf & Meier, 1993). Kochanska (1991) observed children between the ages of 1.5 and 3.5 years in the strange situation. Two patterns emerged: (a) Children retreated from the stranger and were wary and timid in response to her (social inhibition or shyness), and (b) there was little or no exploratory behavior of the room (nonsocial inhibition). The children were observed again at age 5 years, this time interacting with an unfamiliar peer (Kochanska & Radke-Yarrow, 1992). A shyness factor, which consisted of staring, being unoccupied, and not talking to the peer, was strongly predicted by the social inhibition (shyness) observed in the earlier study. The nonsocial inhibition first identified in the earlier study predicted the quality of group play at 5 years. The authors concluded that "the present findings confirm the empirical and conceptual validity of a more differentiated conceptualization of children's inhibition to the unfamiliar" (Kochanska & Radke-Yarrow, 1992, p. 332). Said another way, the shyness young children display is different from nonsocial inhibition. The concept of behavioral inhibition appears to be generalized fear of novelty, both social and nonsocial.

During the preschool years, shy children continue to be silent, rigid in posture, and uneasy when exposed to social novelty. In a previously mentioned study, when shy children were allowed to play with an unfamiliar child, they kept their distance and played only in parallel, not interactively (Asendorpf & Meier, 1993). When in a group of children, they hung back and remained isolated.

Elementary School

Some shy children are so afraid of social novelty that they balk when it is time to attend kindergarten. With parental pressure and some coaxing, they do start school, but on the 1st day, they encounter three kinds of novelty: the building, the teachers, and the students. This triple dose of novelty might make any child wary, but it is truly frightening for shy children. As the months pass, the strangeness gives way to familiarity and shy behavior wanes, but for some children, it does not disappear.

A longitudinal study identified withdrawn (shy) children at age 5 years and followed them for 6 years (Rubin, 1993). At age 7, they had negative perceptions, their peers saw them as shy and afraid, and their parents reported that they were withdrawn. At 11 years, the shy children reported being lonelier and more depressed than did their peers and said that their peers disliked them.

When at home and asked to meet an unfamiliar adult, shy children turn away when the stranger looks at them. This tendency may continue throughout development, especially for males. Beginning at 8 to 10 years, shy children were followed for up to 30 years (Caspi, Elder, & Bem, 1988). Shy girls had few problems in adjusting to the adult world, but when shy boys reached adulthood, they were late in marrying, having children, and moving into stable career paths. A subsequent longitudinal study in Sweden reinforced these findings: "In this sample, too, shy boys were slower to marry and start families but shy girls were not" (Kerr, 2000, p. 65). Beyond shyness, boys and men seem slower to mature socially and have more difficulty in one-on-one situations with unfamiliar girls or women. In marriage, shyness correlates strongly with marital dissatisfaction for both sexes (Baker & McNulty, 2010), suggesting that shyness poses a problem even in familiar social situations.

Adolescence

Starting high school may be a repeat of starting elementary school, but for shy adolescents, the triple novelty of a new school (often distant from home), new classmates, and new teachers poses an especially difficult challenge. All this occurs in the midst of the rapid bodily changes as childhood yields to maturity while the adolescent psychologically is partly child and partly adult. Adolescents have more freedom of choice both personally and socially but may not know how to navigate these uncharted waters.

At this age, individuals are expected to know how to pay attention without excessive staring, how to respond appropriately to keep the conversation going, how to ask about getting together again, how to politely refuse a request, and how to respond to their request being turned down. Shy adolescents are less likely to have acquired these skills because they have avoided contact with unfamiliar people. Alternatively, they may possess the skills but are too socially anxious to perform them. Either way, they know when they have botched a social encounter, which reinforces their negative self-cognitions.

The need for adequate social performance wanes as strangers turn into acquaintances, who turn into friends. Girls hang out with each other, as do boys. The problem for shy adolescents is that they are likely to be excluded from such groups (Gazelle & Rudolph, 2004).

Social novelty returns again for new college students who are away from home and who therefore are often lonely. This problem is acute for shy students, who are considerably more lonely than unshy students not only at the start of college but even 18 months later, when the novelty should have worn off (Asendorpf, 2000).

Dating is an especially daunting problem. It starts with the possibility of rejection. If there is acceptance, how to behave on the first date? Among friends, there is always implicit evaluation of peers' behavior and personality, but on dates, it is explicit. Dating the opposite sex is typically novel, but there is also an elephant in the room. It is sex: how to initiate, how to respond, how far to go, and how to deal with rejection. These issues pose difficulties for any adolescent, but for a shy one, they are excruciating. One solution, now becoming more common, is for groups of mixed sex to go out together to a mall, movie, or party. All these problems are minimized, and the most relieved adolescents are the shy ones. However, they must still acquire the requisite knowledge for one-on-one contact with the opposite sex, and as we saw earlier, this is more difficult for males.

Perspective

There is a consensus that shyness starts as infants' fear of strangers, so it is only a small step to suggest an evolutionary basis for this fear, as reflected in the following facts summarized by D. M. Buss (2008, p. 95): It occurs in a variety of cultures; in both primates and humans, infants are more likely to be killed by strangers; and male strangers are more dangerous to infants. The adaptive aspect of the last fact is that men may not want to waste their resources on other's children, who might compete for resources with men's own offspring.

Certain brain mechanisms are involved in shyness on the assumption that it is the same as behavioral inhibition. The facts suggest that the two are different, as I discussed earlier, and what follows seems better applied to fear. Kagan (2000) reported on earlier work with colleagues in which they presented 4-month-olds with a range of novel stimuli: "About 20% of infants show a combination of vigorous motor activity and crying to these stimuli because, we believe, they have low thresholds of excitability in the amygdala and its projections. These infants are called highly reactive" (Kagan, 2000, p. 24). This highly reactive group of infants tended to be more fearful at 21 to 24 months, were more socially subdued at 4.5 years of age, and displayed more social and nonsocial fear at 7.5 years of age. There was confirmation of a sort in a longitudinal study by Schmidt and Fox (1998). Infants who were highly reactive to novel stimuli at 4 months were reported by their mothers as being shy at age 4 years.

There is more to shyness than stranger anxiety and temperament—recall the negative cognitions of shy people discussed earlier in this chapter. Acknowledging this complexity, Asendorpf (2000) suggested two kinds of shyness:

> *Temperamentally shy* people have a low threshold or a steeper response gradient for behavioral inhibition for physiological reasons and therefore become more easily or more intensely shy in both unfamiliar and socially evaluative situations. *Experientially shy* people have often experienced social neglect or rejection in the past and therefore have higher expectations of being ignored or rejected by others. (Asendorpf, 2000, p. 104)

There is a *self-presentation* theory that assumes people become shy

> when they are motivated to make desired impressions on other people but doubt that they will successfully make those impressions. . . . Thus, self-presentation theory's answer to the question, "What are shy people afraid of?" is that they are afraid of making undesired impressions because doing so leads to unpleasant outcomes. The theory's answer to the second question, "Why are shy people so inhibited?" is that quiet, inhibited behavior

is a reasonable response to situations in which one is afraid of making an undesired impression. (M. R. Leary & Buckley, 2000, p. 139)

This approach assumes that in all social situations, we seek acceptance and avoid rejection, and they are the only motives for being with others. It ignores the intrinsic social reward of responsiveness, as well as cooperation and protective help from others. Yet why are we shy with strangers when we are likely never to see them again and so need not be concerned about acceptance and rejection? Self-presentation does not account for shyness in infants or the young of other social mammals, none of whom are involved with making desired impressions. Its best sphere of application is another kind of shyness, self-conscious shyness, which is discussed in Chapter 7.

Finally, this chapter has dealt only with children in Western cultures, which value modesty and social caution less than Asian cultures, so shy behavior is likely to be more common in Asian cultures. Accordingly, even Chinese children born in Canada are more shy in school than native Canadian children (Chen & Tse, 2008). A review of research comparing Canadian and Chinese children concluded that "shyness was associated with positive peer relationships, school competence, and psychological well-being in China" (Chen, 2010, p. 222). As for the broader disposition of behavioral inhibition, inhibited Chinese 2-year-olds were found at age 7 years to be more cooperative, better liked, and generally better adjusted (Chen, Chen, Li, & Wang, 2009). These facts are a reminder that whatever the biological default produced by our genes, we are cultural animals.

4

TEMPERAMENT II: SOCIABILITY AND IMPULSIVENESS

We are primates and as such are a highly social species. Our closest relatives are chimpanzees, about whom a pioneer observer of chimpanzees wrote,

> I have never met a naturally and persistently unsociable chimpanzee. Even in its relation with humans, once timidity and natural caution have been replaced with confidence and trust, sociability and friendliness of a young ape are very impressive. Evidently they spring from a hunger or need for social stimulation which is comparable in importance with nutritional, reproductive, and like organic urges. (Yerkes, 1943, p. 42)

In this highly social species, as in our species, there are individual differences in this motive, the trait of sociability.

SOCIABILITY

Social Rewards

Why do we want to be with each other? One set of answers is obvious. Cooperation allows us to better defend the group, obtain food, care for the young, and build shelter. These activities may also be achieved without others, sometimes abetted by tools and machines, but they clearly are improved by cooperation with others. However, being with others helps us to achieve the goals that do not necessarily require interaction, and therefore these social rewards are extrinsic to social interaction.

The other set of rewards are *intrinsic social* in the sense that the social activity is itself reinforcing. The first is the *presence of others*. It may appear strange to label the presence of others as a social reward when it is a necessary condition for social behavior and therefore part of its definition. However, humans and other social animals seek it, are reinforced by it, and find its absence aversive, as parents who use time-out as punishment for their young children are well aware.

Normal members of our species do not voluntarily become hermits, shut off from all contact with others. Instead, we prefer to be with others, especially when we are anxious. For example, in his classical experiment on affiliation, Schachter's (1959) subjects were told that they would receive a painful shock and were then given a choice of waiting alone or with others. These fearful subjects preferred to wait with others. In everyday life, fear undoubtedly plays a similar role. Most children are afraid to be left alone, and many adults, especially anxious adults, feel the same way.

The presence of others may be regarded as a dimension. The lower end, complete absence of others for an extended period, is unpleasant for most people. The isolation cell is regarded as the worst punishment for prisoners short of torture. The opposite pole of the dimension is anchored by an excess of people. No one likes to be jammed up against others on a bus or elevator. Excessive crowding causes invasions of personal space, that envelope of space necessary to maintain an adequate distance from strangers or acquaintances (E. T. Hall, 1966), but even when there is no crowding, the mere presence of others may be aversive when privacy is paramount.

The second intrinsic social reward is *sharing an activity*: eating, working in an office, attending a movie, singing in a group, or just watching a lovely sunset. This reward involves no back-and-forth interaction, just people engaging in an activity in parallel. Somehow, just the fact that someone else is engaging in the same activity makes it more pleasant even when there is no conversation or other social interaction. Most children would rather play in a nursery filled with children than alone at home. Many people like to watch sports on television in a group, and most religious people would rather pray together than do it alone. City folk like to stroll among crowds, joggers like to run together, and museum-goers like to browse in the company of others. Those who eat together consume more food (Herman, Roth, & Polivy, 2003), those who work together produce more work (Bond & Titus, 1983; Zajonc, 1965), and audience members laugh louder at humor than a solitary person.

However, sharing activities is no longer rewarding when there are too many people. In a packed movie theater, people may talk during the film, to the annoyance of others. When a cafeteria table is loaded with people, there may not be enough room to eat. If there are too many children in a playground, there will be a long wait to use the swings or slides. The intrusive sharing of activities is aversive.

Sharing an activity is not enough in most social situations because we also need attention. Being ignored causes hurt, anger, or both. This is common knowledge, but there is laboratory confirmation. Fenigstein (1979) had subjects wait for an experiment, during which time they were ignored by other "subjects," actually experimental accomplices, who talked to each other even though they were supposedly strangers. The shunned subjects were made uncomfortable and felt rejected by the strangers. A modicum of attention is the norm, and its absence implies that something is wrong with the person being shunned. Shunning as a tactic belongs under the heading of *relational aggression* (Crick, 1995; Crick, Ostrov, & Werner, 2006)

Of course there is a negative side to attention. People do not enjoy being stared at, the implication being that something is wrong with their appearance or behavior. Being conspicuous may also cause self-conscious shyness (Schmidt & Buss, 2010).

The last intrinsic social reward is *responsiveness*, in which what one person says influences what the listener will say. Responsiveness cannot occur, of course, unless the activity is shared and each attends to the other. The interplay involved in responsiveness is stimulating for the same reason that practicing tennis with another player is more stimulating than practicing against a backboard. In a conversation, if one person knew exactly what the other person would say in reply, it would be too dull to be continued, a problem for some long-married couples.

Like other primates, we seek novelty in social behavior. Mason (1970) raised monkey infants without a real mother, instead substituting robot mothers that were either immovable or allowed to swing free. When the monkeys touched or backed into the free-swinging robot, it rebounded, and this minimal responsiveness was enough for it to be preferred over the immovable robot mother.

These four intrinsically social rewards may be aligned on a dimension of increasing social stimulation. Mere presence of others represents a minimum of social stimulation. Doing things in parallel is more stimulating. Receiving attention appears to heighten arousal, but there is even greater stimulation in the back-and-forth interaction that occurs when people are responsive or when they initiate. Thus, each successive reward in this sequence intensifies social stimulation, an issue related to the trait of sociability. Although these social rewards are universal, those high in sociability strongly prefer the more stimulating social rewards.

Sociability and Shyness

Is shyness nothing more than low sociability? Once, no one asked this question, probably because the concept of introversion dominated our thinking. Introverts tend to be reticent with strangers and casual acquaintances, probably for two reasons: They prefer their own company to that of others (low sociability), and at least some of them are tense and inhibited when with others (shyness). The link between shyness and (low) sociability was assumed without question so that, for example, on the sociability scale of the EASI (Emotionality, Activity, Sociability, and Impulsivity) Temperament Survey (A. H. Buss & Plomin, 1975), we included an item, "I tend to be shy."

However, several years later I questioned whether shyness was equivalent to low sociability, which meant devising separate measures of them. Items were written separately for inhibition, tension, and awkwardness when with people (shyness) and the motivation to be with people (sociability; Cheek & Buss, 1981). The correlation between the two scales was −.30, so it is clear that although shyness and (low) sociability are related, they are distinguishable.

Other researchers constructed a questionnaire consisting solely of items tapping low sociability, examples being "It's not important to me that I spend a lot of time with other people" and "I usually prefer to do things alone" (N. Eisenberg, Fabes, & Murphy, 1995). This low sociability scale correlated .13 with shyness. There were other self-report questionnaires and laboratory procedures, yielding the findings that "reported shyness was associated with high physiological reactivity, negative emotional intensity, dispositional negative affect, and personal distress, whereas sociability was not" (N. Eisenberg et al., 1995, p. 513).

Schmidt and Fox (1994) reported that frontal brain wave asymmetry was related to sociability (less power in the left hemisphere than the right for those high in sociability), but no relationship was found between such asymmetry and shyness. Shy, sociable subjects had a higher heart rate and left frontal electroencephalogram than shy, unsociable subjects: "These sets of findings taken together suggest that different types of shyness are distinguishable on a behavioral, cortical, and autonomic level" (Schmidt & Tasker, 2000, p. 37).

This and more recent evidence deriving from varying methods of study, reviewed in Schmidt and Buss (2010), demonstrate the importance of keeping the two traits separate. Sociability refers to the motive, strong or weak, of wanting to be with others, whereas shyness refers to inhibited behavior when with others as well as feelings of tension and discomfort.

The distinction is underscored by the concept of *social withdrawal* (Rubin & Asendorpf, 1993). One kind of withdrawn child engages in solitary play and would just as soon be with toys or books as with other children (unsociable). The second kind wants to play with others (sociable) but is reluctant to do so (shy).

We are now in a position to understand why shyness and sociability are (negatively) correlated. Unsociable people, by definition, have a relatively weak tendency to associate with others. They are in fewer social situations and therefore are less likely to habituate to novel situations, which are known to be a cause of shyness. Furthermore, those low in sociability, having less contact with others, are less likely to acquire the social skills that might make them feel confident with others.

The direction of causality, however, might go from shyness to low sociability. The intrinsic social rewards are not as powerful for shy people, and they report being uncomfortable when with others, especially strangers and casual acquaintances. Such discomfort surely weakens their motivation to be with others. Thus, social interaction is both less rewarding and more punishing for shy people, causing their sociability to wane.

Given the correlation between sociability and shyness—in the negative .30s—it is not surprising that there are people who are both sociable and shy, as well as people who are both unsociable and unshy (Cheek & Buss, 1981; Schmidt & Buss, 2010). Sociable-shy people want to be with others but hold back in the presence of strangers. Unsociable, unshy people are not strongly motivated to be with others but have no trouble dealing with strangers.

Differentiation of Sociability

Sociability involves the motive to be with others and the tendency to be responsive to them. Thus, the trait differentiates into *gregariousness* and *warmth*. Most sociable people show pleasure when with others (warmth) by being accessible, open, genial, welcoming, receptive, and even convivial. They are attentive and responsive, for example, more likely to turn their head toward others and gesture more in conversation (Gifford, 1991).

Gregarious people need to be with others and suffer from loneliness when forced into solitude. They tend to join groups, like to go out with others, and prefer to study with others. This social motive may be satisfied with two kinds of interactions. One kind involves just one other person or just a few people, who self-disclose and welcome disclosure from others. The alternative is a few people or a group who are involved in a common pursuit, either work or play. These alternatives represent differentiation into *interpersonal behavior*—specifically, conversing and sometimes exchanging confidences—versus *sharing an activity*, such as working together and playing games.

These differentiations occur only at the high end of the sociability dimension. Sociable people may be gregarious or warm. Those low in sociability tend to be more solitary and are more reserved when with others. Gregarious people tend to engage in close interpersonal behavior or share activities with others.

In brief, sociability may differentiate in two ways, the first of which is motive (gregariousness) versus the response (warmth). The second, interpersonal versus shared activities, involves a sex difference. In reviewing research and discussing their own findings, two researchers wrote that men's friendships "may be characterized by shared activity and . . . lower scores on items tapping mutual concern, emotional attachment, verbal expressions of affection, shared personal information, confiding and understanding the other" (Parker & deVries, 1993, p. 623). If men's friendships are less interpersonally close, they are likely to be more tolerant of each other, a hypothesis bolstered by a study of college roommates (Benenson et al., 2009).

To some extent, this sex difference may be part of our primate heritage. Consider male and female roles in primates:

> In general, females occupy themselves with interpersonal matters involving face-to-face encounters and focusing on subjects that have to do with the bearing, nurturing, and training of the young. . . . By contrast, males involve themselves with groups and activities that extend to the whole community. (Tiger & Fox, 1971, p. 104)

No one will be surprised at evidence that in our species women are more nurturant than men (Feingold, 1994).

Aside from sex differences, most sociable children prefer the group play of a playground to sitting alone and watching television or reading a book. Sociable adults gravitate toward professions that involve groups of people, such as a teacher, a coach, or an interviewer. Those high in sociability like team sports (baseball or soccer), and they are especially motivated to seek out games involving responsiveness (tennis or chess). They are likely to join clubs or political parties and tend to be active in them.

Those who are low in sociability are more likely to choose solitary professions (astronomer or mathematician). Having only a weak need to be with others, they are likely to choose as avocations such as long-distance running, solitary fishing, or hunting. Indoors, they might do crossword puzzles, play solitaire, or choose to reflect and introspect.

Gormly (1983) had fraternity members rate each member for sociability. These subjects were then asked whether they preferred to watch a socially interactive videotape or a less interactive videotape. The trait of sociability correlated .53 with choosing to watch the more interactive tape.

Those low in sociability set the tone of conversation by talking less, using fewer gestures, and, in general, displaying less animation in their conversations. Less responsive to others, their conversations are subdued and may lag or peter out. Sociable people tend to be responsive, reinforcing the liveliness of others, and the participants seem to enjoy the interaction. In the Cheek and Buss (1981) study mentioned earlier, there were several pairs of unfamiliar women who were both sociable and unshy. They immediately started lively conversions, and in one instance, a woman reached over to the other's necklace to remark on its beauty. In the pairs that were unsociable and shy, both were reluctant to initiate conversation, which was desultory.

In their need to be with others, those high in sociability tend to modify the environment—for example, overcoming the temporary unavailability of others through advances in technology, especially cell phones, smart phones, and Facebook. The Internet is especially kind to shy sociable people who need contact with others but are reticent in face-to-face interactions with strangers.

Unsociable people do not ordinarily need to modify the environment. If they are already alone, that satisfies them because they prefer solitude (Coplan & Weeks, 2010). Confronted with too many people or too much interaction, they just leave. They will of course use the Internet for information but not to reach out to others.

Development

Infancy

> When a baby is born, he cannot tell one person from another and indeed, can hardly tell a person from a thing. Yet by his first birthday he is likely to be a connoisseur of people. (Bowlby, 1967)

Newborn infants are curious about all kinds of stimuli, including human and nonhuman stimuli. It takes only a few weeks for infants to reveal their highly social nature by preferring humans to things. Beginning with the 2nd month of life, infants increasingly spend more time looking at humans, seek them more often, appear more satisfied when they are present, and cry more when they leave. Not coincidentally, social smiling starts at about the same time. During the 1st half-year of life, infants smile not only at their parents but other humans as well. Infants also like a preverbal analogue of conversation in that they are delighted to give an adult a toy, which is given back, and the sequence starts over again.

By then, individual differences in sociability become especially apparent. Sociable infants do not like to be left alone, smile more often, tend to cuddle more, and respond with more pleasure to being held and stroked even when they are able to walk. Unsociable children do not cuddle or smile as much, do not mind being left alone as much, and are not responsive to babysitters. These differences in sociability tend to be stable (Clarke-Stewart, Umeh, Snow, &

Peterson, 1980). Watch infants sitting in their mother's carts in a supermarket, and the sociable ones respond to a stranger's smile with their own smile. The unsociable infants remain solemn, not because they are insecure or shy—they continue to look at the stranger and do not try to withdraw—but because they are socially less responsive.

Preschool

At this age, there is increasing contact with peers in preschool and outside the home generally. Although shyness plays a role, sociability helps determine the range of friendships and the amount of time spent playing with other children. Recall that we value others for sharing activities and being attentive and responsive, so when these social rewards are offered to sociable children who especially value them, they are happy to respond in kind, setting up a positive cycle. Unsociable children value these rewards less and therefore are unlikely to respond in kind, setting up a negative cycle.

However, two kinds of children play alone: *solitary* children, who build blocks, draw, and generally play constructively but alone, versus *reticent* children, who remain on the fringe of play groups as onlookers (Rubin, 1982). Reticent children are more fearful, suggesting that they are shy, whereas solitary children are just low in sociability (Henderson, Marshal, Fox, & Rubin, 2004).

Elementary School

Although solitary children in play tend to talk less to other students, teachers rate them as no less socially competent than more sociable children (Harrist, Zaia, Bates, Dodge, & Pettit, 1997; Rubin, 1982), but there are qualitative differences. Children who were classified as high or low in the sociability were observed during and after school (Asendorpf & Meier, 1993). Compared with unsociable children, sociable children spent more time with friends but less time with siblings, and they talked less during school but talked more after school and during free time, leading to the conclusion that "Unsociable children may satisfy their social needs through a few, easily available persons such as siblings. Sociable children seek out for more interaction partners and often find them outside the home (Asendorpf & Meier, 1993, p. 1081).

Truly unsociable children tend to be loners. There has been concern in the mental health community about socially isolated children. It is true that psychologically disturbed children tend toward social isolation, but so do normal children who merely represent the low end of the distribution of the trait of sociability.

A gender difference in sociability becomes evident late in this era. Girls want a best friend to share feelings and secrets, and boys want a best friend who is a reliable playmate. Even when girls get together, there is closer interaction as they try on clothes, talk about their family, or gossip about other girls. When boys get together, they are more likely to hang out together or be part of an athletic or social group.

Adolescence

During childhood, children are expected to garner information about social behavior. They gradually learn distinctions involving status and deference, how to behave with the opposite sex, and, generally, the unspoken rules that govern social behavior (Argyle, 1969; Tuckerman & Dunnan, 1995). By adolescence, they should have acquired complementary social skills: how to make friends, put someone at ease, make small talk, and deal with rebuff. Sociable children, by definition, have been strongly motivated to engage in social behavior. Other things being equal, by adolescence they are more likely to have acquired the requisite social information and skills. Unsociable adolescents, by definition, have been less motivated to seek out others, and they spend less time with others, so they are less likely to possess these social skills. Like shy adolescents, they tend to have more difficulty in opposite-sex interactions.

There is still a sex difference in how sociability is expressed. Adolescents were asked to describe their friendships (Blyth & Foster-Clarke, 1987). Girls focused mainly on personal closeness and how they supported each other. Boys described their friendships in terms of shared activities and cooperation in these activities. These differences in the degree of sociability and how it is expressed are likely to continue into adulthood. They would be reflected in the occupational and recreational choices mentioned earlier.

Perspective

As long as there have been questionnaires, going back to the early twentieth century, sociability has been studied as an aspect of personality. Personality psychologists have written about the prominent role of sociability in extraversion, and they have noted the positive correlation of sociability with warmth and its negative correlation with shyness. Their research seems to have ended with two kinds of people who constitute the majority: those who are sociable, warm, and unshy, and those who are unsociable, cold (or cool), and shy.

However, as was documented earlier, there are people who are both sociable and shy. They desperately want to mix with others and are lonely when they cannot, but they clam up and retreat when with others. It has been suggested that this conflict might account for the fact that shy–sociable subjects have more mixed handedness (less cerebral asymmetry) than other combinations of sociability and shyness (Spere, Schmidt, Rinolo, & Fox, 2005). Their opposites, unshy–sociable people, can take or leave others but when with people, they are warm and friendly.

The zeitgeist about sociability as a trait has also prevented most personality psychologists to ask why we want to associate with others beyond the obvious rewards for doing so, such as cooperation and the potential for dominance. I delved into the issue and came up with the aforementioned presence of others, sharing an activity, attention, and responsiveness. These rewards are available from acquaintances or even strangers, but there is another class of social rewards available only from friends, lovers, or family. These are *praise, sympathy,* and *affection–love,* which deepen and cement relationships. There is also *respect,* which is seen as reflecting "Not one but two distinct dimensions of social evaluation: status (perceiving the group judges oneself to be a valued or worthy member) and liking" (Huo, Binning, & Molina, 2010, p. 203). Unsociable people want these social rewards as much as sociable people, and shy people want them just as much as unshy people, but they are unsure of ever receiving them.

IMPULSIVENESS

There may be no better description of this trait than this one from more than 7 decades ago:

> The tendency to respond quickly and without reflection. It is a rather coarse variable which includes: (1) short reaction time to social press, (2) quick intuitive behavior, (3) emotional drivenness, (4) lack of forethought. . . . Deliberation is easier to observe than Impulsion. It is marked by: (1) long reaction time to social press, (2) inhibition of initial impulses, (3) hesitation, caution, and reflection before action, (4) a long period of planning and organizing before beginning a piece of work. (H. A. Murray, 1938, pp. 205–206)

Impulsive people tend to act quickly, which raises the question of whether it is the same as the tempo component of activity. They are not the same. The focus in impulsiveness is on the time it takes to *start* a response, such as deciding to buy an item seen in a shop window. The focus in tempo is on the *pace* of behavior once it is set in motion, such as striding quickly into the shop. There are people who are deliberate—the opposite end of the impulsiveness dimension—but once they decide to act may do so in a hurry (fast tempo). When the two traits are assessed by self-reports, they turn out to be uncorrelated (A. H. Buss & Plomin, 1975).

Differentiation

In discussing the differentiates of impulsiveness, I refer to its opposite pole of the dimension *deliberateness,* calling them control, discipline, and reflection. The impulsive pole refers to the lack of these three.

The first is *control*, but what is being controlled? We socialize our children to control emotions and motives. Temper tantrums must be inhibited, hunger must await the time to eat, and temptations must be resisted. Both emotions and motives represent internal pressure to act, whereas temptations represent an external pull on behavior. Impulsive people have difficulty in resisting these pressures, and people at the opposite pole of the dimension (deliberates) exercise control.

The second differentiate is *discipline*. Does the person stay with the task until completion, however long it takes? Are there tenacity, perseverance, and a dogged, single-minded pursuit of the goal? If the answer is yes, such people represent the deliberate end of the dimension.

At the opposite extreme are those who start a new pursuit before a previous one is finished. Their motivation appears to be transient and mercurial, and their erratic behavior often seems capricious and whimsical. They tend to be the first to adopt the latest fad and the first to abandon it.

Disciplined people maintain their focus, but impulsive people tend to be distractible. Their attention strays and is easily diverted by extraneous stimuli. Their low-impulsive opposites concentrate so hard, sometimes for hours, that they are unaware of their surroundings.

The remaining aspect of discipline is *impatience*. Young children have trouble enduring long waits, but so do impulsive adults. They are restless, and the wait time presses down on them. They also have trouble delaying gratification, opting for the immediate reward when delay would reap a larger one. In brief, lack of discipline has these aspects: failure to complete tasks, distractibility, and impatience.

The third differentiate, *reflection*, refers in part to one's ability to plan. Many situations in life require preparation, but impulsive people do not prepare adequately. If they are students, they register late and leave required courses for their last semester. When taking a trip, they just get in the car without a map or global positioning device and start driving. They have little idea of what they will be doing next year, next month, or even next week.

At the other extreme are those whose detailed itinerary is mapped out weeks or months before the start of a trip. They register early for classes, buy tickets in advance for concerts, and schedule vacations months before they begin. Their calendar is filled in carefully, and they know precisely what they will be doing next month or next vacation.

Another aspect is making decisions. Impulsive people act on the spur of the moment and cannot spend time weighing the costs and benefits of deciding on a course of action. The appropriate proverb for them is "Act in haste, repent at leisure." Consider the way such a person reacts to a beguiling advertisement for a vacation in the Caribbean: He jumps at the chance. His opposite, a deliberate person, considers the cost, the time away from the job, and the reliability of the travel company. There may be too much of a good thing, however, as when excessive rumination leads to indecisiveness.

The concept underlying these three differentiates is *inhibition:* of emotions or motives, of distractions and boredom, and of rash impulses. Lack of inhibition defines one end of the trait dimension of impulsiveness, and firm inhibition defines the other end.

Two personality traits are relevant to differentiation. Emotionality and activity tilt toward the need for control. Emotionality and activity are metaphorical engines, respectively, driving the need to express emotion and the need to expend energy. These engines require inhibitory control—the metaphorical brakes.

Person and Environment

Impulsiveness is the prime target of socialization. We train children to damp down emotional outbursts, practice patience, and delay gratification. Strict and enduring the efforts by parents, teachers, and other socializing agents push children toward the deliberate pole of the impulsiveness dimensions. Weak and lenient socialization practices allow children to continue the childish tendency to act on impulse, and here social class is relevant. Middle-class parents are more likely than lower class parents to teach their child control, persistence, and planning.

The personality trait of impulsiveness also determines how people respond to the societal demands for inhibition. Impulsive people have trouble resisting temptation—for example, buying expensive things they cannot afford—whereas those low in impulsiveness find it easier to avoid such tendencies. Those who are low in this trait (the deliberate end) have an easier time learning the lessons of socialization because they are primed in the direction of inhibition. Impulsive people, however, tend to lack inhibition and so have a steeper road to climb. Just because socialization agents are sending messages does not mean that that impulsive children are receiving them.

Impulsive people tend to choose environments that allow at least some uninhibited behavior. They prefer informal contexts in which status is of no consequence and there are few rules to govern social behavior. The vocations they seek are marked by some chaos and spur of the moment decisions, so they are likely to choose a job that requires little planning, brief encounters with others, and work that involves a quick turnover of customers.

People at the deliberate end of the impulsivity dimension tend to find quieter jobs that involve routine, demand planning and patience, and require caution. Low-impulsive people prefer more formal social contexts in which they know what to wear and how to behave. They like to invite others for dinners that are planned well in advance. If they are extreme in these tendencies, their lives lack the spontaneity that is the hallmark of those high in impulsiveness.

Development

Infancy

Newborn infants are essentially reflexive organisms with an unusually immature nervous system, a product of our evolutionary history. We are large-brained, but bipedal locomotion has narrowed the size of women's birth canals so that human infants are born with what is essentially a fetal brain. The higher brain centers crucial to inhibition are the least developed, but during the 1st year of life, infants start to gain control over motor patterns and response to stimuli (Scheibel & Scheibel, 1964). It is too early for individual differences in inhibitory control to appear, and there is little pressure for parents to inhibit their infants' behavior.

During the 2nd year of life, parents start to rein in temper outbursts and insist on regular bedtimes. Infants low in impulsiveness tend to go along with these demands, but the high-impulsive infants cannot control their tantrums and are more likely to resist going to sleep.

Preschool

Parents are now less tolerant to failures to inhibit emotions and motives. Three-year-old children still tend to grab toys from others, break things, get into the cookie jar, throw occasional temper tantrums, and become extremely impatient when asked to wait. During the 4th and 5th years, most children start to resist temptation. In a laboratory paradigm called *delay of gratification*, children can choose an immediate tempting reward or wait for a better reward to be given later (Mischel & Metzner, 1962). In this paradigm, children could not resist temptation until roughly age 4 years (Mischel, 1974). This kind of task was adopted later as one of those that define *effortful control*, a concept to be discussed in the Perspective section. For example, preschool children were asked to delay eating an M&M candy sitting in front of them or not to peek at a wrapped present (Kochanska, Murray, Jacques, Koening, & Vandegeest, 1996).

Of course there are great individual differences the development of inhibitory control. At one extreme are precocious children who seem like little adults with respect to impulsiveness, and at the other extreme are children who are no less impulsive than infants. Lack of control in 3- to 5-year-olds predicted violent crimes at age 18 (Henry, Caspi, Moffitt, & Silva, 1996). Preschool lack of control also predicted nonviolent crime at 18 when one parent was missing, so parents do have an impact. Delinquent behavior was again predicted by impulsiveness in kindergarten boys (Tremblay, Pihl, Vitaro, & Dobkin, 1994).

The impact of parents is presumably through parental practices, which assume greater importance for impulsive children. Parents who insist on strict discipline have continued tussles with their impulsive children, who resist the insistence on inhibition, but strict discipline is usually effective in damping down impulsiveness. Leniency avoids friction but often only at the expense of having a spoiled, immature child.

Kohlberg's (1981) stages of moral development are relevant to this era. The first stage, *premoral*, involves obedience to authority, avoiding trouble, and being good because it is rewarded. Obeying rules, however, is difficult for impulsive children.

Elementary School

This era offers challenges to children beyond controlling emotions and motives. Now they are expected to resist distractions, persist in completing even boring tasks, and tolerate waiting. These challenges are especially salient during school hours, and in this era, children are expected to sit at their desks, focus on the learning task at hand, and resist the urge to play during class hours.

As cognitive development proceeds, children become more aware of the consequences of their actions and can anticipate later rewards and punishments (Mischel, 1974). This future orientation helps to delay gratification, inhibit immediate expression of anger, and maintain persistence, all of which are typical of children low in impulsiveness. The advanced cognitions, however, have less impact on highly impulsive children who remain slow to develop the required inhibition of behavior. Parental strictness continues to play a role, and now teachers' strictness becomes important.

At this point, Kohlberg's (1969) second stage of morality comes into play. Children become more sensitive to others' reactions, especially parents and teachers. They know which behavior is expected of them and may experience shame if they disappoint others. As might be expected, impulsive children have trouble learning these implicit rules.

Adolescence

Modern technology has entered the picture, as adolescents tweet each other, which requires brevity and a short attention span. They engage in *multitasking* such that an adolescent may be rapidly switching attention back and forth from a cell phone, a computer, and a television set. It will be interesting to see the enduring impact of these activities on attention span and, more generally, the differentiate of discipline.

As for resisting taboo motives, Kohlberg's (1969) third stage, essentially adult morality, is relevant because it involves internalization of moral rules involving obligations, sharing, and not harming others—in other words, conscience. Impulsive adolescents have learned these rules, but their lack of inhibition sometimes overwhelms their cognitions.

Beyond morality, there are everyday temptations in the form of unaffordable credit cards and an "I must have it now" mentality: "I can't be the only one without an iPod, cell phone, or Facebook account." Then there are the challenges of getting schoolwork done, planning ahead for the postschool world, and delaying immediate gratification in the service of future goals. These challenges are especially difficult for impulsive adolescents. For example, the trait of impulsiveness predicted such acts as theft, vandalism, and physical aggression in adolescents (Luengo, Carill-de-la-Peña, Otero, & Romero, 1994).

Perspective

Impulsiveness as a trait has been part of personality questionnaires since the middle of the 20th century, starting with Guilford and Zimmerman (1956) and the Eysencks (S. B. G. Eysenck & Eysenck, 1963). Barratt (1959, 1983) constructed impulsiveness scales and factor analyzed them, revealing factors that roughly match the three differentiates of impulsiveness: lack of impulse control, little discipline, and the absence of reflection. A subsequent study found essentially the same second-order factors (Patton, Stanford, & Barratt, 1995), and an even later study factor analyzed nine impulsiveness questionnaires and came up with four factors (Whiteside & Lyman, 2001): lack of control over emotions and temptations, inability to remain focused (discipline), lack of deliberation, and sensation seeking. Meanwhile, two differentiates of impulsiveness—self-discipline and deliberation—have appeared as facets of the Big Five superfactor of *conscientiousness* (Costa, McCrae, & Dye, 1991).

In the first temperament book I wrote with Robert Plomin (A. H. Buss & Plomin, 1975), we reviewed the research on the inheritance of impulsivity and found it mixed. It was still mixed almost a decade later (A. H. Buss & Plomin, 1984), so we eliminated it as one of our temperaments with the proviso that later research might cause a revision. It did. A review of subsequent research clearly established the heritability of impulsiveness (Zuckerman, 2005, p. 171).

Research on impulsiveness eventually moved in two directions. One was to link it with sensation seeking because the two traits do overlap (Zuckerman, 2007). The second direction was to embed impulsiveness within the broader concept of effortful control (Derryberry & Rothbart, 1997). Although impulsiveness is part of the concept, *effortful control* is more broadly defined as "the ability to inhibit a dominant response, to perform a subdominant response, to detect errors, and to engage in planning" (Rothbart & Rueda, 2005, p. 169). Given the overlap in constructs, we should not be surprised that boys are both more impulsive and lower in effortful control than girls (Kochanska, Murray, & Harlan, 2000; Li-Grining, 2007) or that effortful control, like impulsiveness, has been linked to the inhibition of such motives as sex and aggression (MacDonald, 2008). Whatever the overlap between effortful control and impulsiveness, however, there is evidence that they are different constructs (N. Eisenberg et al., 2004; Kochanska et al., 2000; Li-Grining, 2007).

THE CONCEPT OF TEMPERAMENT

The history of temperament begins more than 2,000 years ago with the Greek physician Galen, who linked personality types to body substances. The *sanguine* person, having an excess of blood (sanguine means bloody), tends to be lively and upbeat. The *phlegmatic* person, having an excess of phlegm, tends to be slow-moving and controlled. The *melancholic* person, having an excess of black bile (melancholy means black bile), tends to worry and be sad. The *choleric* person, having an excess of bile, tends to be excitable and angry.

The idea that body fluids determine personality was discarded long ago, but the four types of personality persisted into the 20th century. Hans Eysenck (1947) arranged the four types of personality in a circle with two axes: extraverted–introverted and emotionally stable–emotionally unstable. Thus, the sanguine person is extraverted and emotionally stable, the melancholic person is introverted and emotionally unstable, and so on. He moved on to his theory of extraversion, neuroticism, and a third concept, psychoticism.

Stagner (1948) used two dimensions to derive the four personality types: high activity–low activity crossed by approach–withdrawal (withdrawal implies unpleasantness). As modified by Diamond (1957), the classification works this way:

Sanguine: approach and high activity
Phlegmatic: approach and low activity
Melancholic: withdrawal and low activity
Choleric: high activity and withdrawal

Conditioning and the Nervous System

The Russian physiologist Ivan Pavlov (1927) was also influenced by Galen's typology, and his ideas gave rise to modern approaches to temperament. He viewed personality as reflecting three properties of the central nervous system: strength, balance, and excitation–inhibition. These properties were used to account for the four types of temperament:

Sanguine: strong, balanced, excited
Phlegmatic: strong, balanced, inhibited
Melancholic: weak, unbalanced, inhibited
Choleric: strong, unbalanced, excited

Arousal

The Polish psychologist Jan Strelau (1983) used Pavlov's theory as a springboard for his own conception, although he discarded Pavlov's fourfold classification of temperaments. His major concepts are *energetic level* and *temporal characteristics*. Energetic level embodies Pavlov's concepts of strength and balance of the nervous system. It consists of both activity and reactivity. Activity is manifest in the amount and range of activities in which the individual engages, and reactivity also has two facets: threshold of stimulation and intensity of the reaction. Temporal characteristics roughly match Pavlov's mobility of the nervous system. A central concept involves the optimal level of arousal:

> Activity is regarded as the temperament trait that plays the primary regulatory function in providing an optimal level of arousal. Reactivity and, especially, activity maintain arousal at an optimal level by regulating the stimulative value of behavior and situations the individual is confronted with. (Strelau, 1989, p. 41)

Optimal level of arousal will come up again in the next chapter as part of Zuckerman's (1979) theory of sensation seeking.

Self-Regulation

Rothbart's (1989, 2004; Rothbart & Derryberry, 1981) model of temperament, although not derived from Strelau's, is similar in emphasizing *reactivity* and *self-regulation*. Reactivity, which involves arousal, may be positive and induce approach behavior, or it may be negative and induce withdrawal behavior. Low stimulus intensity tends to elicit positive reactivity, and high stimulus intensity tends to induce negative reactivity. Self-regulation refers to approach, involving stimulus seeking and seeking excitement, and withdrawal, which involves avoidance and seeking comfort. This model has led to research on infants, children, and even adults (Derryberry & Rothbart, 1988).

Rothbart (1989) also proposed a tentative model of temperament development during the eras of infancy and preschool and beyond. As an example of her model, what follows are selected temperament components that emerge during infancy:

> Newborn: distress, activity, attention, and approach–withdrawal
> Early infancy: stimulus seeking, avoidance
> Late infancy: inhibition, fear

These components of temperament are clearly different from mine, and one of Rothbart's (1989) chapters on temperament is important in dealing with the complex issue of stability during development. By suggesting which components of temperament emerge during each developmental era, she adds specificity and detail to our understanding of the developmental course of temperaments.

The Pediatric Approach

Modern research on temperament in the United States began with the work of Alexander Thomas, Stella Chess, and their colleagues (1963, 1968), who called their project the New York Longitudinal Study. Thomas and Chess, pediatric psychiatrists, were dissatisfied with the psychoanalytic approach to children's problems that predominated after World War II. They interviewed parents, who described their children's behavior, and an armchair analysis of 22 interviews led them to offer nine categories or dimensions of temperament. The examples start in infancy and continue through childhood:

1. Activity level: wriggles when diaper is changed, walks rapidly
2. Rhythmicity: the regularity of cycles of eating and sleeping
3. Approach–withdrawal: approaches strangers, tries new foods, went to camp happily
4. Adaptability: change in response to novel stimuli or situations
5. Intensity of reaction: gets excited easily
6. Threshold of responsiveness: startles to loud noises, cannot be left with strangers
7. Quality of mood: is upbeat, smiles, and is friendly
8. Distractibility: loses interest in a toy after a few minutes, reacts to extraneous stimuli
9. Attention span and persistence: looks at a book for a long time, works on a puzzle for a long time

Some of the categories overlap, notably the last two, which is not surprising because these nine categories were the result of examining only a small number of protocols of parental interviews about infants' behavior. A practicing pediatrician then constructed parental ratings for each of the nine categories, the Infant Temperament Questionnaire (Carey, 1970), and he later

revised it (Carey & McDevitt, 1978). This codification of the categories offered quantification of parental reports, leading to the widespread use of this pediatric approach to temperament. For example, Kristal (2005) used the nine categories to study infants, toddlers, preschoolers, and school-age children and revealed the interaction of these temperaments and parental ways of dealing with them. A questionnaire extended the use of the nine categories through adolescence (Windle & Lerner, 1986).

A. Thomas, Chess, and Birch (1968) introduced the idea of goodness of fit between child and environment. They offered a dimension of *easy-to-difficult* children based on five of the nine temperament categories. The goodness-of-fit concept, adopted by other researchers of temperaments, appropriately emphasizes person–environment interaction:

> As a consequence of their physical and behavioral individuality people evoke differential reactions in their significant others; these reactions constitute feedback to people and influence their further interactions (and thus enhancing their development). The "goodness of fit concept" allows the valence of the feedback involved in these circular functions to be understood. (Lerner, Nitz, Talwar, & Lerner, 1989, p. 510)

Evolution

Diamond (1957) described four temperaments shared by primates (including our species) and perhaps some social mammals: fearfulness, aggressiveness, affiliativeness, and impulsiveness. He conducted no human research, nor did he offer specific means of testing his hypotheses. In the 1950s, psychologists showed little interest in an evolutionary approach to personality, and Diamond's ideas were at first neglected.

However, I found his ideas fascinating, and eventually Robert Plomin and I built on them to formulate our own theory (A. H. Buss & Plomin, 1975). We kept impulsiveness and broadened his affiliativeness, which he saw as the seeking of attachment, to become our sociability, the preference for being with others. We expanded fear to the broader category of emotionality, and we added activity. We also added the concept of differentiation, which this book develops further, and we retained an evolutionary approach, which is expanded and considerably more explicit here.

Critique

The concept of temperament is built on a set of assumptions, which have been challenged by Rutter (1989): (a) there are innate dispositions that do not appear until long after infancy, (b) the evidence for heritability is based on fallible measures, and (c) there is little stability of personality during development. There is truth in each of these statements, which calls into question the concept of temperaments, and therefore each requires a response.

First, that there are innate dispositions that do not appear later in childhood is not under dispute, but the dispositions I define as temperaments are the inherited ones that first appear during infancy.

Second, measures of temperament are fallible, especially those relying exclusively on parental reports. However, these reports have been supplemented by observations of behavior by trained observers, by laboratory research, and, in some instances, by physiological and neural research. Any particular method of studying personality has its limitations, which is why we theorists look to aggregate across methods.

Third, there is reasonable stability during development for some temperament traits but not for others, which is also true of other of later-developing personality traits. There are also individual differences in the stability of personality traits generally, which is a matter that requires research. However, there is a more general problem for studying the development of any personality trait. It is that the measures used for adolescents are necessarily different from those used for infants. Whether the measures are comparable is not a question easily decided, although for IQ the issue seems to have been decided in favor of stability.

This critique is a reminder to psychologists who study temperament to examine our assumptions, the way we do research, and whether the empirical results support our assumptions. There is another issue, however: How much does each approach add to our understanding of temperament? The ones reviewed in this chapter—arousal, pediatric, and evolutionary—offer three perspectives on temperament, each complementing the others.

Rutter's critique of temperament raises important issues, but he took the sting out of his negative comments with this conclusion: "There is support of the key elements involved in the construct. . . . That is, it is clear that there is behavioural individuality, that there is a significant constitutional component, that there is moderate consistency in individual differences after infancy" (Rutter, 1989, p. 467).

5

LATER DEVELOPING TRAITS: SENSATION SEEKING, AGGRESSION, AND DOMINANCE

Recall that temperaments are traits observed in infancy, even during the first months of life. The traits in this chapter are first observed only in the preschool era, but like temperaments, they have a genetic component.

SENSATION SEEKING

We all need stimulation, but sensation seekers need more than most of us because they get bored easily, and there is evidence that their brains are underaroused (Zuckerman, 2007). They are likely to habituate to their surroundings and even to some of the exciting things they do. Habituation sets up a cycle of seeking excitement, finding it, and needing more intense excitement.

Excitement seekers are the adventurers who want to explore the unknown, regardless of the hazards—indeed for some people, *because* of the hazards. Many excitement seekers love to skate on thin ice or take a leap in the dark, displaying either great courage or reckless disdain for danger. They want the spine-tingling adventure that adds spice to their lives.

Other sensation seekers look around the house, and somehow the still-usable furniture seems stale and out of fashion, so they itch to redecorate. Still others feel they are in a social rut and attempt to develop a new circle of friends. It may be temporary: a vacation at the shore or a trip to New Zealand they have always dreamed of. It may be more permanent: sell the house, move to a distant city, exchange city life for a farm, or move back to the city.

People low in the trait of sensation seeking have little need for excitement; in fact, too much excitement is upsetting. They are comfortable with familiar things and places and seem not to get bored easily. They seek familiarity, regularity, continuity, and stability.

However, even people who are only moderate in their sensation seeking still need novelty or an occasional thrill because the brain needs invigoration. Those high in sensation seeking are especially motivated to obtain excitement, and many sources are available, a fact that opens up the possibility of differentiation of the trait.

Differentiation

Arousing *body sensations* can be obtained through sheer speed (a fast motorcycle), through stimulating drugs ("uppers"), or merely by spinning around until one becomes dizzy. The excitement may arise from *taking risks:* dangerous pursuits such as skydiving, rock climbing with no equipment, high-stakes gambling, or illegal acts or forbidden pleasures that threaten relationships. *Novelty* can be a source of excitement. Sensation seekers regularly need a change of jobs, location, or even close relationships—been there, done that. *Suspense* is a source of excitement—for example, being in a contested athletic event.

All these sources typically involve sensation seekers as participants, but excitement may be obtained vicariously by being a spectator—of a football game, a suspenseful novel, or a horror movie. Vicarious sensation seeking suggests a lower level of the trait because ultimately there is no risk or negative consequences of actions. High sensation seekers tend to be participants, not spectators.

In brief, sensation seeking may differentiate into body sensations, risk taking, novelty, suspense, and vicarious excitement. Notice that some these sources overlap, but distinguishing among them offers a finer grained understanding of the trait.

Tilts

Several personality traits affect sensation seeking. *Active* people, virtually by definition, gravitate toward energetic excitement seeking, and inactive people are likely to seek arousal passively, perhaps through drugs or as spectators. *Sociable* people seek excitement in the presence of others, and unsociable people prefer to do it alone. *Emotional* people, by definition, are easily aroused, although the arousal is unpleasant, so they either do not seek excitement or choose the safe kinds, especially vicarious excitement.

Impulsive people tend to act without forethought, which means that impulsive sensation seekers tilt in the direction of risky behavior. Recall that impulsive people tend to become bored easily, which is also a characteristic of sensation seekers. This overlap poses problem for personality researchers, who reasonably prefer neater, sharper distinctions between traits. However, both impulsives and sensation seekers do become bored easily, a fact that cannot be ignored. This is not a unique case because other personality traits overlap, such as dominance and self-esteem. Dominance enhances self-esteem, and being high in self-esteem makes is easier to attempt to dominate others. The overlap is real, not the result of any particular theory or the way the traits are assessed.

Gender is a strong tilt in the direction of more excitement seeking in males, especially in taking risks, a sex difference that may be part of our evolutionary heritage (D. M. Buss, 2008). As child bearers, women have more to lose than men. In competing for status, men are willing to take risks to obtain the rewards of higher status: better access to women and food.

Person and Environment

High-arousal environments are not forced on people; rather, sensation seekers choose them because they are highly motivated to escape boredom. The choice involves two related issues: the degree of excitement sought and whether it is obtained through body sensations, risk taking, novelty, or suspense.

Sensation seekers also may modify the environment. If they are playing penny-ante poker, they try to raise the stakes. They might convert an ordinary street into a venue for drag racing. On a steep roller-coaster, they take their hands off the safety handles, and when skateboarding, which is safe on a level surface, they do flips.

Development

Preschool

The opportunities for seeking sensations are limited in 2-year-olds. They can spin around until they are dizzy or pedal too fast on tricycles. They can and do explore every nook and cranny they can reach because strong exploratory drive is part of the trait. They are similar to other children in being delighted for a new toy but different in becoming bored with it sooner. They are bored by routine activities and make more demands on their parents for novelty.

Those low in sensation seeking are easier for parents to handle. These preschoolers do not mind routine—indeed, they may take pleasure in it. Because they do not need constant stimulation, they are easier on parents.

Older preschool sensation seekers are willing to put up with being just a little frightened because the arousal is so pleasurable. They prefer the highest, steepest slide and are eager to jump off the diving board into the pool. They like a challenge that involves some peril, such as climbing to the top of a monkey bar in a playground or to a precarious perch at the top of a tree.

For those low in sensation seeking, the down side of becoming scared has no upside because there is no particular urge to arouse the brain. They limit themselves to the lower rungs of the monkey bar and the lower teeter-totters. The sensation seekers suffer from wanderlust and are likely to get lost. Those low in sensation seeking stay close to home and thus are easier on their parents.

Elementary School

Children age 5 years completed a self-report questionnaire on sensation seeking that is worded simply enough for young children (Putnam, 1998). Included are items tapping four of the sources (differentiates) of sensation seeking:

1. Novelty: try a food never before eaten
2. Body sensations: ride a fast-galloping horse
3. Risk: go down a slide head first
4. Vicarious excitement: watch a video of a car exploding

As the years pass, sensation-seeking children may engage in activities such as going to a dangerous part of town, which involves both risk and exploration. They try hazardous tricks on skates or bicycles and will not be stopped by bruises or even broken bones. They want to climb the tallest tree or ride the steepest roller-coaster. Low sensation seekers are content merely to watch their siblings or friends do these things because there are other, low-key sources of enjoyment.

Engaging in forbidden behavior is exciting. Sensation seekers enjoy sneaking around and doing something frowned on by parents and teachers. It may be pilfering inexpensive objects, part of the reward being the spice that they might be caught, a spice that may extend to adventuring into forbidden parts of town.

School-age children are reading, which offers adventures to be shared vicariously through the lives of characters in books and comic books. Most children like ghost stories or viewing horror movies. They want to be scared, which is especially rewarding for sensation seekers.

Adolescence

Most adolescents are bored with at least one subject in high school, and perhaps a majority find high school too constraining. Sensation seekers are so bored that some tend to cut classes and even quit school.

With more freedom, adolescents have the broader opportunities to seek sources of excitement that are available to adults. When they are away from parental supervision, they can indulge in the more intensely arousing activities, including those deemed unacceptable by parents. For older adolescents, these include unusual sexual activity, gambling, flouting authority, going into dangerous neighborhoods, stealing, using illegal drugs, and bouts of drinking. Running away from home now seems to be a more realistic option for them. Alternatively, those bitten by wanderlust might go across the country solo or partake of adventurous sightseeing in distant lands.

Those low in sensation seeking are much easier on their parents. The do not seek risk and are less likely to gamble and engage in illegal activities. When they watch a scary movie, they cover their eyes when the dangerous scenes come on the screen.

Perspective

For a historical perspective on individual differences in sensation seeking, let us start with the concept of excitement seeking, which was promulgated many decades ago under the heading of *activation* (Maddi, 1961). Activation refers to a preferred level of alertness, attentiveness, tension, or subjective excitement. This level might be obtained through physical intensity, meaningfulness, or variation in stimuli. Stimuli might also activate people by deviating from prior stimuli, novelty, or being unexpected. When the level of excitation is too low, the person seeks stimuli of greater impact. When the level of excitation is too high, the person seeks stimuli of lower impact. Presumably, there are individual differences in the preferred level of subjective excitement:

> That the need for variation can be considered an aspect of personality is suggested by the observation that individuals show reliable differences in the intensity and quality of their variation-seeking. Some people are simply more interested in, and disposed toward, the occurrence of change, novelty, and the unexpected than others. (Maddi, 1961, p. 273)

No instrument for measuring these individual differences was developed, so the concept of activation, although still prominent in biopsychology, was not assessed as a personality trait. However, starting with sensory-deprivation research, Marvin Zuckerman (1971, 1979, 2007) independently investigated sensation seeking as a trait. His research on sensation seeking and his theory mark him as the pioneer and still leading scholar on the topic. He and his colleagues developed a questionnaire that assessed individual differences in sensation seeking (Zuckerman, Kolin, Price, & Zoob, 1964), which has been revised several times, finally ending up with its fourth iteration in an attempt to lower the correlations among the subscales (Zuckerman, Eysenck, & Eysenck, 1978). The subscales consist of four factors:

1. *Thrill and adventure seeking* consists of two kinds of items: risk, such as mountain climbing and parachute jumping, and the sensations of speed, such as surfboard riding and skiing down a steep slope.
2. *Experience seeking* consists of items about seeking novelty through trying new foods or hallucinogenic drugs, and exploring a new city.
3. *Disinhibition*, as the term denotes, includes such activities as getting drunk, trying marijuana, going to wild parties, and engaging in illegal acts.
4. *Boredom susceptibility* involves impatience with monotony, predictable events, and boring people.

The experience-seeking and disinhibition factors are slanted toward seriously nonconforming and even deviant behavior (Arnett, 1994). Most of the items refer to activities available only to adults or older adolescents, not to children. In thinking about the development of sensations seeking, I needed to come up with a conception that would apply to children. Once I concentrated on development, it became clear that body sensations and risk taking are distinguishable and that suspense and vicarious excitement are important sources of arousal. Then I could specify the developmental era when each source would become available and how sensation seekers would choose and modify environments.

However, what we know about adult sensation seekers derives from research with the sensation-seeking questionnaire (Zuckerman, 1979). Skydivers, rescue divers, and firemen score higher. High scorers also include men with wider sexual experience, drug users, and volunteers for experiments involving drugs, hypnosis, or transcendental meditation. Sensation seekers also prefer complex and asymmetrical designs and drawings in contrast to simple and symmetrical designs and drawings, which are preferred by those low in sensation seeking.

These personality attributes were only part of Zuckerman's contributions. He investigated the psychobiological aspects of sensation seeking in an initial theory (Zuckerman, 1979) and eventually a revised theory (Zuckerman, 1995, 2007), the latter involving three behavioral systems: "High sensation seeking is a function of strong approach and weak inhibition and arousal systems" (Zuckerman, 2007, p. 27). Notice that it is a distant cousin of Strelau's (1989) temperament theory.

AGGRESSIVENESS

Anger

Recall that the trait of anger is considered to be a component of emotionality, but its discussion was delayed until now because of its close association with aggression. If they are closely associated, how are they different? Anger is one of the emotions, involving physiological arousal, particular facial and body expressions, and cognitions, whereas aggression is interpersonal behavior directed at a victim.

Physiological arousal is part of the ancient innate preparation for flight or fight, in this instance, fighting to rid the person of any threat or, more generally, the source of the anger. This arousal is the same as that in fear (flight): mobilizations of the body's resources for massive action. The arousal typically is a brief, emergency reaction that exhausts the body, which soon must replenish itself. The angry person is often aware of the physiological arousal and the facial and bodily changes during anger (feelings).

The *expressive* aspects of anger are open to observation by others and may even function as a threat: The fists are clenched, the mouth is grim, the teeth may be bared, and the nose is flared. Darwin (1883/1955) suggested that the human expressions of anger are highly similar to those observed in primates and hence are part of our evolutionary heritage. Consistent with this assumption, the human face in anger is essentially the same all over the world (Ekman, 2003).

Beyond these expressions of anger, which were prominent in Ekman's (2003) photographs, there are facial expressions of anger, usually observed in frustrated children: pouting, sullenness, and sulkiness. In brief, anger consists of three components: physiological arousal, awareness of the arousal, and expressions of anger. During the course of development, these components are expected to differentiate such that one component, say, physiological arousal, might be primary in some people and another component, say, expressiveness, might be primary in other people.

Hostility

Hostility is here regarded as the residual left after anger cools down. Anger is part of our evolutionary heritage, an emergency reaction to threat, and emergency reactions cannot endure. When anger ebbs, it often leaves behind the negative cognitions called *hostility*, as reflected in the variations of language used to describe it: *ill will, animosity, resentment, bitterness, jealousy, spitefulness, loathing, malice.* Hostile people harbor resentment or loathing for years.

Anger and hostility obviously overlap, but it is still worthwhile to distinguish between them, as follows:

1. Anger is observed in other animals and in human infants; hostility is seen only in humans and not until the preschool era.
2. Anger is transient; hostility is enduring, as in vendettas.
3. Anger involves intense physiological arousal; hostility involves little or none.

The distinction has implications for health. Although hostility is an important predictor of cardiac mortality (Matthews, Gump, Harris, Haney, & Barefoot, 2004), a meta-analysis revealed that anger is a risk factor for coronary disease (T. W. Smith, Glazer, Ruiz, & Gallo, 2004).

This research used trait measures of anger and hostility, often two scales of The Aggression Questionnaire (A. H. Buss & Perry, 1992) The Anger scale contains such items as "I flare up quickly but get over it quickly." The Hostility scale has such items as " I wonder why sometimes I feel so bitter about things" and "I am suspicious of overly friendly strangers." Another frequently used measure is the State–Trait Anger Inventory (Spielberger, 1988).

Aggressive Behavior

Aggressive behavior is directed toward another person or an animal with the intent to cause hurt or harm, or at the very least to threaten to do so. When the aggressive act is delivered, its object is caused hurt or harm, physically or psychologically. So aggression consists of actions, in contrast to anger, which consists of emotional outbursts. What about a temper tantrum, when a furious man hurls a dish at the wall, shattering the dish? Because the wall cannot be considered a victim, the tantrum is an expression of anger, not an aggressive act.

Aggressive behavior has many forms, which boil down to a few categories. The most obvious is *physical aggression*, which we share with our animal ancestors: biting, punching, kicking, and wrestling. We are the quintessential weapon makers, which leads to further differentiation of aggression into minor components, so that there are aggression specialists in shooting, knifing, clubbing, garroting, or poisoning.

As speakers of language, we engage in *verbal aggression*, which, as the only animal with spoken language, humans have refined into several specialties: curses, insults, jibes, sneers, and taunts. It may also include criticizing others and sarcasm (Moskowitz, 2010). These may vary in the intensity with which they are delivered—by shouting or screaming, for example.

Another variety of aggression is *threats*. They are typically delivered verbally, as in the motion picture *The Godfather:* "I'll make him an offer he can't refuse," a threat to kill. However, the threat may also be physical, as in pulling out a gun or knife or making a fist in readiness to punch. Even the expressions of anger may serve as threats in both humans and animals.

We humans also go one better than animals in devising yet another variety of aggression, namely, *indirect aggression,* in which the attacker gets at the victim in a roundabout way. He may let air out of the victim's car tires, steal his mail, or deface the walls of his house—all forms of physical aggression. Alternatively, he may spread nasty gossip about the victim or blackmail the victim by exposing secrets damaging to the victim's marriage or his or her vocational reputation—all forms of verbal aggression. Two items of the Indirect Aggression subscale of the Aggression Questionnaire are "I sometimes spread gossip about people I don't like" and "I like to play practical jokes" (A. H. Buss & Warren, 2000). Such indirect attacks have also been conceptualized as *relational aggression* (Crick, 1995; Crick, Ostrov, & Werner, 2006).

Tilts

In brief, aggression may differentiate into these dichotomies: physical–verbal, actual–threat, and direct–indirect. There are not only individual differences in the predilection for one or the other of these differentiates but also group differences.

One individual difference is gender. Being male strongly tilts toward physical and direct aggression. For example, men who are hostile to women, when provoked in the laboratory, aggress more intensely to women than to nonhostile men (Anderson & Anderson, 2008). Men who are physically aggressive are likely to be verbally aggressive too; however, some men are aggressive verbally but not physically. Being female tilts toward indirect aggression, the reason being greater fear of retaliation if the victim is a man.

We know from observations of animals that larger animals within a species tend to be more aggressive, and in our species, larger size is also a tilt toward aggression for both sexes (Tremblay et al., 2004). In a longitudinal study, larger body size at 3 years of age predicted the level of both physical and verbal aggression at 11 years of age (Raine, Reynolds, Venables, Mednick, & Faringon, 1998)

Sociologists have documented the greater incidence of wife beating, assaults against strangers, and murders among those of the lowest social stratum. Thus, social class constitutes a tilt toward physical aggression. Beyond that, middle-class children are socialized to avoid direct aggression, so being middle class is a tilt toward indirect aggression.

As a differentiate of emotionality, anger is expected to correlate with emotionality, and it does: .37 for men and .28 for women (A. H. Buss &

Plomin, 1984). Thus, emotionality tilts toward anger, and anger tilts more toward *angry aggression*, which is motivated by a desire the hurt the victim, than toward instrumental aggression (more on the distinction between angry and instrumental aggression in the Perspectives section). Activity is a tilt in that increased vigor intensifies any response, including aggression. This is true especially at the high end of the trait of activity because young male bullies tend to be hyperactive (Pulkkinen & Tremblay, 1992). Impulsiveness, specifically, the lack-of-control component, also tilts toward anger being expressed as a tantrum or as angry aggression.

Person and Environment

Environment Affects Person

Mothers of 4-year-olds were asked whether an adult had ever harmed their children (Dodge, Bates, & Pettit, 1990), and a minority admitted that they had harmed their children. All the children were observed and their behavior rated by preschool teachers. The harmed children were observed to be more aggressive than the unharmed children, which tells us that an abusive environment is a source of aggressiveness. Family environment also establishes expectations for each sex. Boys reported that they expected no censure from parents if they retaliated against a boy who had attacked them, but there was no similar expectation by girls (Perry, Perry, & Weiss, 1989).

Part of family environment is the presence or absence of siblings. It turns out that having siblings available as targets of aggression is a tilt toward aggressiveness (Tremblay et al., 2004).

Reflect for a moment about how much violence occurs in the media. Television news supplies details of the bloodbath of suicide bombers, movies and television portray the violence of heroes and villains and the bloody outcome, and video games tend to depict one killing after another. One result of this saturation is expected to be habituation to all this displayed aggression, inuring viewers to any emotional impact that might diminish anger or upset. Such habituation to video aggression was documented many decades ago in elementary school children (Cline, Croft, & Courrier, 1973; M. H. Thomas, Horton, Lippincott, & Drabman, 1977) and in college students (Geen, 1981).

Exposure to violence in the media causes habituation not only to violence but also to *imitation*. In movies, television, videos, and computer games the hero, heroine, and villains all engage in beating, knifing, or shooting people. The main characters serve as aggressive models to be copied by the onlookers. Two reviews of research concluded that in Western countries, television violence makes a clear, if modest, contribution to children's aggressiveness (Eron, 1982; Eron, Gentry, & Schlegel, 1994).

A more serious problem is the enduring impact of television violence. As a longitudinal study of aggressive behavior revealed, the television viewing of 8-year-olds correlated strongly with the aggressive behavior of 30-year-olds (Eron, 1987). In subsequent research over a 5-year period, television violence again led to an escalation of aggressiveness (Huesmann, Moise-Titus, Podolski, & Eron, 2003).

Another longitudinal study, this one brief, is especially relevant in today's world (Anderson et al., 2008). In both Japan and the United States, youngsters who played violent video games many hours per week early in the school year tended to be more physically aggressive late in the school year.

What can we conclude from all this research on media violence? First, it affects everyone by habituating them to violence. Second, it increases aggression in youngsters who are already aggressive by presenting models to be imitated.

The other psychological mechanism, *instrumental conditioning,* may be summarized in two words: aggression pays. In an experimental situation in which the only reward was obtaining correct responses from the other person, college students willingly escalated the intensity of aggression to obtain that reward (A. H. Buss, 1971). The rewards of everyday life are of course much bigger. In both humans and animals, the rewards for aggression may be attention from and domination over others; better access to food; and, for males, better access to females.

Aggressive children find instrumental aggression especially rewarding. More than nonaggressive children, aggressive children are confident that they have the requisite ability to aggress, that it is easy to do but hard to inhibit, and that it leads to rewarding outcomes (Perry, Perry, & Rasmussen, 1986). Compared with nonaggressive children, aggressive children value their control over the victim more and are less concerned with retaliation or the victim's suffering (Boldizar, Perry, & Perry, 1989).

Aggressive behavior is not always successful and might even be punished by retaliation from the target, a consequence that diminishes aggressiveness. When the punishment is by a parent, it may have two opposite effects. One is the drop in aggressiveness just mentioned. However, when the parents use physical punishment, they also serve as a model to be imitated, a model who is in the house all the time. The issue of punishment raises the issue of how parents socialize their children to inhibit aggressive tendencies.

In all cultures, adults do not stand by and allow children to have temper tantrums or engage in excessive violence. Infants start with temper tantrums, and when they have sufficient motor control, they are capable of hurting others, in some instances injuring them. Accordingly, as socialization agents, the parents have two tasks. One is to offer themselves and others as models of nonaggressive behavior and to suggest peaceful ways of solving conflicts. The other is the more immediate task of asserting discipline in dealing with the child's aggression.

At first glance parental behavior appears simply to range from laissez-faire to extremely controlling, but observations of parental discipline revealed three clusters of such behavior (Baumrind, 1971). One cluster occupies the *permissive* end of the spectrum, with few demands made of children and the use of using reason instead of punishment. At the other end of the spectrum, *authoritarian* parents are strict, demand respect, and try to instill high standards of behavior in their children. There is little use of reason, and aggression is punished. A third cluster of parents, called *authoritative*, occupy the middle of the dimension. They set standards and occasionally use punishment, but they first try reasoning instead of punishment. As might be expected, the extremes of parental control were related to the aggressiveness of the children, but this held true only for boys. Children of permissive parents tended to show more anger. Children of authoritarian parents went in one direction or its opposite: obedience versus rebelliousness.

It is not surprising that both extremes affect aggressive behavior and do so mainly for boys, who generally are more aggressive than girls. This sex difference alerts us to the issue of direction of effects. In research on parents and children, psychologists often take the adult's view of the interaction, but C. C. Lewis (1981) took a child's perspective in interpreting the impact of parental discipline. For example, in firm control, the parents use reason and respect their children's decisions, so the children might think, "My parents withdraw their demands after I convince them with my arguments" (from "respects child's decisions"); or "Since we handle things by discussing them, my parents never attempt to get their way by coercing me" (from "use of reason to obtain compliance"; C. C. Lewis, 1981, p. 561).

Person Affects Environment

"Highly aggressive individuals to a considerable degree actively select and create the kinds of situations in which they are often observed" (Olweus, 1979, p. 873). Let us start with *choosing environments* that foster aggression. Some men deliberately drink at bars known for the brawls that occur immediately outside. Spoiling for a fight, they sometimes convert peaceful interactions into violent ones. In some cities, certain streets are known as a place to fight later at night, and those who go there expect a battle. In Europe, there are so-called soccer hooligans who go to soccer matches prepared to fight partisans of the opposing team. The larger issue is that aggressive people set up a cycle of aggression to retaliation to more aggression

As for children, recall the link between television violence and aggression. It is just as likely that aggressive boys choose to watch these programs as it is that these programs escalate aggressiveness. We need both perspectives.

Aggressiveness may set the tone of a social interaction. Grade-school boys watched videotapes and were asked about the intentions of the characters on the videotapes (Dodge & Somberg, 1987). Aggressive boys thought that the intentions of the televised characters were significantly more hostile than did nonaggressive boys. Even when aggressive boys did not attribute hostile intent to the characters, the boys thought that the characters would be likely to aggress. In other words, aggressive boys tend to be hostile and believe that those around them are aggressive even when they are not.

The anger-prone person starts off by glaring, scowling, and becoming piqued or by being grouchy, sullen, or surly. People eaten up by jealousy or envy set the stage for others to be annoyed and ready to be angry in return. Some aggressive men stare challengingly at other men as if daring the others to start a fight. Their opposites set an entirely different tone by smiling, adopting a welcoming look, and generally being peaceable.

Aggressive children tend to experience more turmoil and receive more aggression from others. They are not trusted, are strongly disliked, and sometimes receive open displays of hatred (Dodge, 1983). The way they set the tone of an interaction may enhance their original aggressiveness. These bullies have been described this way:

> The bullies were distinguished by strong aggressive tendencies and a weak control of such tendencies, if activated. They clearly had a more positive attitude toward violence and violent means. . . . Moreover, they felt fearless, confident, tough, non-anxious, and had, on the whole, a positive attitude toward themselves. (Olweus, 1984, p. 62)

There are always victims available as easy targets for aggressors. It starts in the preschool period when children who are picked on give in quickly or even cry (G. R. Patterson, Littman, & Bricker, 1967). There is a second kind of victim, however, angry children who retaliate when they are attacked (Perry, Kusel, & Perry, 1988). These authors also suggested that roughly one child in 10 is a victim during the elementary school years.

In addition to victims, there are people who are able to modify the environment away from aggression. They assume that others' intentions are peaceful and respond to disputes by attempting to mediate them.

Development

Infancy

How can we tell whether the 2-month-old baby is angry or merely distressed? It is not the emotional expression because in both emotions, there is a red face and howling. The distressed infant cries loudly for reasons parents can only guess at and discover by trial and error, but the infant just sits there and emotes vigorously. The angry infant, within the limits of primitive muscular control, also engages in instrumental behavior by attempting to get rid of the source of anger: the mother who is pushed away, the cereal bowl that is knocked over, or the offending toy that is hurled away. Only by later in the 1st year will there be the specific facial expressions of anger, which more sharply distinguish it from fear as the years pass, until by adulthood anger is universally recognized (Ekman, 2003).

Babies differ considerably in their proneness to anger. Some are placid and hardly complain at all. Others have a low threshold for being annoyed and are too ready to have a temper tantrum, kicking, screaming, and fighting off attempts to placate them. They are the ones labeled *difficult* (A. Thomas, Chess, Birch, Hertzig, & Korn,1963).

In the 2nd year of life, infants start trying to do things beyond their capability, so they become frustrated and angry. They may demand exclusive affection, and their jealousy sometimes shows up as head banging and throwing clothes around.

Angry aggression requires sufficient control of arms and legs and therefore does not show up until late in infancy. However, it is sporadic and not yet stable enough to be called a trait.

Preschool

Toddlers now have sufficient motor control to shove, punch, or kick another child or an adult. It can be angry aggression (wanting to hurt the victim), or it can be instrumental aggression (e.g., hitting another child to seize a toy or a piece of candy). As motor control matures, children become adept at punching, wrestling, jumping on others, and generally a widening repertoire of physical aggression. Mothers were asked how often their children, 17, 30, and 42 months of age, kicked, bit, fought, or bullied (Tremblay et al., 2004). Trajectories of high, medium, and low aggressiveness were identified, and the odds of being in the high aggressive trajectory multiplied by roughly 11 times when both the children were larger and their mothers had engaged in antisocial behavior in high school.

During this era, children with uncontrollable anger are likely to be referred to psychiatrists. Compared with nonreferred children, referred children have higher rates of these symptoms of *oppositional defiant disorder*: defies adult's requests, loses temper, angry and resentful, and spiteful and vindictive (Keenan & Wakschlag, 2004). Notice the link between anger and hostility (resentment and vindictiveness).

By late in the preschool era, fighting may become a means of achieving dominance or may be intrinsically rewarding as an end in itself. Meanwhile, outbursts of anger still occur, although with diminishing frequency and intensity. There is strong parental pressure to inhibit explosions of temper, espe-

cially in girls. Individual differences in anger now show up more clearly. Children low in the trait of anger have no problem adjusting to parental pressure, but those high in the trait cannot help but resist parental efforts to eliminate expressions of childish fury.

There are interesting gender differences in how preschool children deal with their anger when there is conflict with another child. Children were observed in free play over a 3-month period, and their anger and angry aggression were observed: "Boys were proportionately more likely than girls to vent their feelings when angered, whereas girls were more likely than boys to utilize active resistance (such as verbally asserting themselves)" (Fabes & Eisenberg, 1992, p. 125). By 4 years of age, children engage in relational aggression—for example, the threat of exclusion—and girls do it more than boys (Murray-Close & Ostrov, 2009).

Elementary School

At the start of this era, children have mastered the most important elements of language. Having previously heard verbal aggression from older children, adolescents, and adults, they are ready to try it for themselves: name-calling, cursing, derogating, ridiculing, teasing, and taunting. Verbal aggression becomes increasingly sophisticated as the years pass, allowing the flowering of indirect aggression. Girls, more than boys, pass on malicious gossip or even initiate nasty lies about casual acquaintances or rivals.

For boys the indirect aggression typically is physical. They steal or destroy others' toys, comic books, or games and, in the later years of childhood, may even ruin clothes and furniture. Being rejected and receiving relational aggression led to increases in relational (indirect) aggression only in girls, but rejection and physical aggression led to increases in physical aggression only in boys (Werner & Crick, 2004). For both sexes, children rejected in the 6- to 8-year-old range became more aggressive when they were 10 to 12 years old, but this held only for children originally above average in aggressiveness (Dodge et al., 2003).

In the elementary school era, there are additional sources of anger. Other children tease children about their appearance, speech, or even clothes, and boys do it more frequently than girls (Keltner, Capps, King, Young, & Heery, 2001). When the anger dies down, there is often residual dislike, even hatred, as well as envy and resentment about not getting a fair share or at being negatively compared with other children.

By 8 years of age, the trait of aggressiveness has been firmly established for many years. Using the entire second-grade class in a U.S. elementary school, Eron, Walder, and Lefkowitz (1971) identified which children were aggressive and which were not, and 22 years later, one third of the cohort was located (Huesmann, Eron, Lefkowitz, & Walder, 1984). The children identified as aggressive at age 8 tended to still be aggressive at age 30 and were above average in punishing their children and in frequency of criminal offenses. When the longitudinal study continued until the subjects were 48 years old, those high in aggressiveness earlier were still high, and those low were still low (Huesmann, Dubow, & Boxer, 2009).

Eight years of age was also the starting point for a longitudinal study in Finland that sampled peer nominations and teacher ratings at 8 and 14 years and checked on adjustment problems at 20 and 26 years (Pulkkinen & Pitkanen, 1993). Aggressiveness at 8 and 14 years predicted aggression and adjustment problems.

In a study conducted in Canada (Brame, Nagin, & Tremblay, 2001), boys' physical aggression was tracked from age 6 years to late adolescence. Although there was little stability for the group as a whole, the authors noted that "boys with higher physical aggression trajectories are far more likely to transition to a higher-level adolescent trajectory than boys with lower childhood physical aggression trajectories" (Brame et al., p. 510). This study illustrates yet again the need to examine segments of a trait distribution.

Adolescence

Boys' bullying continues into adolescence (Ahmad & Smith, 1994; Olweus, 1993), but in school at least, there is a downward trend from 8 to 16 years in reports of bullying (P. K. Smith, Madsen, & Moody, 1999). In this study, interviews with children and adolescents revealed two causes: Younger children have many more older, stronger children around them, and younger children lack the skills to deal with bullying.

Young adolescents may engage in *sexual bullying*, which involves inappropriate body touching or nasty sexual comments. Young adolescents who saw themselves as attractive tended to engage in more sexual bullying (Cunningham et al., 2010). In a survey, more than half of adult respondents said that while in high school, they had engaged in sexual harassment—for example, calling someone gay or lesbian (American Association of University Women, 2001).

Modern technology has offered another outlet for bullies: the Internet. To cite just one study, traditional bullying was a predictor of online bullying (Raskauskas & Stoltz, 2007).

Teasing and gossiping continue and are more hurtful in this era of greater dependence on the good will of peers. A tiny segment of adolescent males react with such anger and hatred to being excluded (and being bullied) that they plan deadly attacks on their tormenters, and a few execute these plans, notably in recent years at Columbine High School in Colorado, at Virginia Tech, and at Northern Illinois State University.

A new source of anger emerges within the family. Adolescents typically want greater freedom from parental supervision without taking on new responsibilities, but parents want to keep a rein on their adolescents and want them to take on more responsibility. This conflict accounts for some adolescent sullenness and rebelliousness, and these reactions are more intense in the adolescents who are already predisposed toward anger.

In some South American adolescent gangs, there is an initiation in which gang members beat and kick the pledge unmercifully for 45 seconds, and he must take it. Young men who want to join such gangs typically are aggressive, a tendency intensified by the beating. In this country, recruits to fraternities, sororities, bands, and other clubs are routinely bullied and degraded in the name of tradition and with the aim of instilling group loyalty. At the individual level, so-called practical jokes are just another name for socially acceptable aggression.

Perspective

Aggression, Anger, and Hostility

The distinction among these three traits dates back half a century: "Aggression is an instrumental response that administers punishment; anger is an emotional reaction with prominent autonomic and skeletal-facial components; hostility is a negative attitude defined in terms of implicit verbal responses" (A. H. Buss, 1961, p. 1). It was empirically sustained by a factor analysis that yielded factors of behavior (physical and verbal aggression, anger, and hostility; A. H. Buss & Perry, 1992), and the same three factors emerged from a different inventory (Martin, Watson, & Wan, 2000).

Instrumental and Angry Aggression

In its enduring influence on the topic of aggression, the book *Frustration and Aggression* (Dollard, Doob, Miller, Mowrer, & Sears, 1939) deserves the historical importance it is generally accorded. In asserting that frustration is the cause of aggression, the authors assumed that only when frustrated do people aggress. I have challenged this assumption, using a behaviorist vocabulary:

> The Dollard et al. approach emphasizes *angry aggression*, which is usually reinforced by the victim's pain, but it neglects an entire class of aggressive responses. These are *instrumentally aggressive* responses, which are reinforced by the same reinforcers that follow any instrumental responses: food, sex, money, approval. (A. H. Buss, 1961, pp. 2–3)

Said with another kind of vocabulary, the intent of the angry aggressor is to hurt the victim, so the reward is intrinsic to the act. The intent of the instrumental aggressor is obtaining any of the rewards mentioned above, which may be acquired by nonaggressive behavior: the reward is extrinsic to the act. This distinction was adopted first by Feshbach (1964), who used the terms *hostile aggression* and *instrumental aggression*, and subsequently with usage that continued in later literature (Anderson & Bushman, 2002; Baron & Richardson, 1994).

Others narrowed the distinction with their own variations on it. Scott (1958), who studied aggression in animals, came up with *affective aggression* (hot-blooded) and *instrumental aggression* (cold-blooded). Zillman (1979) separated *annoyance-motivated aggression* from *incentive-motivated aggression*. Dodge and Coie (1987) distinguished between retaliating against a threat (*reactive aggression*) and aggressing in an attempt to attain one of a variety of specific outcomes (*proactive aggression*), and several measures of the two have been developed (Hubbard, Morrow, Romano, & McAuliffe, 2010). How close is this distinction to angry versus instrumental aggression? Here is the answer: "In children, reactive aggression is displayed as anger or temper tantrums, with an appearance of being out of control. Proactive aggression occurs usually in the form of object acquisition, bullying or dominance of a peer" (Dodge, 1991, p. 205). This reactive–proactive distinction is also similar to that between *offensive* and *defensive aggression* (Pulkkinen, 1987). In offensive aggression, the aggressor initiates the attack, whereas in defensive aggression, the angry victim retaliates. In brief, the original distinction between angry and instrumental aggression endures in the form of different terminology and in further distinctions by later researchers on aggression.

Indirect Aggression

When the distinction between direct and indirect aggression first appeared in my book the *Psychology of Aggression* (A. H. Buss, 1961), it was of no particular interest to those who studied aggression, but many years later, European researchers asked whether indirect aggression was more typical of girls (Lagerspetz, Bjorkqvist, & Peltonen (1988). The answer was yes, but more on sex differences shortly. Equally interesting was the previously mentioned concept of *relational aggression*, which consists of shunning, spreading nasty gossip, and humiliating others (Crick, 1995; Crick, Grotpeter, & Bigbee, 2002). I view relational aggression as a differentiate of indirect aggression, representing the social aspects of indirect aggression, in contrast to the physical aspects (destroying another's possessions or harming another person's relatives).

Stability of Aggressiveness

Aggressiveness is expected to vary over the course of years, but as a trait we expect it to have at least a modicum of stability. A review of early longitudinal studies on boys over intervals of several years found that aggressiveness was nearly as stable as IQ (Olweus, 1979). However, stability is likely to drop as the interval increases, so for example, there is less stability when the longitudinal comparison is between children and adults (Olweus, 1979).

In three studies, the interval ranging from 6 to 10 years, the correlation coefficients were in the mid to high .30s (Cairns, Cairns, Neckerman, Ferguson, & Gariepy, 1989; Huesmann, Dubow, & Boxer, 2009; Lefkowitz, Eron, Walder, & Huesmann, 1977; Pulkkinen & Pitkanen, 1993). This certainly is modest stability, but as we saw earlier, children high and low in aggressiveness tend to have more stable trajectories than those in the middle range.

Sex Differences

There is a clear sex difference in victims. Men who are hostile specifically toward women and who are provoked in the laboratory aggress more intensely against women than against men (Anderson & Anderson, 2008). We also know from police reports that within families, it is overwhelmingly the women who are physically abused. Why are women the targets of aggression more than men? One obvious reason is that, like other mammalian females, women are on average smaller and weaker than men.

As for why men are more aggressive than women, this is a hotly debated topic, and there are two seemingly irreconcilable positions. One emphasizes the contributions of socialization—specifically, culturally defined sex roles—and the other position emphasizes the contributions of biology—specifically, hormones and inheritance.

First, however, consider the facts of sex differences. When preschoolers' reactions to anger were observed during play, boys reacted more often with physical aggression than girls; there was no other sex difference in aggression (Fabes & Eisenberg, 1992). On the most popular aggressiveness questionnaire, men are clearly and significantly higher than women mainly on physical aggression (A. H. Buss & Perry, 1992). Research with this and another questionnaire confirmed a large sex difference in physical aggression, a smaller one for verbal aggression, and no sex difference for anger or hostility (Archer, Kilpatrick, & Bramwell, 1995).

There are other ways of studying aggression, however, and other sex differences might appear when other methods are used. In the most complete review that included various methods, Eagly and Steffen (1986) concluded that men are generally more aggressive than women by about one third of a standard deviation. The difference was larger for physical aggression than for verbal aggression; recall that it is physical aggression that we share with other animals. As for indirect aggression, a meta-analysis found that among children and adolescents, the sex difference in favor of girls is trivial (Card, Stucky, Sawalami, & Little, 2008).

Hormones

There is basis for implicating the male sex hormone testosterone in the greater aggressiveness of males because it is well known that castrated animals become less aggressive, which is why steers are herded rather than bulls. Can we extrapolate to human males? Virtually all the research is on the relationship between level of testosterone and aggressiveness in men, and the findings are mixed.

Several studies, however, yielded positive results. Violent criminals have a higher level of testosterone than nonviolent criminals (Dabbs & Dabbs, 2000; Dabbs, Frady, Carr, & Besch, 1987). Normal adolescent males who were reported to act out and misbehave had higher levels of the male hormone androstenedione than those who did not act out (Susman et al., 1987). A large-scale review of this literature concluded that there is a low correlation between testosterone and aggression in males (Archer, 2006).

Socialization

This approach emphasizes social roles:

> Like other social behaviors, aggression can be viewed as role behavior and therefore regulated by the social norms that are applied to people based on the roles they occupy. To account for sex differences in aggression from this perspective, we must understand the ways in which aggression is sustained or inhibited by the social roles occupied mainly or exclusively by persons of each sex. (Eagly & Steffen, 1986, p. 310)

One socialization theory emphasizes how the two sexes respond to their own anger:

> Women cry rather than hit not because of their hormones, their reinforcement history, or their role as carers but because they see aggression as a personal failure; and the safest release for their anger, when they deny themselves blows, is tears. Men hit not because their testosterone makes them, or because their mothers didn't punish them enough . . . but because when they are publicly humiliated by another male, they believe that aggression will restore the status quo. (A. Campbell, 1993, p. 85)

Cultures vary in the social roles assigned to each sex, so if social roles determine aggressiveness, it follows that in some cultures, men will be more aggressive. In Kenya, boys assigned to feminine tasks were found to be less aggressive than boys assigned to typical masculine tasks (Ember, 1973). In this country, men are expected to be more aggressive (Cicone & Ruble, 1978), and men view violence on television and war more favorably than do women (T. W. Smith, 1984).

So there is evidence for the socialization position. Of course, it might be argued that socialization practices merely follow the dictates of biology, reflecting an innate sex difference in aggression caused by testosterone. This argument neglects both the importance of culture and the extremely long period of human childhood. It seems more reasonable to suggest that socialization practices may enhance or diminish the biological sex difference in aggression.

Evolution

Sex differences in aggression are assumed to start with reproduction. Females can produce a limited number of offspring and must expend time and energy in lactation, whereas males are free to produce huge numbers of offspring. Elephant seals keep harems, and their human counterparts, Eastern potentates, once kept harems and sired hundreds of children. At a more modest level, some men have children by several wives (*polygyny*), and because there are roughly as many men as women, some men are denied reproduction.

It is known that adolescent mammalian males fight to establish dominance, one of the major reasons being that dominant males have better access to females. In our species, dominance means having more resources, which attract women. So males are more aggressive than females to avoid being shut out of reproduction completely and to achieve a position leading to better access to multiple women: "In essence, polygyny selects for risky strategies, including those that lead to violent combat with rivals and those that lead to increased risk taking to acquire the resources needed to attract members of the high-investing sex" (D. M. Buss, 2008, p. 297).

The evolutionary approach to sex differences, by rooting men's greater aggressiveness in different reproductive strategies, connects us with our animal ancestors. The explanation applies to all cultures, regardless of cultural differences in sex roles. More specifically, it ties the sex difference in aggression to dominance.

DOMINANCE

A little more than 70 years ago, Maslow (1937) distinguished between two kinds of dominance. *Cultural dominance*, which is established through a title, wealth, or status in a work setting, occurs only in our species. *Personal dominance* occurs in both our species and other animals, and this kind of dominance is the focus of this section.

As examples of dominant behavior, consider these acts nominated by college students (D. M. Buss, 1981): I told her to get off the phone so that I could use it; I chose to sit at the head of the table; I decided which programs we could watch on TV. Subjects in this study were also administered a dominance questionnaire, which revealed sex differences:

> Men expressed their dominance in the entire range of dominant acts. They reported more often taking the lead in the group, initiating group activities, and talking considerably in public. . . . Dominant women reported expressing their dominance primarily in group-oriented actions: settling disputes among group members, introducing people, involvement in community activities, and organizing projects. (D. M. Buss, 1981, p. 151)

Another questionnaire contained these items (Ray, 1981): I'm the sort of person who likes to get my own way; I tend to dominate the conversation; I tend to boss people around. Domineering (bossy) people are so strongly motivated to have their own way that, unlike most of us, they are always insistent. Like an admiral of the navy, they assume command. On the positive side, they will offer help when you need it; on the negative side, they will insist on helping even when you do not want it.

The personality trait of dominance in humans is best regarded as a dimension. *Domineering behavior*, the high end of the dimension, consists of direct and emphatic control over the behavior of others: telling them what to do, when to do it, and how to do it. The clearest examples of this extreme of control by one adult of another may be found in the military or in prisons. Parents, in their roles of caretaker and disciplinarian, exercise a similar degree of control over young children, though it is more benevolent and flexible.

One response to domineering behavior is *resistance*. If both people are domineering, there is a contest of wills, showing up as verbal or physical aggression. But what if one of them has neither the strength nor the status to fight back but still will not submit? One option is *negativism*, which is tapped by these items on a questionnaire (A. H. Buss & Durkee, 1957):

- When people order me around, I take my time just to show them.
- Unless someone asks in a nice way, I won't do what they want.
- When someone makes a rule, I am tempted to break it.
- When people are bossy, I do the opposite of what they ask.

The alternative to resistance and negativity is of course *submissiveness*, the bottom of the dimension. One reason people are submissive is a lack of confidence, which causes them to back off when being confronted. Another reason, connected to the first, is an inherited tendency to be low in dominance, which usually leads to a history of submission.

Assertive behavior, the middle of the dominance dimension, consists of insisting on having your voice heard, of having your way occasionally, and of going along at other times. Assertive people tend to resist being dominated if they feel strongly about an issue. They neither fight back nor submit but insist on being autonomous. The bottom of the dimension is *submissive behavior*.

Paths to Dominance

Among highly social mammals, dominant status is achieved through aggression, as it is in our species. Dominance imposes social order among animals by minimizing aggression. When animals are of equal status, they are likely to aggress, as may be seen in these chimpanzees:

> Dita and Fifi, both aggressive adult females, long acquainted but usually living apart, struggle for dominance whenever they are cages together. . . . Dita has the advantage of greater size and strength but Fifi by fearless and persistent attacks can sometimes achieve mastery. So evenly matched are they that neither may confidently assume superior status, for it is usually challenged by the other. (Yerkes, 1943, p. 47)

If these chimpanzees were living together, the aggression would continue until one was clearly dominant over the other, ending the conflict.

In many species, wolves and gorillas especially, once conflict over status ends, the dominant animal is also the leader who decides when to stay, when to go, and where food is likely to be available. In our species, the most aggressive person may be the one who leads, but not always. Leadership in the absence of aggression is an alternative path to dominance, one of the ways we are unique as a species.

Leadership

Here are some examples of leadership, as reflected in these items from the "directiveness" part of a dominance questionnaire (Lorr & Moore, 1980):

- I work best when I'm the person in charge.
- I seek positions where I can influence others.
- I am usually the one who initiates activities in my group.
- In an emergency I get people organized and take charge.

Notice that the third item involves *taking initiative*, which "consists of the ability to be motivated from within to direct attention toward a challenging goal" (Larson, 2000, p. 170). This is the first step to becoming a leader, the one who says which way to go when the path is not clear. Such a person must have knowledge and be enough of a risk taker to point the way ahead when no one else does. The last item, taking charge, suggests the other personal quality of a leader, *decisiveness*. Leaders may be selected because they have already been accorded prestige on the basis of high intelligence, inventiveness, or other valued abilities; read more about prestige in the section on adolescence.

Competitiveness

Competition is another path to dominant status, which typically is accorded to the winner. The trait of competitiveness has been assessed by Spence and Helmreich (1983), who offered these items:

- I enjoy working in situations involving competition with others.
- It is important for me to perform better than others on a task.
- I feel that winning is important in both work and games.
- It annoys me when people perform better than I.
- I try harder when I'm in competition with other people.

Competitive people thrive on matching themselves against others. They seek the clarity of knowing there is a definite winner and loser. They enjoy being in the midst of a contest in which there is suspense about the outcome. As the foregoing items suggest, winning is important, but there is also the thrill of the contest itself. Some competitive people thrive on betting money, so that if someone remarks that it might rain that day, the reply might be, "Want to bet?"

In the context of dominance, competitiveness comes into play when a leader is needed. There are usually rules for competition, and the winner assumes dominant status, for example, an election.

Differentiation

In brief, there are three paths to dominance, each involving a personality trait: aggressiveness, leadership, and competitiveness. The most powerful path is aggression because it guarantees control over others when it is successful. Leadership is not as powerful because others may choose not to be led. Finally, winning in competition does not necessarily lead to dominance because losers may rationalize their loss, and others simply choose not to compete. Nevertheless, when people compete successfully, they tend to dominate others.

The way these paths play out in everyday life is more complicated than just the power to dominate because they differ in their social acceptance. Thus, aggressiveness is condemned, but leadership and competitiveness are praised.

There are a few studies that bear indirectly on this account. Feedback to subjects that they were perceived as leaders made them feel dominant (M. R. Leary, Cottrell, & Phillips, 2001). Subjects tended to confer higher status on those who delivered angry opinions (Tiedens, 2001). To the extent that anger is associated with aggression to aggression, this finding suggests that aggressive behavior is a path to dominance, but followers are likely to prefer leaders who are not aggressive or angry.

The study bearing directly on differentiation was on how the three postulated traits relate to the trait of bossiness (Gallaher & Buss, 1987). The three paths were intercorrelated, so the correlations among them were partialled out to yield these correlations with bossiness: leadership, .50; aggressiveness, .40; competitiveness, .29. A dominance questionnaire that emphasized the bossiness end of the dominance dimension—items such as "I demand respect from my peers"—correlated with hostility and was unrelated to testosterone level (Johnson, Burk, & Kirkpatrick, 2007).

Regardless of which path is taken, there is always at least one target. Adults obviously are more likely to dominate children than other adults, some adults dominate only children, and older children dominate their younger siblings. Women who dominate other women may be reluctant to dominate men (Megargee, 1969), and, rarely, there are men who dominate other men but are submissive to their wives.

Person–Environment Interaction

Environment Affects Person

We know from research on animals that males compete for dominance, which gives them greater access to food and females. In complex human cultures, especially individualist cultures such as our own, the tendency to compete is amplified, and in the modern era, this extends to females. Competition in sports and even in beauty and talent contests starts in the preschool era and continues into adult life. Winners are feted and losers are regarded as, well, "losers." Pressure to win enhances competitiveness in winners and decreases it in losers—common sense, but true.

Like our animal forebears, there is a strong sex difference in humans because of the greater size and strength of males, but this difference amplified in cultures with traditional sex roles. We occasionally forget that our culture once denied women the right to vote, although women now head corporations and occupy high government office because of an environment that allows women to assume positions of high status.

Person Affects Environment

Those high in the subtrait of bossiness may seek positions that allow them to dominate others—that is, they typically choose their environments. Coaches tell their players exactly how to play, and judges are all-powerful in their courtrooms. Bossiness obviously is the not the only reason people seek these positions, but having powerful control over others sets up a cascade of dominance from person to environment, back to person.

Of course, the target of bossiness may not accept being dominated. One option is to rebel and openly challenge the domineering person, which produces strong interpersonal conflict. As we shall see in the Development section, such conflict is particularly relevant when children challenge parental authority.

Competitive people are attracted to social contexts that involve head-to-head contests, but not necessarily violent ones. Many free-time pursuits feature such competition: poker, bridge, rummy, and other card games; checkers, chess, dominoes, and other table games; and tennis, squash, golf, and other sports. Competitive people are also drawn to vocations that offer the excitement of competition, such as professional gambler, athlete, or trial lawyer. They choose the very environment that canalizes competitiveness.

There is a sex difference here, illustrated by a laboratory study. Men and women worked on a noncompetitive task for which there was no sex difference in performance (Niederle & Vesterlund, 2007). When next given the option of working on a competitive task, three quarters of the men chose to do so but only about one third of the women.

Those high in the subtrait of *leadership* somehow manage to find themselves in groups they can lead. They are the ones who run for office, start a new business, take over a failing business, or become religious leaders. Such people are complemented by those low in leadership, many of whom want to be led. Erich Fromm (1941) was so struck by what he saw as a pervasive human tendency to follow strong leaders, even at the cost of independence, that he wrote a book called *Escape From Freedom*.

Dominant people tend to have an appropriate personal style: erect posture with head held high, looking down at another person, and a loud confident voice (Argyle, 1969, 1990). They talk louder and interrupt more (J. A. Hall, Coats, & Lebeau, 2005). There is also a personal style associated with submissiveness: slumping posture, head slightly down, and a voice that is anything but self-assured. These opposites in the trait of dominance set the tone at the start of a social interaction, thereby to some extent determining their own social environment.

Development

Preschool

For the first 2 years of life, the only conflicts between parents and infants tend to be over food and sleeping. Defiance and rebellion start for most children at or after 2 years of age, aptly characterized as the "terrible twos." Toddlers have heard the word *no* often enough, and now they start using it in response to parental requests of command. The parent places a new food in front of the child, and she refuses to eat it. The parent asks the child to wash her hands, and she refuses. The occasional resistance to parental dominance is one aspect of the assertion of self, the first stirrings of autonomy.

Some children show up as especially strong willed, assertive, and even opinionated. These are the ones who have an inherited tendency to be dominant and therefore refuse to be submissive. They are in no position to dominate, so the only option is determined resistance. This is the season of negativism.

Other children might be described as mellow. They have no strong motive for independence and are willing to tolerate parental command and go along with requests. Being low in the trait of dominance, their twos are not terrible.

The type of parenting is important here. Recall that authoritarian parents tend to have boys who are either obedient or defiant (Baumrind, 1971). Such parents may have an opposite impact on toddlers who differ in the trait of dominance, the result being that submissive boys become more obedient and dominant boys more defiant. For both sexes the combination of an authoritarian parent and a dominant child may set up a cascade: a command to the child, who resists, causing the parent to become even more demanding, so that the child becomes so rebellious and resistant to all authority that teachers label the child as a troublemaker (Bates, Maslin, & Frankel, 1985)

Once children are playing outside the home, there are conflicts with peers, and many of these conflicts are aggressive. In groups of older preschool children, the dominance hierarchy predicted 96% of physical attacks, 80% of threats, and 76% of struggles for a toy (Strayer & Strayer, 1976). In the playroom behavior of preschool children, most pairs had a stable pattern of one dominating and the other submitting (Gellert, 1961). This pattern has also been observed in siblings, the older one dominating. It even occurs in some identical twins, one taking the role of follower in the interest of harmony.

Toward the end of the preschool era, a sex difference in play appears. Like their primate cousins, boys delight in rough-and-tumble play much more than girls (DiPietro, 1981). An example of this kind of dominance game, which seems to appeal only to boys, is King of the Hill, an apt metaphor for dominance.

Elementary School

In elementary school, children are thrown together in larger groups. There is jockeying in the school hallways to be head of the line. In the playground, under more lax supervision, fights break out, many as part of conflicts over dominance. A dominance hierarchy was found to develop in previously unacquainted first- and third-grade boys after just a few hours of plays sessions, the dominant boys being more aggressive (Pettit, Bakshi, Dodge, & Coie, 1990).

Older, stronger boys, and sometimes girls, bully the younger, weaker children, who are in no position to resist. Older siblings also may bully, but at home their targets can resist by getting their parents to intervene. As in similar conflicts, exerting power may have opposite effects, making submissive children more submissive, and making dominant children more rebellious and determined to even the score when they are older.

At the elementary school level, there are opportunities for leadership, as clubs and athletic teams form, and the potential for leadership can be actualized. In some instances, the teachers appoint the leaders, presumably based on the attributes of leaders. In other instances, leaders are elected, and attractiveness and initiative are expected to play a role. The experience of being a leader surely leads to better competence at leading and the confidence to try it again. These are the familiar elements of a cascade: the attributes of a leader to becoming a leader to gaining more attributes that result in subsequent leadership.

For those low in leadership, this tendency is deepened by two experiences during this era. They discover that others have much more of the preferred attributes of leaders, so it might be useless to seek leadership. They also learn to modulate even a modest desire to lead in the interest of harmony.

When there are clubs and teams, there will be competition to represent the group in contests. There are also individual events, especially in athletics, but also in spelling bees and games of chess. Thus, there are ample opportunities for children to fulfill a desire to compete. Winning, of course, strengthens personality trait, but the minority of extremely competitive children will persevere even in the face of repeated losses.

Parents encourage their children to win in competition, sometimes to the point of letting it dominate the lives of both them and their children. One reason is the potential for athletic scholarships to college and perhaps a professional career. Another reason is the parent's own competitiveness, which is lived out in the activities of the child.

In this era, a sex difference appears in competitiveness. Starting in the second grade and continuing through the 12th grade, boys seek competition more than girls (Ahlgren & Johnson, 1979).

Adolescence

Since the Ahlgren and Johnson (1979) study appeared, there has been increasing pressure to succeed in competition in school and on the athletic field. Students planning to attend college, especially one of the better institutions, need not only good grades but also additional advanced placement courses. Athletics has expanded in both intensity of competition and breadth of activities.

Being a successful athlete clearly can lead to dominance, at least for most of high school. During the freshman, sophomore, and junior years there is a strong correlation between athletic ability and leadership, but it drops off sharply in the senior year (Weisfeld, Omark, & Cronin, 1980). The opposite trend holds for the relationship between intelligence and leadership, which is unrelated through the first 3 years but strongly related in the senior year, perhaps because many students are thinking ahead about college.

Intelligence and athletic ability are prized in most cultures, where they accrue prestige (Henrich & Gil-White, 2001), which is likely to result in leadership, a path to dominance. Distinguishing between dominance and prestige helps us understand the difference between domineering and dominant behavior (Johnson, Burk, & Kirkpatrick, 2007): The domineering kind of dominance was related to physical and verbal aggression, but prestige was not.

In a rare study of adolescents living together for 3 weeks, Savin-Williams (1976), acting as a counselor, observed 13-year-old boys in a summer camp and obtained peer nominations for dominance. At first there were some disagreements as the boys sorted out differences in status. These disagreements largely vanished by the 3rd day, when a stable dominance hierarchy was established among these boys who had entered the camp as strangers. Those who ranked higher—they were more athletic, assertive, and aggressive—received relatively scarce rewards at the camp: a cot nearer the counselor, a better seat when they ate, and a better chance to eat preferred food. The submissive boys at the bottom of the hierarchy slept farther from the counselor and fared worse in the dining hall.

In a subsequent camp study with both boys and girls, housed separately, the age range was 12 to 14 years (Savin-Williams, 1979). The results for boys were much the same as in the earlier study, but the dominance hierarchy was not as stable for girls. The more dominant girls established their status by bossing others or shunning them. Girls in the 16- and 17-year-old range still had a dominance hierarchy, which could be predicted from athletic ability (Paikoff & Savin-Williams, 1983).

Perspective

As a personality trait, dominance may be found along with other traits in the superfactor of extraversion, for example, as assertiveness within the extraversion factor of the Big Five (McCrae & Costa, 1985). Dominance has a long history of being examined on its own, however. Leadership in preschool children was systematically observed more than 70 years ago (Parten, 1933). A factor analysis of children's behavior yielded a factor called *ascendance-submission* (dominance; Williams, 1935). In adolescents, Tryon (1939) also found a factor called *ascendance*.

Hormones

It has been established that testosterone is a crucial determinant of dominance in animals (see the review by Ellis, 1986). Virtually the only path to dominance is aggression, so the testosterone–dominance connection may derive solely from the role of hormones. However, as we have seen, there are other paths to dominance in our species.

Research with humans has shown a direct connection between testosterone and success in competition. In their own research and a review of others' research, Mazur and Booth (1998) reported that testosterone rises in the male winners of athletic contests, and even chess matches, and drops in the losers. However, it is questionable whether the personality trait of dominance is related to testosterone (Sadalla, Kenrick, & Vershure, 1987).

Evolution

Recall that males fight to attain dominance to obtain better access to females, but there is a related reason: Females prefer dominant males. Is this true of our species? Mating preferences in 37 cultures were collected and analyzed, and women but not men had a strong preference for a partner with status (D. M. Buss, 1989, 2003). To the extent that dominant men are likely to have high status, these data suggest that women prefer dominant men.

In a previously mentioned study (Sadalla, Kenrick, & Vershure, 1987) in each of several experiments, college women were given vignettes of men who were described as dominant or nondominant. The dominance vignettes contained such words as *powerful, commanding, strong,* and *competitive.* The nondominant descriptions contained such terms as *yielding, obedient, not competitive,* and *not authoritative.* Women found the dominant man to be more sexually attractive than the nondominant man. There was an alternative dominance vignette in which the man was described as aggressive, and female subjects showed a weaker preference for this man. This finding is consistent with the earlier suggestion that followers are likely to prefer leaders who are not aggressive or angry.

In a follow-up study, a control condition was added: men described without reference to dominance (Burger & Cosby, 1999). Few women saw dominant men as desirable, instead preferring men who were confident and assertive. Evidently, women want status in their partners but not necessarily dominance.

Socialization

This approach assumes that the young are socialized to prepare them for an adult world in which men have higher status than women. Each sex has its own role models in everyday life and in the media, with men assuming leadership and women becoming followers, and there is evidence consistent with this assumption. In a previously mentioned experiment, two subjects were to decide who would be the leader and the follower in a task (Megargee,

1969). In mixed-sex pairs, when the man was high in the trait of dominance and the woman was low, the man was chosen roughly nine times out of 10. When the woman was dominant and the man was not, the woman was chosen only one time in five. Their conversations were recorded, which revealed that when a high-dominant woman was paired with a low dominant man, she almost always appointed him the leader. This finding suggests that in the presence of men, women wish not to be seen as leaders.

A follow-up experiment tested this idea (Snodgrass & Rosenthal, 1984). This time the experimenter decided which of two subjects would lead, and the leader's behavior during the task was watched. Observers saw no difference in dominant women, whether they led a man or a woman, but women leaders rated themselves as less dominant when they led men than when they led women. The authors suggested that dominant women experience conflict when they are called on to lead men because their personality disposes them to be dominant but such behavior with men is inconsistent with their traditional sex role.

What about leadership? An extensive review of the literature concluded that when the group has a specific task, men are chosen to lead, but when the goal is harmony, women are likely to be chosen as leaders (Eagly & Karau, 1991).

All this research was done in Western cultures, and we expect that in cultures we regard as sexist, men would dominate across the board. That cultures differ in this way is evidence for the socialization approach, as is evidence that in United States, the sex difference in status has diminished over the past several generations. However, the socialization and evolutionary perspectives are not mutually exclusive, and indeed, they may be regarded as complementary: Again, socialization might amplify or diminish evolutionary tendencies.

III

THE SELF

6

SELF I: SELF-CONSCIOUSNESS

It might seem obvious in retrospect, but 35 years ago it was not at all apparent to two graduate students and me that there are two kinds of self-consciousness. We discovered this distinction when we factor analyzed a questionnaire designed to as assess self-consciousness as a personality trait and derived factors of *private self-consciousness* and *public self-consciousness* (Fenigstein, Scheier, & Buss, 1975). The two scales correlated in the .30s.

PRIVATE SELF-CONSCIOUSNESS

The following section briefly explores aspects of private self-consciousness.

Self-Focus

People who are high in the trait of private self-consciousness try to figure themselves out, reflect on themselves, scrutinize themselves, and examine their motives. Those low in private self-consciousness do not have a similar self-focus. It follows that those high in private self-consciousness know themselves better and produce self-reports more in line with their behavior.

College men and women filled out a questionnaire on the trait of aggressiveness, and later their instrumental aggression was assessed in the laboratory with the aggression machine (Scheier, Buss, & Buss, 1978). The correlation between self-reports of aggression and aggressive behavior in the laboratory were .66 for those high in private self-consciousness and .09 for those low in this trait.

Instead of self-reports, subjects were asked to make up stories about how dominant they would be and told to be as assertive and dominant with others in a real group situation in which they were observed (Turner, 1978). Dominance in the stories correlated with behavioral dominance .67 for those high in private self-consciousness and .33 for those low in the trait. In a subsequent experiment, subjects self-reported on altruism and were given the opportunity to offer help (J. D. Smith & Shaffer, 1986). For those high in private self-consciousness, the correlation between self-reported altruism and helping behavior was .56, and for those low in private self-consciousness, it was .12. In brief, people high in private self-consciousness know themselves better and as a result supply more veridical self-reports.

Self-Reflectiveness and Internal Self-Awareness

Further psychometric research on private self-consciousness revealed two factors (Burnkrant & Page, 1984), shown in Exhibit 6.1. Notice that the self-reflectiveness items contain the words *always, a lot, often,* and *constantly,* which suggest an excessive attention to the self. The internal state awareness items involve a neutral kind of introspection (*introspectors*).

The two factors correlate .54, which is hardly surprising because they were combined into one factor in our original study (Fenigstein et al., 1975, a finding confirmed by Bernstein, Teng, & Garbin, 1986). However, the presence of two factors of private self-consciousness was replicated several times in

EXHIBIT 6.1
Two Factors of Private Self-Consciousness[a]

Self-Reflectiveness
1. I'm always trying to figure myself out.
2. I reflect about myself a lot.
3. I'm often the subject of my own fantasies.
4. I'm constantly examining my own motives.
5. I sometimes have the feeling I'm off somewhere watching myself.

Internal State Awareness
1. I'm generally attentive to my inner feelings.
2. I'm alert to changes in my mood.
3. I'm aware of the way my mind works when I work through a problem.

---

[a]The two reversed items in the original private self-consciousness factor were dropped.

the 1980s. Subsequent research showed that high scorers on internal state awareness, called *ruminators*, tend to obsess about themselves (Creed & Funder, 1998). Trapnell and Campbell (1999) constructed their own rumination scale—for example, "I always seem to be rehashing in my mind recent things I've said or done"—and found that rumination is correlated with neuroticism. The autobiographical memories of ruminators are affectively loaded (Teasdale & Green, 2004), so we should not be surprised that rumination correlates with neuroticism (Teasdale & Green, 2004; Trapnell & Campbell, 1999), as well as sadness and anxiety (Mor & Winquist, 2002). These findings with the rumination items may account for the following results, derived from studies with all the private self-consciousness items: (a) Under conditions of noise and time pressure, workers high in private self-consciousness reported more stress and somatic symptoms than those low in the trait (Frone & McFarlin, 1989), and (b) diarists high in private self-consciousness reported more frequent negative moods than those low in the trait (Flory, Raikkonen, Matthews, & Owens, 2000). The focus of introspectors is considerably more positive in that it correlates with superfactor of Openness (Trapnell & Campbell, 1999).

Thus, there are two successive differentiations involving self-consciousness. First, attention is directed to either the private aspects of the self or the public aspects, a crucial distinction. Next, private self-consciousness differentiates into either a darker, ruminating self-focus or a more benign introspectiveness.

Development

Infants are attuned only to the world around them, but toddlers start on the road to covertness. They gradually learn to inhibit their rage and panic, which leads to growing awareness between the inner experience of the emotion and the external expression of it. As their cognitive development continues, they learn by roughly 4 years of age that the minds of others are different from their own. They discover that others lie, and they start to lie themselves, which increases awareness of an inner self that is not available to others.

Fantasy also plays a role. The play of infants typically is entirely overt: handling objects and playing such games as peek-a-boo. Gradually, children start using fantasy in play, and a stick becomes an imaginary horse. Later, all the overt elements may be dropped in place of play that occurs entirely in the imagination. Even more relevant to the private self are wish-fulfilling fantasies that occur with the self as hero.

When infants first learn speech, they sometime practice it alone, talking to themselves. As the years pass, the motor elements slowly disappear and the lips no longer move, as self-talking becomes entirely covert. Talking to oneself, fantasies about oneself, and inhibition of emotions are all aspects of the trend toward covertness. The biological basis of this trend is the continuing development of the frontal and prefrontal cortex. The psychological bases are (a) increasing awareness that the minds of others are different from their own (theory of mind) and (b) increasing awareness of the difference between inner feelings and overtly expressed emotion and between knowing the truth and lying about it. These are slowly developing during the preschool era, but these young children "are largely unaware of their ongoing inner speech and may even not know that speech *can* be covert" (Flavell, 1999, p. 39).

Some elementary school children keep a diary, but it typically is the record of external, daily events, although some children might occasionally focus inward. However, the *trait* of private self-consciousness awaits late childhood or even adolescence, and not until adolescence does it differentiate into self-reflection and internal state awareness. We await research on the determinants of the latter differentiation.

PUBLIC SELF-CONSCIOUSNESS

The focus of attention here is not on the private aspects of the self but on the observable aspects. There is a keen awareness of how we are coming across to other people, but we are not attending to them so much as to ourselves.

The first study to use the public self-consciousness scale was on shunning in a laboratory setting (Fenigstein, 1979). There was a real subject and two other women (experimental accomplices) who were waiting for the experiment to begin. Those high in public self-consciousness reacted more intensely to being ignored, avoiding those who shunned them and reporting more dislike for them.

A social psychologist emphasized the negative side of self-consciousness, but he included something else: "Self-consciousness also has a purely cognitive component—the extent to which a person focuses his attention on how [he thinks] others see him, rather than on how he sees them" (Argyle, 1969, pp. 360–361). Viewed in this context, self-consciousness heightens one's feeling of being observed. Subjects were asked whether they felt more observed than observing in several social contexts (Argyle & Williams, 1969). Women felt more observed than men, and both sexes felt more observed when with elders. These authors suggested that there are individual differences in how much people feel they are being observed.

This suggestion proved apt, as revealed 25 years later in research on people as targets. *Public self-consciousness* is defined as having an intense awareness of oneself as a social object, so people high in this trait might feel targeted. Small groups of students were told that some of them had been chosen randomly for an experiment and were asked to indicate privately the probability that they had been selected (Fenigstein, 1984). The probability of being targeted correlated .34 with public self-consciousness. Next, a questionnaire was constructed about public events that might be attributed to a self-focus. On each question, subjects could answer that they would be the target of attention or not. Subjects high in public self-consciousness endorsed more of the self-as-target answers.

Fenigstein and Vanable (1992) carried this idea one step further with this line of reasoning:

> To see oneself as an object of attention, especially to others, may leave one susceptible to the idea that others are more interested in the self than is the case; the self-referent perceptions of the behavior of others is one of the hallmarks of paranoid thought. (p. 136)

These authors constructed a paranoia scale, a typical item being "Someone has it in for me." It correlated with public self-consciousness from .37 to .41 over four successive samples of subjects. Suspiciousness and resentment make up the Hostility scale of an aggression questionnaire (A. H. Buss & Perry, 1992). The correlation between public self-consciousness and hostility is .32 for men and .49 for women. Clearly, a strong sense of oneself as a social object leads to a feeling that one is the center of attention, which for some people involves suspiciousness. Consistent with this idea is the fact that drinkers who were high in public self-consciousness remembered more negative consequences of their drinking (LaBrie, Pederen, Neighbors, & Hummer, 2008).

People high in public self-consciousness are expected to have better knowledge about how they come across to others, and in fact women high in public self-consciousness are better at predicting the impression they would make than those low in the trait (Tobey & Tunnell, 1981). It follows that such self-awareness should lead to better knowledge about one's style of behaving. Observers watched subjects moving about and rated them for expressiveness—for example, lots of gestures—and expansiveness—for example, broader gestures (Gallaher, 1991). The subjects also rated themselves for these two stylistic features. For subjects high in public self-consciousness, the correlations between observers' ratings and self-reports were .67 for expressiveness and .55 for expansiveness. For those low in the trait, the correlations were, respectively, .07 and −.05, suggesting that people who are unaware of their social selves are ignorant of the stylistic aspects of their personality.

Part of awareness of oneself as a social object is a concern with appearance. Public self-consciousness correlated .32 with women's use of makeup, as judged from photos, and .40 with subjects' belief that makeup enhances appearance and social interactions (L. C. Miller & Cox, 1982). Consistent with these findings, a questionnaire tapping the importance of hair, face, and body proportions correlated .48 with public self-consciousness (Cash & Szymanski, 1995).

Men's awareness of appearance may cause them to be concerned about baldness, a concern that correlated .48 with public self-consciousness (Franzoi, Anderson, & Frommelt, 1990).

Being made aware of one's appearance affects self-consciousness When subjects were shown photographs of highly attractive people, their public self-consciousness scores rose (Thornton & Moore, 1993).

Development

The first step is the ability to take the perspective of others to learn how they see you, an ability that starts late in the preschool era. Flavell (1968, pp. 164–168) asked children to select gifts for themselves and older family members. The 3-year-olds selected gifts for others that they themselves wanted— something like a man who buys his wife a box of cigars for her birthday. Some 4-year-olds, many 5-year-olds, and all 6-year-olds chose gifts appropriate for older members of the family, demonstrating increasing ability to take the perspective of others.

Children probably learn to take this perspective by imitating parents who remind them of how others will regard them. After many repetitions, it is as if the parental question, "What will people think of you?" is being repeated inside the head of the child.

Parents vary considerably in how intensely they socialize their children. At one extreme, they lay down strict rules of appearance and deportment. Children's attention is firmly directed toward themselves as social objects. Such children are likely to become high in public self-consciousness. At the other extreme are parents who are casual about appearance and demeanor. They are more likely to value independence in their children and only minimally direct attention to the externals of self. Such children are expected to remain low in public self-consciousness.

Aside from explicit socialization, consider the social environment of children of ministers, politicians, and media stars. Family life is something like living in a fishbowl. There is a stream of visitors or paparazzi, and the public is intensely curious about everyone in the family. These children learn early that others will examine them closely. As a result, most of them become high in public self-consciousness and retain it beyond adolescence.

Puberty is marked by rapid body growth and development of secondary sex characteristics. The adolescent body feels and looks different from the child body—not only to the adolescents but to everyone else as well. Parents, siblings, and friends comment on the rapid changes, often in a teasing fashion. Keenly aware that they feel different and look different, adolescents are certain that everyone is looking at them and examining them. When strolling down the street, they have something in common with movie or rock stars: a belief that they are the center of attention. For some adolescents, the attention is welcome, and they may even show off, perhaps with a female hip swing or a male swagger. For many of them, the attention is distressing, making them feel naked and exposed.

Whether the reaction is positive or negative, public self-awareness reaches its peak during adolescence. Public self-consciousness was assessed in 13- and 14-year-olds and then continued for 4 more years (Rankin, Lane, Gibbons, & Gerrard, 2004). It was highest in the 13- and 15-year-olds and diminished subsequently.

In some cultures, heightened public self-awareness is a way of life. Japan is a country in which *face*, the public persona presented to everyone, is so crucial that loss of face may lead to suicidal thoughts and even suicide. Japanese public self-consciousness far exceeds Western self-consciousness:

> An external frame of reference leads Japanese to have a heightened awareness of their audience. . . . In this way, rather than being seen as subjects, they may more aptly be viewed as imagined objects in the eyes of others. (Heine, Lehman, Markus, & Kitayama, 1999, p. 8)

Divergence

A keen awareness of oneself as a social object may be used in the service of *self-presentation*, which involves projecting an image of yourself to others, a topic to be discussed in the Perspective section. Alternatively, a keen sense of yourself as a social object may cause you to feel embarrassed, which is self-conscious shyness.

SELF-CONSCIOUS SHYNESS (EMBARRASSMENT)

Awareness of oneself as a social object may be simply a mild feeling that others are looking at you, perhaps inspecting you. It evolves into shyness when public self-awareness is so acute that you feel exposed, awkward, and uncomfortable. Blushing does not occur every time embarrassment is experienced, but it is an unequivocal sign of it. So far as is known, we are the only species that blushes—or as Mark Twain said, "Man is the only species that blushes. Or needs to."

One way to study blushing is to have nonmusical subjects sing a song they know, such as their national anthem, and then have them watch a video of their performance (Shearn, Bergman, Hill, Abel, & Hinds, 1992). When the subjects and others watched the video together, the larger this audience, the more intense the blushing. Beyond that, blushing was uncorrelated with a rise in skin temperature; people can feel their face being hot without it becoming red.

The same paradigm was used to study empathic blushing, this time with the subject and a friend watching the video, and both blushed (Shearn & Spellman,1993). Given the human capacity for empathy, we are sometimes embarrassed at another's embarrassment (R. S. Miller, 1996, 2007).

Causes

A prominent cause of embarrassment is a feeling of being conspicuous, usually because of excessive attention from others. Alternatively, this feeling may arise in the rare situations in which a person is remarkably different from the others present. Visualize being in an elevator with members of professional basketball team or entering a costume party in formal dress.

Everyone knows the difference between public and private behavior. When the barrier between private and public is violated, that is, when private behavior occurs in public, the outcome is usually embarrassment. Three such breaches of the private–public distinction may be summarized as the social requirements of privacy: to be unseen, unheard, and untouched. The most frequent and perhaps most intense embarrassment occurs over body modesty. If you are the one who is not fully clothed, you may be the only one who becomes embarrassed, or both you and the other person become embarrassed.

The *physical privacy* just described involves the social self, which is relevant to public self-awareness, but there is also a covert self that is relevant to private self-awareness: thoughts, feelings, ambitions, love, and jealousy. This *psychological privacy* may be breached when you inadvertently blurt out a hidden feeling or make a Freudian slip, which is then interpreted by others.

The staring of others, causing conspicuousness, has already been mentioned, but there are more active behaviors by others that cause shyness. The most serious is *teasing*, which causes considerable discomfort to the victim to the considerable amusement of onlookers (Keltner, Capps, King, Young, & Heery, 2001). Just telling people that they have blushed increases blood flow to the face (M. R. Leary, Britt, Cutlip, & Templeton, 1992), especially in those with a propensity for blushing (Drummond et al., 2003).

Even pleasing social behavior may cause embarrassment. *Overpraise* is evidently a case of too much of a good thing—that is, compliments causing mild distress. As to why, one reason is the feeling of being conspicuous, but there is more to it (L. Buss, 1978). Subjects who received excessive praise became more embarrassed than those who were merely made conspicuous.

Development

The earliest study used parental reports of blushing or any other signs of embarrassment observed during the past 6 months (A. H. Buss, Iscoe, & Buss, 1979). The frequency of reported embarrassment followed this developmental course: 3- and 4-year-olds, 26%; 5-year-olds, 59%; and 6-year-olds, 73%. Thereafter, the percentage of children displaying embarrassment remained stable the rest of childhood. As in most aspects of development, some children are precocious, first displaying embarrassment at 3 years of age, but it shows up for most children by 5 years of age. The reports were retrospective, covering the previous 6 months, which means that the ages reported here are on the high side by 6 months or more.

More controlled research clearly was needed. It was supplied by Michael Lewis and his colleagues (M. Lewis, Sullivan, Stanger, & Weiss, 1989), who had mothers bring their infants into the laboratory. In two experiments, the infants were exposed to procedures designed to induce mild embarrassment. In the first one, the infants were placed in front of a mirror, and several signs of embarrassment were recorded: smiling, gaze aversion, and nervous movements of the hand. These frequencies of embarrassment were observed: in ages 9 to 12 months, 22%; in ages 15 to 18 months, 30%; and in ages 21 to 24 months, 63%. In the second experiment, infants averaging almost 2 years of age were exposed to the mirror situation, were excessively complimented, and were asked to dance by both the experimenter and the mother. The frequencies of embarrassment, expressed in percentages, were as follows: mirror, 25%; compliment, 32%; dance for mother, 23%; and dance for experimenter, 32%. The conclusion was that first appearance of embarrassment was roughly 2 years. However, another researcher of embarrassment reviewed this study and reached a different conclusion: "Thus when some 2-year-olds appear coy in response to their reflections, I'd not call them embarrassed, at least not in any adult sense of the emotion. They are self-conscious and conspicuous, however" (R. S. Miller, 1996, p. 86).

So perhaps embarrassment occurs later in development. Children were to imagine knocking cans over in a crowded supermarket or singing to an audience (Bennett, 1989). The frequency of reported embarrassment at each age was as follows: 5 years, 13%; 8 years, 44%; and 11 years, 75%. Children were then asked the same question, except now the imaginary audience would be ridiculing them. The reported frequencies of embarrassment were as follows: 5 years, 44%; 8 years, 75%; 11 years, 88%. The data on the 5-year-olds are especially interesting. For virtually all them, singing to an audience would not be embarrassing, but for almost half of them, ridicule would be embarrassing.

With regard to developmental processes, all children are taught the ways of their group through various kinds of learning, specifically instrumental conditioning; imitation; and cognitive learning, especially perspective taking. A child's prosocial behavior is reinforced with praise and affection. Behavior that opposes or ignores the goals of socialization is punished by isolation, loss of privileges, and verbal admonitions. The most potent verbal punishment consists of laughter, teasing, and ridicule. Once the child acquires public self-awareness, such punishment tends to embarrass the child. During the 2nd or 3rd year of life, children are initiated into toilet training, and by their 3rd year, they are often teased for "accidents" involving bladder or bowels.

Laughter and ridicule also start early with respect to modesty. Children are taught about being clothed, and when they violate taboos involving body privacy, they are often made to feel silly or foolish.

Starting in the preschool era, children are introduced to manners and etiquette. They are taught appropriate social behavior in more formal contexts, and they learn the difference, for example, between eating at home and eating in a restaurant. Again, the penalty for mistakes is often ridicule and teasing, and children become embarrassed when others laugh at them.

During the preschool era, children develop the cognitive ability to take the perspective of others (Flavell, 1992, 1999; Wellman, Cross, & Watson, 2001). This ability underlies being able to perceive oneself as a social object, so these findings are consistent, with age 4 years as the time when the conditions required for true embarrassment are in place. However, even 4-year-olds are only at the beginning of the ability to take the perspective of others, as was demonstrated when they had difficulty explaining to a confederate how to play hide-and-seek (Peskin & Ardino, 2003).

Somewhat later in childhood, usually in elementary school, children are teased and ridiculed for another kind of immodesty: bragging and conceit. In our society, if people tout their own accomplishments, others typically react with raucous laughter, sarcastic remarks, and caricature—all of which tend to cause embarrassment.

Gradually, children learn about two other kinds of privacy. They learn that certain activities must be clandestine: plotting and scheming with others; masturbation; and reading about, talking about, or viewing sexual behavior. The other kind of privacy involves the private self—fantasies, feelings, ambitions, and memories that are known only by oneself. Children learn caution about disclosing them because peers and unsympathetic adults might laugh or ridicule them.

Vicarious embarrassment requires two cognitive advances fostered through socialization practices: empathy and taking the perspective of another. Those are the necessary conditions. The sufficient condition is our own previous experience of embarrassment. Then when we observe another person being embarrassed, we share a part of the same feeling.

The dichotomy between a primitive self and an advanced self bears directly on the concept of public self-awareness. Infants can recognize themselves in the mirror (primitive self-awareness) without being aware of themselves as social objects (advanced self-awareness). Thus, a 2-year-old clearly has achieved self-recognition but not the advanced cognitions and the extended lessons of socialization that result in public self-awareness. Lacking public self-awareness, a 2-year-old human infant has no more reason to become embarrassed than does a chimpanzee. When 2-year-olds recognize themselves in a mirror, they obviously are self-aware, but it is not the advanced, public self-awareness necessary for embarrassment to occur. By age 3, some children have a sufficient sense of themselves as social objects and have undergone sufficient socialization to display. The majority of children are unlikely to show embarrassment until age 4.

Although instances of embarrassment are rare, they increase in frequency throughout childhood. Children become more adept at teasing and ridicule—to the discomfort of their victims—and familiar adults seem to enjoy teasing children. Children also become ever more aware of the private–public distinction, an important source of embarrassment, and these trends reach a peak in adolescence. Elementary school, high school, and college students were asked to recall their earliest embarrassing experience (Horowitz, 1962). The highest frequency of embarrassment was reported for the 11- to 15-year period of adolescence.

After adolescence, social situations become familiar, the pressures of socialization abate, and adults become more adept at handling teasing. As a result, the frequency of embarrassment wanes as the years of adulthood pass, and blushing is self-reported to decrease in frequency during adulthood (Shields, Mallory, & Simon, 1989). Older people are rarely embarrassed.

ANXIOUS VERSUS SELF-CONSCIOUS SHYNESS

This chapter has approached shyness as acute and uncomfortable awareness of oneself as a social object, but in Chapter 3 of this volume, shyness was discussed as social anxiety. Why have the same name, *shyness*, for two kinds of behavior? One reason is that both involve discomfort, avoidance, and inhibition of normally expected social behavior. Another reason is that both kinds of behavior are included in most psychologists' descriptions of shyness. So why distinguish two kinds of shyness? I do so because in several respects they differ.

Anxious shyness has the following characteristics:

- It starts at roughly age 1 year.
- It is caused by novelty: strangers and unfamiliar social settings.

- In adolescence it is caused by novel social roles and by social evaluation
- Its developmental causes are heredity, social isolation, and insecure attachment.
- The emotion is fear.

Self-conscious shyness, on the other hand, is characterized as follows:

- It starts at roughly age 4 years.
- It is caused by conspicuousness and breaches of privacy.
- Later in childhood, it is caused by overpraise, minor social mistakes, and teasing.
- In adolescence, it is caused by strong awareness of secondary sexual characteristics.
- Its developmental cause is excessive socialization.
- The emotion is embarrassment.

There have been only few studies on the distinction between the two kinds of shyness (reviewed by Schmidt & Buss, 2010). College women who identified themselves as shy were asked when they first experienced this (Cheek, Carpentieri, Smith, Rierdan, & Koff, 1986). Roughly four fifths said that their shyness started after age 6, which presumably is self-conscious shyness, and the other fifth said it started before age 6, which presumably is anxious shyness.

College students were divided into two groups of subjects: high fear, low public self-consciousness (anxious shyness), and low fear, high public self-consciousness (self-conscious shyness; Bruch, Giordano, & Pearl, 1986). Most of the anxious shy subjects reported that their shyness started before elementary school, but most of the self-conscious shy subjects reported that their shyness started after they began elementary school. In addition, anxious shy subjects reported physiological arousal more frequently than did self-conscious shy subjects. Anxiously shy subjects were found to have lower self-esteem than self-consciously shy subjects (Schmidt & Robinson, 1992),

These findings support the distinction between two kinds of shyness, but they were based on retrospective reports. Such research needs to be supplemented by longitudinal studies. We already know that anxious shyness starts in the 1st year of life, when it is called *stranger anxiety* or *inhibition*, and that self-conscious shyness starts a few years later. Thus, the distinction is important in childhood, but is it important later in development—that is, does it make a difference whether adults are anxiously shy or self-consciously shy? To find out, we need to track both kinds of shy children through to adulthood.

Self-conscious shyness, which occurs because of socialization training and a history of teasing, is likely to be more easily overcome than anxious shyness, which has an inherited component and therefore may be more resistant to change.

If the problem is anxious shyness, the therapy would be similar to that used in other kinds of anxiety. It might be systematic desensitization, flooding, or a variety of cognitive behavior modification techniques. The emphasis would be on coping with anxiety and diminishing it. As in other kinds of anxieties, one problem is that clients may focus on the physiological components of fear, which is *private* self-awareness.

If the problem is self-conscious shyness, clients are focusing too much on the *public* aspects of the self. One way to deal with this problem is to teach clients to direct attention elsewhere, for example, by moving the conversation to topics other than the self ("Are you wearing a new outfit?") or by having pictures or other objects that listeners might examine. Another way is to have clients learn that most of the time they are not the focus of attention, for example, by showing them videotapes of themselves in social interaction. A third option is to have clients learn to direct attention away from the self by concentrating on the current topic of conversation or on the physical and psychological characteristics of those around them. When attention is directed toward the social environment, there is a double benefit. Self-awareness is necessarily diminished, and people can more comfortably deal with the social context because their focus is where it belongs: on being socially responsive and on their social skills.

People who seek help for their shyness might be both anxiously and self-consciousness shy. If so, both kinds of therapy would be needed. The larger point is that differentiating between the two kinds of shyness suggests two kinds of psychological treatment.

PERSPECTIVES ON THE SELF

Self-Consciousness

One theory, *objective self-awareness*, with a nod to cognitive dissonance, assumes that self-awareness is at least mildly aversive (Duval & Wicklund, 1972; Wicklund, 1979). The putative sequence proceeds from self-awareness to self-evaluation, which consists of comparing present behavior to a standard. Most behavior does not meet the standard, yielding a negative discrepancy, and the dominant response is escape by leaving the situation or directing attention elsewhere. If escape is not possible, the only option is to reduce the discrepancy between the behavior and the standard.

There is some evidence that self-awareness is aversive. As reviewed by Carver and Scheier (1981), subjects try to escape self-awareness when they are negatively evaluated, fail on a task, or asked to contemplate death. However, all these experimental situations cause sadness or anxiety, so there is ample reason for subjects wanting to stop thinking about them. Beyond that, there is no aversiveness when subjects look at nude pictures or, when angered, aggress against victims; more generally, self-directed attention is not necessarily aversive.

Comparison with a standard is also fundamental to the *control theory* of Carver and Scheier (1981, 1998). A standard develops when

> behavioral specifications are encoded in memory in the same fashion as is other information. As schemas develop for the recognition of event categories, some schemas . . . include behavior-specifying information. . . . When a schema that includes such information is accessed and used in the classification of a stimulus input, the response-specifying information may also be accessed as part of the schema. That information, then, constitutes the behavioral standard. (Carver & Scheier, 1981, p. 121)

These standards or set points are familiar: "Attitudes, for example, provide behavioral standards. Desires represent standards" (Carver & Scheier, 1981, p. 120).

The generation of standards is the first part or system of control theory, setting up goals for behavior or at least guides. The second system "reduces discrepancies between an existing state and the previously evoked standard" (Carver & Scheier, 1981, p. 117).

There are major differences between objective self-awareness theory and control theory. First, objective self-awareness theory insists that a discrepancy between behavior and a standard is aversive, but control theory denies this. Second, objective self-awareness theory does not specify what a standard is, whereas control does. Third, objective self-awareness theory clearly belongs under the rubric of cognitive dissonance theory, whereas control theory places itself in the context of the test–operate–test–exit model of cybernetics theory (G. Miller, Galanter, & Pribram, 1960). Fourth, objective self-awareness has no place for self-consciousness as a trait, whereas control theory finds the trait important. Fifth, objective self-awareness theory makes no distinction between private and public self-awareness, whereas control theory does.

Self-Presentation

Recall that one outcome of awareness of yourself as a social object is *self-presentation*, which may account for the paucity of research on public self-consciousness. Most psychologists, especially social psychologists, ignore public self-consciousness and prefer to use the concept of self-presentation.

Interest in self-presentation started with an aptly named book, *The Presentation of Self in Everyday Life*, written by a sociologist (Goffman, 1959). He suggested that we are essentially actors who by our dress, speech, and gestures portray ourselves in the roles we play in everyday life. He introduced the concept of *demeanor:* "that element of the individual's ceremonial behavior typically conveyed through deportment, dress, and bearing, which serves to express to those in his immediate presence that he is a person of certain desirable or undesirable qualities" (Goffman, 1959, p. 77). He added a caveat: "A psychology is necessarily involved but one stripped and cramped to suit the sociological study of conversation, track meets, banquets, jury trials, and street loitering" (pp. 2–3).

Despite this "cramped psychology," the approach has been widely adopted by researchers on social behavior, some of whom equate self-presentation with impression management. Sometimes the terminology of the stage is used: "Assertive impression management refers to those behaviors initiated by the actor to establish particular identities or attributes in the eyes of another" (Tedeschi & Norman, 1985, p. 295). Some adherents suggest that self-presentation is ubiquitous in social behavior, which may make sense in a culture like that of Japan but not in more individualist Western culture.

To continue the stage metaphor, when the play is over, the actors leave the stage, shuck their costumes, and return to their unscripted everyday selves. Similarly, as acquaintance grows, if there has been self-presentation, it is usually replaced by usual and typical behavior that reflects both the actors' personality and their relationships with others. There may be no self-presentation even when interacting with strangers because there are individual differences here (Lennox & Wolfe, 1984; M. Snyder, 1974). At one extreme, some people are frequent self-presenters who may even persist in this behavior as acquaintance grows, as if they were always on stage. Consistent with this idea, people high in public self-consciousness tend to make socially desirable responses (Lalwani, Shrum, & Chiu, 2009, Study 4). At the other extreme are those who seem to always be off stage. They are low in public self-consciousness and high in expressive behavior: What you see is what you get.

Embarrassment

Self-presentation lends itself to explaining embarrassment by specifying the kinds of social mistakes that lead to embarrassment (M. R. Leary & Kowalski, 1995; Schlenker & Leary, 1982). The basic idea is that people try to present themselves as mature and capable, and when mistakes are made or social accidents occur, the wished-for image crumbles, and embarrassment ensues. Becoming embarrassed is a signal to others that the person is aware of the social mistake and takes responsibility for it, thereby avoiding social punishment. One theorist (Edelmann, 1987) offered this sequence:

1. People attempt to present images of themselves to others in accord with standards or goals.
2. Any social mistake means that an undesired image is being projected.
3. Awareness of this fact focuses attention on the self.
4. A real or imagined audience focuses attention solely on the public self.
5. The self-focus intensifies embarrassment.

This approach was used to suggest two kinds of embarrassment. Children in the 4- to 7-year range are assumed to display an early kind of embarrassment. They are aware that

> certain behaviors provoke ridicule and teasing while others do not. This may well see the emergence of a "primitive" embarrassment, which involves being embarrassed by others' reactions without being fully aware of why the reactions occur. From the age of 8 years it is more likely that the child will wish to convey a particular impression of self, recognizing the impression that he/she creates for others. As the child's motivation to manage impressions and his/her awareness of how these impressions are viewed by others increases the "mature" embarrassment is a much more likely outcome should unintentional transgression occur. (Edelmann, 1987, p. 119)

Self-Reference and Evaluation

One theory suggests that there are two kinds of embarrassment, the first kind starting in infancy (M. Lewis, 1995). This earlier kind, appearing sometime before age 2 years, requires mirror-image recognition:

> Sometime in the middle of the second year, the child develops a sense of self, as evidenced by . . . self-referential behavior. . . . At this time emotions such as envy and empathy emerge. The child will also express self-conscious embarrassment when he or she is looked at, pointed at or singled out in some way. (M. Lewis, 1995, p. 77)

The second type of embarrassment requires internalization of societal standards, rules, and goals, which are assumed to develop as early as the 3rd year of life (M. Lewis, 2007, 2010). It follows that 3-year-olds are capable of evaluative embarrassment.

Consider, however, the experimental manipulation designed to elicit evaluative embarrassment was failure on a timed task, which caused only a minority of the 4-year-olds to display "a smiling facial expression, gaze aversion, and nervous touching of the hands to the body or face" (M. Lewis & Ramsey, 2002, p. 1037). These behaviors may just as easily be interpreted as children being disappointed at failure and displaying a downcast appearance, but they are not necessarily embarrassed. This interpretation is strengthened by the fact that some of the children in the study showing signs of shame after failure in the task.

Appeasement

Finally, it has been suggested that blushing is an involuntary appeasement gesture:

> Those who are blushing are somehow saying that they know, care about, and fear others' evaluations and that they share those values deeply; they also communicate their sorrow over any possible faults or inadequacies on their part, thus performing an acknowledgement, a confession, and an apology aimed at inhibiting others' aggression or avoiding social ostracism. (Castelfranchi & Poggi, 1990, p. 240)

These authors hypothesized that blushing evolved before our species differentiated into different races. Said another way, blushing is an evolutionary adaptation, a hypothesis that Darwin (1853/1955) denied.

This evolutionary approach was taken a step further in offering embarrassment as similar to the submissive gestures of primates and other animals: "Blushing, then, may be a social attention diversion or distraction mechanism comparable to nonhuman appeasement displays. Besides their shared functions of remediation or appeasement, both are elicited by undesired attention from conspecifics and typically deflect it" (M. R. Leary et al., 1992, p. 455).

Subsequently, Keltner (1995) theorized about appeasement, and he and his colleagues wrote,

> Reactive forms of appeasement follow actual, discrete events, such as transgressions of morals or conventions, that disrupt social relations and require immediate response. Reactive forms of appeasement, therefore, are likely to be discrete and state-like in nature and engage humans in brief emotional exchanges. Embarrassment and shame are two forms of reactive appeasement that redress different kinds of transgressions. (Keltner, Young, & Buswell, 1997, p. 362)

They mentioned research demonstrating that people who display signs of embarrassment or shame are treated better or at least less harshly than those who do not, leading to the conclusion that embarrassment "is an adaptation to a problem related to physical and social survival: the restoration of relations following a social transgression" (Keltner & Buswell, 1997, p. 263).

Embarrassment may serve an appeasement function for minor social mistakes, but people also become embarrassed when they have not erred and have nothing to apologize for. Recall situations in which innocents tend to blush: the woman who is in the bathroom when a man inadvertently enters, the speaker who is overpraised, or the adolescent whose crush on another person is disclosed. The victims have not transgressed—only the private–public barrier has been breached—so there is no need for appeasement. These facts do not deny the value of the appeasement approach but emphasize the limits of its application.

There remains the question of why our species would need an additional display of appeasement when we already have available kneeling and groveling, as well as verbal apology. If embarrassment is not an adaptive display of appeasement, there is another evolutionary account of it, as follows.

Highly social mammals, such as wolves and chimpanzees, have two of the requirements needed for embarrassment to occur. They have bonds of attachment that extend beyond the mother–offspring relationship, which, incidentally, can spur jealousy. They also socialize their offspring to promote harmony among adults. However, they never display any embarrassed behavior, only the submissive posture necessary to appease an angered dominant member of the group, which means that this first set of features is necessary but not sufficient.

So which features of our species set us up for embarrassment?

1. We have considerably more intense socialization of the young.
2. We teach the young complex social rules, such as the private–public distinction, which they absorb because they have the cognitive ability to do so.
3. We are able to focus attention to the self well beyond mere mirror-image recognition.
4. When this self-focus involves the self as a social object and a social rule has been broken, we experience embarrassment.

Other social mammals do not have this second set of features (the necessary ones) and so cannot be embarrassed. This approach to embarrassment emphasizes our advanced cognitive ability and socialization of the rules that promote group harmony.

7

SELF II: SELF-ESTEEM AND IDENTITY

On his radio show *A Prairie Home Companion*, the humorist Garrison Keillor regularly reports the news from a fictional town in Minnesota called Lake Wobegone, where "all the women are strong, all the men are good looking, and all the children are above average." Like all spoofs, it has a kernel of truth because Americans, especially those high in self-esteem (Beauregard & Dunning, 2001), tend to inflate their abilities and endorse a variety of virtues as applying to themselves (Dunning, 1999). This self-serving tendency is crucial to understanding the mass of research that has been done with U.S. subjects, which is placed in the broader context of cross-cultural research in the Perspectives section in this chapter.

SELF-ESTEEM

Like other personality traits, self-esteem may wax and wane from day to day or week to week, but over time it is consistent enough for differences among people to be significant. The consistency appears to derive from self-esteem being in part inherited (Raevuori et al., 2007) and from cognitive mechanisms that maintain a given level of self-esteem. We begin with how people with high self-esteem (Highs) and those with low self-esteem (Lows) describe themselves.

Descriptions

If we were to ask people to describe themselves, they would do so in so many different ways that it would be difficult to relate the descriptions to self-esteem. The solution is to have them rate how a set of descriptive adjectives applies to them. When this has been done, Highs have rated themselves higher on the positive adjectives and lower in the negative ones (J. D. Campbell & Fehr, 1990). In subsequent research, Highs rated themselves more favorably on these adjectives: *attractive, capable, good-looking, kind, smart,* and *talented* (Brown, 1993).

In a variation of this method, subjects used percentages to guess where they stood in relation to the general population (Baumgardner, 1990). Highs reported higher percentages than Lows for these adjectives: *able, bright, clever, likable,* and *talented*. Lows reported higher percentages than Highs for these adjectives: *incapable* and *unpopular*. This study also confirmed what other studies implied: that most people believe they are above average on positive attributes. For example, on the adjective *likable* even Lows rated themselves in the 65th percentile, although still lower than the Highs' average rating of 85%.

In brief, individual differences in self-esteem are reflected in the particulars of self-description. The importance of self-esteem, however, extends beyond self-descriptions to how it affects perceptions of others' views of oneself. Pairs of men were asked to get acquainted and afterward completed a likability questionnaire on their partners and themselves (Brockner & Lloyd, 1986). Lows, compared with Highs, liked themselves less but thought their partners liked them less. In fact, the partners liked the Lows just as much as the Highs. Does this false perception occur among pairs who already know each other? Yes; among dating partners and married people, Lows also underestimate their partners' regard for them (S. L. Murray, Holmes, & Griffin, 2000).

Challenges

Performance

How does self-esteem affect the performance of people after they succeed or fail? A review of laboratory experiments conducted in the 1970s and 1980s concluded that failure typically deteriorates the subsequent performance of Lows (Brockner, Derr, & Laing, 1987). These researchers went on to study a real-life situation: college students' exams. Doing poorly on the first exam did not affect the performance of Highs on the second exam, but it caused a significant drop in the second exam's scores for the Lows.

Lows perform poorly after failure perhaps because they conclude they are bound to fail in anything they try (Kernis, Brockner, & Frankel, 1989). Kernis et al. (1989) used an overgeneralization questionnaire, sample items of which are "How I feel about myself overall is easily influenced by a single mistake" and "If something goes wrong—no matter what it is—I see myself negatively." This questionnaire correlated −.61 with self-esteem.

Lows are so sensitive to failure as to be affected even when it is merely hypothesized (J. D. Campbell & Fairey, 1985). In a study by J. D. Campbell and Fairey (1985), the task was arranging letters to make up a word. In the experimental condition, subjects were shown the anagrams, asked to imagine they had taken on the task and done poorly, and asked to explain their failure; then they worked on the task. Control subjects merely performed the task. Lows performed worse than control subjects, but Highs performed better than control subjects. Even hypothetical failure caused Lows to lose self-competence and perform poorly, but Highs tried harder after imagined failure and performed better.

Cognitive Tactics

When people have done poorly in comparison to others, one tactic is to engage in *downward comparison* (Wills, 1981). If you received a C on an exam, for example, you would focus on the number of people who failed. The other tactic, used less frequently, is to engage in *upward comparison*. After failing in a task, subjects could seek upward or downward social comparison (Wood, Giordano-Beech, Taylor, Michela, & Gaus, 1994). Lows sought downward comparison, but the Highs sought upward comparison.

In a similar study, subjects were failed in a task and were then allowed to engage in social comparison (Crocker & Gallo, 1995). Lows reported feeling better and more satisfied with life after downward comparison. A review of literature revealed that Highs benefited from upward comparison (Collins, 1996). In brief, Highs tend to look upward and Lows look downward to assuage their feelings after failure.

Challenges to self-esteem may be met by self-presentation. In a study by Schlenker, Weigold, and Hallam (1990), both Highs and Lows were motivated to impress others. Highs did so by bragging, Lows by being modest.

Another tactic is to place barriers to performance in advance and to use them as an excuse for failure (E. E. Jones & Berglas, 1978). Such *self-handicapping* may be used to enhance self-esteem when the barriers are overcome. Subjects were told that they could practice for as much time as they needed for a subsequent task and were asked about the meaning of their later performance (Tice, 1991). Told that the task would tell who was extremely able, Highs tended to agree with this attribution: "If I do not practice much and do very well in the evaluation, that suggests that I have extremely high ability," an enhancement tactic. However, told the task would identify those of extremely low ability, Lows tended to agree with this attribution: "If I do not practice much and do very poorly, that does not say much about my ability because I might have done better if I had practiced longer," a self-handicapping tactic.

If Highs tend to enhance their self-esteem, they might be more willing to take risks, and if Lows tend to protect their self-esteem, they might avoid risks. In Josephs, Larrick, Steele, and Nisbett (1992), subjects were to gamble for money and could choose safe or risky ways to play. Lows chose safer bets than Highs. In a related study, subjects practiced a video game and then gambled on how well they would perform when playing it again (Baumeister, Heatherton, & Tice, 1993). Compared with Lows, Highs said they would do much better and would be able to make more money. When it was suggested that subjects might choke under pressure, Highs tried for self-enhancement and bet too much, this time losing more money than Lows. In contrast, Lows protected their self-esteem by betting cautiously and therefore lost less money.

We now return to the consequences of failure, this time with an emphasis on cognitive tactics when failure cannot be denied. After failing a so-called achievement test, Highs exaggerated their being altruistic and other social positives, a compensatory tactic (Brown & Smart, 1991). Lows did not use this compensatory mechanism, presumably because they regarded failure as being consistent with their lack of ability. These findings were confirmed when subjects were told they scored low in tests of ability and then guessed about improvement if they took the tests again (Josephs, Markus, & Tafarodi, 1992).

High Versus Low Self-Esteem

In what follows, differences between people high and low in self-esteem are being exaggerated for the sake of exposition. Lows avoid challenges because they are insecure about their abilities. They seek sure bets, tasks that are so easy as to guarantee success. If Highs take the offensive in the expectation of success, Lows adopt a defensive strategy of not failing. Lows do not take chances and desperately try to avoid mistakes they believe are likely to occur. When confronted with a specific inability, they cannot deny its importance. When confronted with failure, they find consolation in the fact that others are inferior (downward comparison) but seem not to benefit from upward comparison. When they fail, they subsequently perform worse and assume they will fail in everything. When rejected, they blame themselves and make negative appraisals (Ford & Collins, 2010).

Highs, being optimistic, seek to enhance their already high self-esteem. Highs are likely to seek challenges because they are secure in their own abilities. Confident of success, they are willing to reach for the brass ring, seeking a risky job but one with a potential for personal advancement. They dismiss evidence of inability as being unimportant. They react to failure by trying harder and by telling themselves and others of their other abilities and successes. Already feeling superior, they cannot benefit from knowing that others are inferior, but they do value upward comparison.

These characteristics, the result of decades of research, suggest that Highs and Lows follow different paths over time. Lows set themselves up for failure or at least not to succeed, and they are ready with excuses when they do fail. Avoiding challenges, they are less likely to acquire the skills needed for success and the confidence that might accompany it. Worse still, they easily accept negative feedback but are reluctant to accept positive feedback (Josephs, Bosson, & Jacobs, 2003).

Highs expect to succeed, are willing to take chances to do so, easily accept positive feedback, assume that any failure is transient, and have cognitive mechanisms for maintaining or even enhancing self-esteem. Over time this cascade is likely to magnify differences between Highs and Lows.

Relation to Other Traits

In my research, I have used a brief questionnaire that is similar to other self-esteem questionnaires and correlates strongly with them (A. H. Buss & Perry, 1991, 1992):

1. I have a good opinion of myself.
2. Overall, I'm glad I'm me and not someone else.
3. I'm fairly sure of myself.
4. I am basically worthwhile.
5. I'm satisfied with who I am.
6. I often wish I were someone else. (Reverse coded)

These items and others assessing several personality traits were administered to 912 college students of both sexes. Self-esteem correlated −.59 with shyness, which confirmed an earlier study with children (Lazarus, 1982). Highs are by definition confident, which means that in a novel social situation they are likely to be relaxed and ready to interact.

Lows expect that others will see them as they see themselves and therefore not accept them, the result being reticence and difficulty in dealing with novel social interaction. They tend to be anxious or self-conscious and therefore back off from strangers and casual acquaintances who are turned off by this lack of responsiveness. The result is fewer friends, more isolation—self-esteem correlates −.59 with social loneliness—and a failure to develop the social skills that might make novel situations rewarding.

Self-esteem is also closely related to optimism, the correlation being .64 (A. H. Buss & Perry, 1991). Highs, other things equal, have good reasons for being optimists, but as we saw earlier, Lows expect to fail or at least not do well, which is a pessimistic outlook. So in a sense, optimism might be regarded as a cognitive consequence of high self-esteem, and pessimism might be regarded as a consequence of feeling unworthy. However, some Highs might set such lofty goals that they might be pessimistic about reaching them, and some Lows might set such modest goals that they might be optimistic about reaching them. So though self-esteem and optimism are closely related, they are not identical.

In fact, Scheier and Carver (1985) reported a lower correlation between self-esteem and optimism, and later research confirmed this lower correlation (Scheier, Carver, & Bridges, 1994). Their research showed that optimism has a positive effect on physical health independent of self-esteem, which is a good reason to separate the cognitive aspect of self-esteem from global self-esteem.

Self-esteem also correlates moderately with Extraversion and more strongly with the Conscientiousness superfactor of the Big Five (Robins, Tracy, Trzesniewski, Potter, & Gosling, 2001). Taken together, these trait correlations and the ones mentioned earlier suggest several tilts in the direction of self-esteem. Dominance, leadership, extraversion, and conscientiousness all tilt toward high self-esteem, and shyness tilts toward low self-esteem

SOURCES OF SELF-ESTEEM

Global self-esteem might be regarded as just the sum of various sources of self-esteem, but perhaps it is not. College students rated themselves for appearance, leadership, emotional stability, and intelligence (Pelham & Swann, 1989). A composite of these sources correlated .50 with global self-esteem, which leaves open two possibilities: (a) Self-esteem is more than the sum of its sources, and (b) there are other sources of self-esteem. In the Perspectives section, I discuss the sources suggested by other psychologists, but what follows is my organization of them. It starts with distinguishing between social sources and personal sources.

Social Sources

Social Rewards

In Chapter 4, I discussed the social rewards of presence of others, sharing, activities, attention, and responsiveness. These rewards are likely to be offered by friends, and there is evidence that people tend to choose friends who are likely to help maintain their self-esteem (M. Snyder, Berscheid, & Glick, 1985; M. Snyder, Gangestad, & Simpson, 1983). However, there is another set of social rewards that are perhaps more familiar. The most obvious one is affection, ranging from the bond of friendship to the love of parents, siblings, and spouses; the others are praise and respect.

Each of these social rewards is best regarded as the positive end of a bipolar dimension, each with its negative opposite: for affection, hostility; for praise, criticism. These opposites tend to lower self-esteem. The positive and negative effects of this set of social rewards on self-esteem may seem obvious, but they need to be stated.

Power

Dominance correlates with self-esteem (M. R. Leary, Cottrell, & Phillips, 2001), but a more detailed study related self-esteem to bossiness, leadership, competitiveness, and aggressiveness (Gallaher & Buss, 1987). Self-esteem correlated moderately with bossiness (dominance), strongly with leadership, and not at all with competitiveness or aggressiveness. We know that bossiness and leadership are related (see Chapter 5), so the correlations between each of them and self-esteem were computed again, using partial correlations. Now self-esteem correlated .02 with bossiness and .38 with leadership. Evidently, the main road to interpersonal power associated with self-esteem is leadership. There may be a cascade here: self-esteem to leadership to higher self-esteem.

It is worth examining the other side of the coin: followers, those who are bossed, and losers in competition or fights. Followers do not necessarily lose any self-esteem, but for the other two, loss of power must diminish self-esteem, especially those whose self-esteem is already fragile.

Leadership results in earned power, but power may also be obtained through appointed status. An officer has power over enlisted men, a policeman over civilians, and a judge over anyone in the courtroom. It may not require any prior self-esteem to attain such power, but asserting it benefits self-esteem.

Social Identity

It is said of descendants of the founding families of Boston that "the Lowells talk only to the Cabots, and the Cabots talk only to God." Think of the Kennedy clan, which has included a president and two highly prominent senators, as an example that membership in a family can be a source of pride. Other examples involve achieving social status—for example, immigrants becoming citizens of the United States, which the rest of us take for granted—and making it through Marine basic training ("We Select Few").

Vicarious Self-Esteem

In identity, the connection is there for anyone to see, but why would the owner of a restaurant want pictures on the wall of a celebrity who might have visited only once? This desire to be associated with success has been labeled "basking in reflected glory" (Cialdini et al., 1976). On the Monday after a victory by the Arizona State University football team, more students wore buttons, jackets, sweaters, or shirts with the name or insignia of the university than on a Monday after a loss; and after those victories, students tended to say *we* in referring to the football team.

Does this hold true for dedicated fans? College students, self-reported as true fans, reported their level of self-esteem during and after live telecasts of their team's basketball game (Hirt, Zillman, Erickson, & Kennedy, 1992). When the team won, self-esteem rose, but when it lost, self-esteem dropped, and the drop after a loss was greater than the rise after a win. When a source of self-esteem is vicarious, it may have costs as well as benefits.

Costs and benefits are especially salient when the source of vicarious self-esteem is a family member, as Tesser (1980, 2000) elaborated in his theory of *self-evaluation maintenance*. The crux is whether there is competition. If there is none, a man can boost his self-esteem because of his brother's success, but if they compete, the man's lack of success lowers his self-esteem unless he has psychological distance from his more successful brother. The more successful brother wants closeness to make it easier to demonstrate his superior ability.

To initially test his theory, Tesser (1980) asked men and women how much they resembled their siblings in ability and ways of thinking. The theory was confirmed only for men. When they reported performing better than a sibling, the men said they felt closer in ability, thereby intensifying the rivalry and elevating their self-esteem. When they reported poorer performance, they felt closer to a more distant sibling than the successful one, thereby minimizing rivalry and maintaining their self-esteem. Next, the biographies of eminent scientists revealed that when their occupations were similar, there was conflict, but there was none when their occupations were different.

When an ability or task is important to the person, Tesser (1980) labeled it *relevance*. In a later study, when the task was relevant, a stranger's performance was perceived as better than a friend's, a tactic that allowed less self-attention to the subject's poorer performance (Tesser & Campbell, 1982). When the task was irrelevant and therefore not a threat to the subjects' self-esteem, he or she saw the friend as performing better. Conversely, when one is better than a friend, it enhances psychological health but only when the comparison is in an important domain (Kamide & Daibo, 2009).

Even when there is no relationship, a peer's doing well can be a threat to self-esteem. In one experiment, when an experimental confederate scored higher on an ostensible IQ test, subjects later rated the confederate's IQ higher than did neutral observers (Alicke, LoSchiavo, Zerbst, & Zhang, 1997). The subjects were maintaining self-esteem by inflating the other person's ability, hence the name of the study, "The Person Who Outperforms Me Is a Genius."

Personal Sources

Appearance

An early summary of research on attractiveness concluded that it was related to self-esteem (Berscheid & Walster, 1978), and there have been reports in the media that good-looking people are liked better and obtain better jobs. Even infants prefer more attractive faces (Langlois, Roggman, Casey, Rieser-Danner, & Jenkins, 1987). Some older adults choose surgery or Botox to smooth their wrinkled faces. Many balding men report being upset at their hair loss and strongly interested in getting their hair back (Cash, 1989), and this is especially true of men high in public self-consciousness (Franzoi, Anderson, & Frommelt, 1990).

There have also been studies on self-esteem and general attractiveness, but in much of the early research, they are both self-reported. This is a built-in confound, which is corrected by having attractiveness rated independently by judges. A meta-analysis of such studies yielded a correlation of .06 between judge-rated attractiveness and self-esteem for both sexes (Feingold, 1992). However, self-esteem correlated .31 with popularity, and we know that popularity is related to good looks. Evidently, looks do make a difference in peer relationships, and when the focus is on one's own body, it contributes to self-esteem, even though general attractiveness and self-esteem appear to be unrelated.

Ability

Many pursuits involve ability, and knowing that you excel at cooking, gardening, or athletics contributes to self-esteem. The broadest ability and probably the one most valued in our culture is intelligence, so it should be an important source of self-esteem. The correlations range from zero to the .50s, but most of them are in the .30s (Wylie, 1974).

If intelligence is so highly prized, why is the correlation not higher? First, for some people, it is not highly valued, although others are delighted to be able to join Mensa. Second, it is more important in education than in other areas of life. Third, IQ may be an important source of self-esteem mainly for the top 15% and bottom 15% of the distribution, which would account for the positive correlation.

Goals and Attributions

"Ah, but a man's reach should exceed his grasp, or what's a heaven for?" The epigram by the poet Robert Browning is entirely appropriate for people who set high goals for themselves. When they succeed, the payoff for self-esteem is considerable, but setting the bar too high risks failure and a loss of self-esteem. At the opposite extreme are people who set low goals for themselves, so that they are likely to succeed, but the payoff for self-esteem is less.

People also differ in the kind of goals they seek (Dweck, 2006; Dweck & Leggett, 1988; Elliott & Dweck, 1988). *Entity theorists* focus on those who seek evidence of their ability in the belief that success depends on innate, fixed ability. They feel good when the task is easy and they make few mistakes, but failure depresses their self-esteem because it indicates a lack of ability. *Incremental theorists* focus on those who attribute success to discipline and learning. When they succeed, they are not satisfied and strive for higher goals. When they fail, their self-esteem is not damaged and the message they receive is to work harder.

Incremental theorists, wanting to improve, use upward comparison to remediate self-esteem, whereas entity theorists use the defensive tactic of downward comparison (Nussbaum & Dweck, 2008). Culture may play a role here because there is evidence that East Asians tend to be incremental theorists who respond to failure by trying harder (Heine & Buchtel, 2009; Heine et al., 2001).

Another dichotomy of attribution is luck versus skill, which applies especially to one-on-one contests. If your self-esteem is high, when you win, you can attribute it to skill, and when you lose, you can attribute it to luck, thereby maintaining self-esteem. There is a sex difference here: In one study, when boys failed, they attributed it to bad luck, and when girls failed, they said it was because of lack of ability (Dweck, Davidson, Nelson, & Enna, 1978). Notice that the boys' attribution for failure resembles that of Highs, and the girls' attribution is like Lows' attributions.

Vicarious Self-Esteem

Some people derive self-esteem from their possessions—for example, first-edition books, rare paintings, fine furniture, or expensive cars. Another example might be the young so-called trophy wives of wealthy older men. The excellence of their possessions appears to reflect on them.

Character and Morality

Character refers to the traditional values that society tries to inculcate in children: honesty, generosity, virtue, and even courage. For most Americans, morality is intertwined with religion. Good Catholics go to confession and try not to sin again, Orthodox Jews keep to the dietary laws and pray every day, and Muslims pray five times a day and fast on holy days. For such people, adhering to the everyday requirements of their religion is the essence of morality and therefore a source of self-esteem.

Beyond religion, being moral is a potential source of self-esteem. What about those who are immoral? If they did not undergo traditional socialization, they care nothing about morality, so their self-esteem is unaffected. Those who do care experience shame or guilt, which lowers their self-esteem, or they rationalize their behavior.

Importance of the Sources

Which sources are important? In one study, several sources were rated for importance, and a sex difference was found (A. H. Buss & Perry, 1991). Men rated intelligence as the most important source, followed by character–morality, being liked, and appearance. Women rated character–morality and intelligence as the most important sources, followed by being liked and appearance. The sex difference was especially clear in the numerical ratings. For men character–morality was a distant second to intelligence, whereas for women, they were essentially equal. Bear in mind that these are averages. For some people, being liked is a more important source of self-esteem than intelligence; for others, physical attractiveness is foremost; and for highly religious people, character–morality is first, with a large gap between it and the other sources.

In everyday life, little attention is paid to the sources of self-esteem, and they become salient mainly when they are lost through such means as the following:

- loss of affection through rejection or divorce,
- threat to ability through low scores on general tests or rejection from college,
- loss of one's job,
- being charged with immorality, and
- loss of physical attractiveness through age or accidental harm.

Self-Competence and Self-Worth

Self-competence is the optimistic feeling that you can meet challenges and solve life's problems. *Self-worth* is the feeling that you are of value, important, and deserve to be loved. Tafarodi and Swann (1995) assessed the two components of self-esteem through self-report. They revised the questionnaire in the quest for a better instrument, and here are two typical items, one for each aspect of self-esteem: I am highly effective at the things I do; I am secure in my sense of self-worth (Tafarodi & Swann, 2001). Both components clearly contribute to global self-esteem, as reflected in their correlation, which ranged in the .50s and .60s.

Tafarodi and Vu (1997) studied whether subjects persisted after failure when they were allowed further work on a task. Although competence had no effect, those low in self-worth demonstrated less persistence than Highs. Next, subjects were asked to remember personality trait terms that applied to them, and two groups of subjects were selected as having paradoxical self-esteem (Tafarodi, 1998). High competent–low self-worth subjects remembered more negative trait terms, and low competent–high self-worth subjects remembered more positive ones.

Thus far, only self-worth seemed to have an impact, but the next study revealed that competence does as well (Tafarodi & Milne, 2002, Experiment 3). Subjects were administered the self-competence–self-worth questionnaire 4 weeks apart and asked the second time to recall negative events of those 4 weeks. Events involving frustration or failure caused a drop in competence, and events involving rejection or personal conflict diminished self-worth. Notice that personal sources affected competence, whereas social sources affected self-worth. There is also evidence that self-competence is higher in individualistic cultures and self-worth is higher in collectivist cultures (Tafarodi & Swann, 1996)

In a study with Norwegian students, self-liking correlated with the Agreeableness, Conscientiousness, and Neuroticism superfactors of the Big Five personality traits, whereas self-competence correlated with Extraversion and Openness (Ramsdal, 2008). However, Norway is part of Western culture. Do competence and self-worth vary across cultures? Yes, in the trade-off between the two, competence is higher in Western cultures and self-worth is higher in East Asian cultures (Tafarodi & Swann, 1996), facts confirmed in a massive study of self-esteem in 53 nations (Schmitt & Allik, 2005). These findings call attention to both the need to look beyond overall level of self-esteem and the strong impact of culture.

Development

Infancy

There is nothing more self-centered than a neonate because an infant does not know how small it is until it stands up. As we saw in Chapter 6, infants also have not yet developed the cognitions necessary for an advanced self, so the concept of self-esteem does not apply to them. For most infants, however, the groundwork is being laid for the later self-worth component of self-esteem. In the first months of life, parents are showering their infants with unconditional love. When conditions are added later, there is still abundant love and care. The outcome is likely to be an enduring sense of self-worth that cannot be communicated until a more advanced self is fully in place.

Preschool

Play and games are now an important part of life, and as children develop motor and cognitive skills, they can take pride in childish accomplishments such as learning to swim, kicking a soccer ball, or assembling a simple jigsaw puzzle. Parents start placing their children's "art" on the refrigerator door and praise them for mastery in general; they hold their children to low standards and praise the children for meeting them. There may be a cascade from success to a greater feeling of competence to accepting greater challenges, resulting in more mastery. For a minority of children, the cascade may be from failure to loss of feeling competent to avoiding developmental challenges to a diminished feeling of competence, resulting in avoiding challenges.

Elementary School

In elementary school, praise from parents continues, although the standards for performance and behavior are higher, especially in school. Now the *competence* component of self-esteem comes into play. Younger children, especially those in the first grade, feel more competent than older children, and boys believe they are better than girls in sports (Eccles, Wigfield, Harold, & Blumenfield, 1993). Competence is based on meeting these higher standards, and the evaluators are teachers and other adults. Now children split between seeking evidence of their ability (entity theorists) and striving to improve (incremental theorists; Dweck, 2006).

Peers enter the picture, offering teasing; sneering; and, in some instances, rejection or even physical attacks. Thus, both self-worth and self-competence are challenged, and how these challenges are met determines self-esteem throughout childhood.

Are the children aware of these issues? Six- and 7-year-olds are too young to reliably answer a self-esteem questionnaire (Davis-Kean & Sandler, 2001), but Harter and Pike (1984) tapped into such children's feelings about their competencies with pictorial scales. Children were able to distinguish between being socially accepted and being competent, but there was no overall factor indicating self-esteem.

Eight-year-old children are mature enough to reflect on sources of their self-esteem, and the results of a questionnaire yielded four factors (Harter, 1982). The first two, intelligence–getting good grades and athletic–games ability, involved competence. One was social: being liked and having friends. The fourth factor involved feeling secure and happy with oneself, which describes self-worth. Thus, even in elementary school both the self-worth and the competence components of self-esteem appear in self-evaluations.

Adolescence

There are new sources of the self-worth component of self-esteem. One is the development of secondary sex characteristics. These body changes, as we saw in Chapter 6, make adolescents more self-conscious and make most feel less attractive, especially adolescent girls. Relationships between the sexes often seesaw between acceptance (raising self-esteem) and rejection (lowering it). There is now also a new source of self-esteem: the school's athletic teams, which can provide vicarious self-esteem.

There is research on the sources of self-esteem in adolescents, although the largest study also includes children (Harter, 1986). It yielded five factors, but of particular interest here, a higher order factor analysis produced two clusters. The first, consisting of appearance, likability, and athleticism, was judged to be more important by adolescents than their parents. The second cluster, good behavior and doing well in school, was judged to be more important to parents than their children. Evidently, the parents focused on success (competence), whereas the children focused on positive evaluation by peers (self-worth). However, grades do play a role in self-esteem of both young adolescents (Dubois, Bull, Sherman, & Roberts, 1998) and college students (Crocker, Luhtanen, Cooper, & Bouvrette, 2003).

Developmental Trends

Longitudinal research offers the best foundation for understanding developmental trends. Simmons (1987) found a gradual increase in self-esteem throughout childhood and confirmed the drop at age 12 years, but only for girls. She went on to count the number of transitions in life at adolescents, such as starting junior high school, moving to a new neighborhood, and family problems. The more transitions, the sharper the drop in self-esteem, but only for girls. However, a large-scale study found that self-esteem drops throughout the high school years for both sexes (Heaven & Ciarrochi, 2008).

Adolescents at age 14 years were followed until they were 23 years old, the measure of self-esteem being how close the self was to the ideal self (Block & Robins, 1993). The self-esteem of most of these adolescents changed by more than half a standard deviation, either up or down. Boys' self-esteem tended to rise, and girls' tended to drop.

Cross-sectional research has also revealed developmental trends. A review of the literature revealed that the gender difference continues throughout adulthood (Robins & Trzesniewski, 2005). As to why women have lower self-esteem than men, there are several possibilities: (a) Women's self-esteem reflects their lower status in society, (b) women are more realistic about their sources of self-esteem, and (c) men engage in more of the self-enhancement and self-protective mechanisms described earlier in the chapter.

Perspective

As in so many areas of psychology, William James (1890) was one of the first to write about self-esteem. He started with the ratio of pretensions to success. Low pretensions virtually guarantee success, leading to high self-esteem. If the pretensions are too ambitious, meeting them is unlikely, which leads to low self-esteem, as in the Greek myth of Icarus, who flew too high. James's ideas are still reflected in the conceptions of Wells and Marwell (1976) and the aforementioned Susan Harter (1999).

James also wrote about the commonsense idea that only important abilities are weighed in evaluating our self-esteem. Perhaps, but more than a century later, the commonsense idea remains controversial (Hardy & Leone, 2008; Marsh, 2008).

Carl Rogers (1951) replaced the concept of pretensions with the broader concept of the *ideal self*. Now the discrepancy is between the ideal self and the real self. When there is little or no discrepancy, people accept themselves (good self-esteem). When the discrepancy is great, people do not accept themselves (low self-esteem), and they need what Rogers called *nondirective psychotherapy*.

Sources of Self-Esteem

Coopersmith (1967) summarized previous research, conducted interviews, and came up with four sources of self-esteem: "the ability to influence and control others—which we shall term *Power*; the acceptance, attention, and affection of others—*Significance*; adherence to moral and ethical standards—*Virtue*; and successful performance in meeting the demands of achievement—*Competence*" (Coopersmith, 1967, p. 38).

I modified this list and added appearance, social rewards, and vicarious self-esteem. These are broad sources of self-esteem, but a list might comprise narrow sources, such as honesty, parents, and skill in problem solving (Marsh, 1986). Between such narrow sources and broad self-esteem is *contingent self-esteem*: "feelings about oneself that result from—indeed, are dependent on—matching some standard of excellence or living up to some interpersonal or intrapsychic expectations" (Deci & Ryan, 1995, p. 32).

The concept of contingent self-esteem was taken one step further (Kernis, Granneman, & Barclay, 1989), linking it to *stability of self-esteem*. As Michael Kernis and a colleague later wrote, "The more that individuals' feeling of overall self-worth are contingent on specific evaluative information, the more unstable their self-esteem is likely to be" (Waschull & Kernis, 1996, p. 4). Stability of self-esteem is sufficiently different from self-esteem—correlations in the −.30s—to make it a topic worthy of study. It was expected that daily events would have a greater impact on people with unstable self-esteem, but that held true only for negative events (Greenier et al., 1999). For a more recent review, see Kernis and Lakey (2009).

Other research on contingent self-esteem has typically involved students needing success in college courses to maintain self-esteem (Crocker & Wolfe, 2001). The self-esteem of some college students may depend on something as specific as doing well in a course of their major (Crocker, Karpinski, Quinn, & Chase, 2003). The results for individual differences in contingent self-esteem follow the same pattern as individual differences in global self-esteem in that Highs tend to strive to do better and Lows feel bad and tend to give up (Park, Crocker, & Kiefer, 2007).

The concept of contingent self-esteem may have derived from the pioneering work of Albert Bandura (1977) on *self-efficacy*. The original concept applied to specific tasks, but it was later expanded to be close to overall competence:

> A strong motive of efficacy enhances human accomplishment and personal well-being in many ways. People with high assurance in their capabilities approach different tasks as challenges to be mastered rather than as threats to be avoided. . . . They set themselves challenging goals and maintain strong commitment to them. They heighten and sustain their efforts in the face of failure. They quickly recover their sense of efficacy after failures or setbacks. (Bandura, 1994, p. 71)

Notice how this formulation overlaps issues already discussed—specifically, the motivation of incremental theorists, who are not satisfied with easy tasks and instead seek improvement through challenge and the response to failure of Highs and those with stable self-esteem.

Self-Esteem as Protection

We are the only species that knows individuals are going to die, which spawns existential anxiety. It has been suggested that one way to tame this anxiety is through self-esteem (Becker, 1962), a starting point for the modern theory called *terror management*, which assumes that self-esteem serves as a buffer to the terror of dying (J. Greenberg, Pyszczynski, & Solomon, 1986). In a series of experiments, reviewed subsequently (Pyszczynski, Greenberg, Solomon, Arndt, & Schimel, 2004), they demonstrated that manipulating transient self-esteem does indeed allay anxiety. They are of course referring to the self-worth component of self-esteem.

It needs to be pointed out that self-worth serves as more than managing terror and is strongly affected by success and failure in events having nothing to do with existential anxiety. For example, the experience of being respected by others derives from both social status and being liked by the group (Huo, Binning, & Molina, 2010).

At the opposite end of the spectrum, no one likes to be rejected or excluded, and this fact has given rise to the *sociometer* theory of self-esteem (M. R. Leary, Tambor, Terdal, & Downs, 1995). It starts with assuming that

all humans need to affiliate with others, and the funct
monitor being accepted or rejected by others. The theory
this way:

> Stated baldly, people do not have a need for self-esteem . . . Rath
> ple only appear to have need for self-esteem, because they typically t
> behave in ways that maintain or increase their relational value to othe
> people. . . . They appear to be seeking self-esteem, because self-esteem is
> the internal, subjective gauge that monitors their success in promoting
> relational value. (M. R. Leary, 2004, p. 376)

The theory was expanded by adding an informational component: whether feedback relating to self-esteem is consistent or inconsistent with one's level of self-esteem (Stinson et al., 2010). The theory suggests that when Lows receive positive feedback—information inconsistent with their self-view—this discrepancy makes them uncomfortable and that feeling good about oneself is wrong. The outcome would be confirmation of their low self-regard, which was documented earlier in the chapter.

Evolution

Lacking cognition, animals cannot have a sense of self-worth, but social animals can behave confidently, as has been observed repeatedly in alpha males. These observations are the starting point for a theory of how self-esteem evolved in our species:

> I am going to argue that natural selection has transformed our ancestors'
> general primate tendency to achieve high social rank into a need to main-
> tain self-esteem. With the development of a sense of self, our ancestors'
> primate tendency would have been transformed. Having a sense of self
> means that self-evaluation is possible. The social dominance imperative
> would have taken the form of an imperative to evaluate the self as higher
> in rank than others: *To evaluate the self as higher than others is to maintain
> self-esteem.* (Barkow, 1975, p. 554)

Different Cultures

As these perspectives demonstrate, having good self-esteem is a positive attribute, which suggests a universal need for self-esteem. We must be careful, however, in generalizing from our individualist culture to collectivist countries. The outstanding example of a collectivist country is Japan, where children are taught humility and self-criticism, far different from what is taught in America. When asked, Japanese say they do not want to be self-confident:

> Conventional theories of self-esteem are based on a North American indi-
> vidualized view of the self that is motivated to achieve high self-esteem.

ntrast, the most characteristic view of the self in Japan (and else-
re) is that it is crucial to developing a worthy and culturally appropri-
e self in Japan. (Heine, Lehman, Markus, & Kitayama, 1999, p. 785)

se authors also reported that as Japanese become exposed to North Amer-
in culture, their self-esteem rises. However, the findings for China, another
ast Asian culture, are different and more complex, self-esteem consisting of
both self-competence and self-worth. The Chinese are too humble socially to
admit to being self-competent, but their self-worth may not be different from
that of Americans (Cai, Brown, Deng, & Oakes, 2007; Cai, Wu, & Brown,
2009). An earlier massive study of self-esteem in 53 countries found that generally positive self-evaluations were universal, with American being most positive and Japan least positive (Schmitt & Allik, 2005).

Another complication is the previously mentioned cultural trade-off,
with self-competence being higher in Western cultures and self-worth being
higher in East Asian cultures (Tafarodi & Swann, 1996). However, cultures
vary in how power is distributed in the population, which turned out to be
crucial: "Power disparities were most closely associated with national variations in self-competence and self-liking, with greater power disparity associated with more self-competence and less self-liking" (Schmitt & Allik, 2005,
p. 637). This research is another reminder of (a) the importance of differentiating self-esteem into components and (b) cultural differences in personality (Heine & Buchetel, 2009).

IDENTITY

Self-esteem and identity are linked in several ways. Both are ordinar-
ily out of awareness but powerful determinants of behavior. Both have multiple sources that may be divided into the categories of social and personal.
These sources can elevate or diminish self-esteem and identity, and recall
that social identity is a source of self-esteem. When threatened, both pro-
voke strong cognitive and behavioral reactions. Whatever the links, however, they are different in ways that help summarize what we know about
identity.

Self-esteem involves how well we play such roles as family member and
teacher, whereas identity involves how committed we are to these roles.
Acceptance by the group makes us feel valued (self-esteem), but it also offers
a stronger sense of belonging (identity). When our group is attacked, self-
esteem is diminished, but group identity is strengthened. Loss of self-esteem
usually involves lack of self-competence, but loss of social identity involves a
feeling of rootlessness. For self-esteem, the basic question is "How worthwhile
am I?" but for identity, the basic question is "Who am I?"

Self-esteem and identity also differ in the way they vary from one person to another. There is a trait of self-esteem but none for identity, although as we shall see, there are individual differences in identity consisting of patterns of the sources of identity. To cite just one example, for some people it is the personality sources of identity—feelings of uniqueness—that are paramount, whereas for others it is the social sources of identity—the sense of belonging to larger entities.

Social Identity

Citizenship and Culture

Being born in the United States automatically confers citizenship, and that includes the children of undocumented immigrants. All children are taught to respect the flag and what it represents. Still, there are individual differences in patriotism as a source of identity. For some people, it is so strong that they fly the flag every day and respond to our country being attacked by immediately volunteering to fight. For others it is unimportant, and they identify more with their hometown or state.

Native Americans and immigrants, especially Muslim immigrants in this century, face a problem called *bicultural identity*, of which two kinds have been distinguished (Benet-Martínez & Haritatos, 2005). One is a conflict between two cultures, with continuing discrimination and strain, as may be seen in many Muslim immigrants. The second kind is cultural distance, for example, adopting American practices at school and Muslim practices at home.

Religion

Most people are born into a religion and receive at least some religious training. The result for some is that religion becomes the dominant source of their identity, and they build their lives around it.

Vocation

We no longer have the medieval guilds that apprenticed young men for a lifetime of skilled work, but we do have a variety of vocations that are analogous, such as plumbers and electricians. The so-called professions require schooling and certification, so, for example, in most states if you want to call yourself a psychologist, you must be certified. It is no exaggeration to claim that for most psychologists, this vocation is an important part of their identity.

Organized Secular Groups

Some adolescents develop a strong identity as members of a street gang, and others strongly identify with their college fraternity or sorority. Intense initiation rites strengthen identity in all these groups, and college itself is a source of identity.

Family

There has always been an interest in ancestry, but in the 1970s, Alex Haley's book *Roots* and then the movie about his African ancestors stirred an immense interest in genealogy. Then Ellis Island registers became widely available, and millions of Americans could trace when their forebears arrived in this country as well as their country of origin. More recently, DNA testing has allowed people to trace back their ancestry even further.

Gender

Throughout childhood, the sexes are sharply differentiated in their clothing, their choice of toys, the violence of their games, and their social behavior. This socialization prepares them for their different adult social roles, hence the difference between male and female *social* identity. For some people, there is a disconnect between their social gender identity and their inner feelings about gender and their sexual outlet, topics to be discussed in the section on personal sources of identity.

Dimensions

The social sources vary along several dimensions, the first of which is their importance for identity. A graduate student and I asked college students to rank the importance of a set of social identities (A. H. Buss & Portnoy, 1967). Men ranked being American first, followed by both gender and religion and, lower down, expected vocation. Women also ranked being an American first, followed equally by gender, religion, and expected vocation, so the only sex difference was that women ranked vocation higher. The other sources—age group, college, club, and state—were ranked so low that we need not consider them here.

I repeated the study 25 years later, with different results (A. H. Buss, 1992). Now gender was ranked barely ahead of being American for men, and gender was ranked far ahead of being American for women. For both sexes religion was a distant third. A comparison of the two studies revealed several major changes that took place during the 25-year time interval. Being an American was now a weaker source for both sexes, and religion dropped in importance. The importance of gender remained unchanged for men but rose sharply for women to be ranked first, far above the second choice, being American.

These were college students, but to the extent that they are representative—and the majority of the population attends college—their choices appear to reflect two trends over the course of a generation or so. The first is the weakening of America as a source of social identity, perhaps because of the impact of the 8-year Vietnam war. A repeat of the study today surely would find a resurgence in American identity in the aftermath of the 2001 terrorist attacks. The second trend is the upsurge in feminine identity, surely a reflection of the more prominent role of women in government and the private sector.

The aforementioned article on social identity (A. H. Buss & Portnoy, 1967) also included an experiment in which pain tolerance was tested twice. Between the first and second tests, the male subjects were told either that Russian men could tolerate more pain than American men or that Canadian men could. Pain tolerance increased sharply when the comparison group was Russian (our Cold War enemy at the time) but hardly at all when the comparison group was Canadian (our friends). Tolerating more pain is just one example of identity translating into commitment, the extent of which is the second dimension of social identity.

The third dimension varies in how much individuals are stuck with the social identity into which they are born. We are born into an immediate and extended family, as well as an ethnic group, and we generally cannot escape. Our social gender is innate and, for almost everyone, unalterable. We are also born into a nationality and a religion, but these can be relinquished or changed.

The clubs and other organized social groups we join are of course voluntary, as is the vocation we selected. Some of them involve face-to-face contact, and others are so large or distant that any contact is rare or indirect. The social self may be regarded as embedded in a network that ranges from close to distant: family, neighborhood, religion, social class, ethnicity, and nationality (Oyserman & Markus, 1993).

None of these characteristics completely determines how committed the person is to any particular social source. Thus, a voluntary source (being a Marine) or a distant source (ancestral roots) might involve more commitment and importance for identity than an involuntary source (ethnic group) or a close source (immediate family).

In brief, the social sources of identity vary along four dimensions, which may be described by these dichotomies: important versus unimportant, commitment versus no commitment, involuntary versus voluntary, and close versus distant.

Personal Identity

Body

Everyone has private sensations that are entirely private and that separate us from everyone else. I can empathize with your pain but not sense it.

Beyond sensations, we have particular, private cognitions about our own bodies that contribute to our *body image*.

Body image remains below awareness until marked change in the body calls it to our attention—normal change that occurs during adolescence or pregnancy as well as disfigurement or amputation.

Personality

Each of us has a pattern of the personality traits, habits, and sources of identity that define our personality, a pattern as distinct as a fingerprint, which makes each of us special. We have daydreams and night dreams known only to ourselves. All this engenders a sense of uniqueness, especially in our individualist culture. But do identical twins feel unique as individuals? Some of them react to their sameness by dressing differently, adopting different hairstyles, and having different friends, all in the service of individuality. Others delight in their sameness, dress alike, have the same friends, and even take up the same vocation. This pattern suggests that they implicitly regard themselves as a unit the way each singleton does—a different kind of individual identity—and a reminder of our feeling of being unique.

Gender

There are marked individual differences in masculinity and femininity. Some men, for example, define themselves primarily by their masculinity, and for a small minority, there is a disconnect between their biological gender and their personal feeling of male identity.

Personal and Social Identity

So far the distinction between personal and social identity has been emphasized, but the situation is more complex. Religious identity is solely social for many people, but for others, it is also personal, so that religion is more than a particular set of beliefs and attendance at a house of worship.

One aspect of both kinds of identity is a sense of *continuity*. Even when enduring sources of social identity are disrupted or lost, there remains a strong sense of continuity, as may be seen in the life of Janusz Kaminski, a Polish-born cinematographer. Comparing his younger and older selves, he has said,

> Of course I can see that we are the same person. . . . but it is a person who has evolved from being a teenager in a Communist country in a very protected environment to a man who is in his 40s who lives in a different country, in a different system, but who still has many of the same values. Now I am in America, but I am still idealistic; I am still romantic; money

still does not dominate my world. I am the same person, but I am still searching. (Lyman, 2006, p. B26).

As this life story reveals, identity may be seen as a narrative of life that offers meaning, purpose, and sense of unity (McAdams, 1997).

Given that identity has both personal and social components, one may predominate over the other. No one wants to be so different as to be considered weird or an outlier, but in our culture especially, there is a strong need for uniqueness (C. R. Snyder & Fromkin, 1980). This need for personal identity may be increasing as telecommunication and national franchises (McDonald's, Walmart) further homogenize the culture.

Angyal (1951) suggested that personal and social identity sometimes act as opposing motives. We want distinctiveness from others and freedom to pursue our own goals with minimal constraints from society, but the need for social identity may be equally strong so that each of us "strives to surrender himself willingly to seek a home for himself and *to become an organic part of something he conceives is greater than himself*" (Angyal, 1951, p. 132, emphasis in original). The issue was later framed in terms of "a tension between our 'individual,' private, interior, unique selves, and the 'social,' public, exterior, collective world" (Kitzinger, 1992, p. 223).

Development

Preschool

Identity starts with toddlers, who develop several sources of identity. The first is gender, as any uncle knows when he teases his nephew about whether he is wearing feminine clothes, whereas girls are more relaxed about the clothing issue. This gender difference about clothes is the start of a stronger need for a male identity.

The immediate family is a source of identity for preschoolers but not the extended family. Minority children are made aware of their ethnic identity through observation, teasing, or simply being told. In each successive era, sources of identity are added.

Elementary School

These children are aware of their religious identity or, for a minority, their nonreligious identity. Their nationality is proclaimed every day at the start of school, and in this country, like most countries, children are taught that we are the best nation. Late in this era, children are capable of understanding their place in an extended family over generations, and for many, this heritage becomes part of their identity.

Notice that all this is *social* identity. Personal identity starts with appearance and a unique combination of personality traits. It continues as older children become aware that their daydreams are special, and the onset of private self-awareness sets the stage for feeling unique about one's private thoughts and feelings.

Adolescence

This awareness of an inner world, which now includes ambition and romantic and sexual feelings intensifies during adolescence, enlarging personal identity. Adding to it is awareness of the relatively sudden appearance of secondary sexual characteristics and its associated focus on gender identity.

This is a particular problem for gays and lesbians, whose sexual outlet does not match that of the majority. Over the past generation, they have been declaring their homosexuality earlier, perhaps because it is more acceptable, and interviews with adolescents suggest that they are more relaxed about their being different (Savin-Williams, 2005).

Some previously adopted adolescents discover for the first time who their biological parents were, and an English study revealed two contrasting reactions (Haimes, 1987). One group needed merely to add the name of their biological parents and said the discovery made little difference in their social identity. The other group changed their name to that of their biological parents and construed their lives differently: original (birth) identity, false (adopted) identity, and now back to the original identity, hence the name of the study, "Now I Know Who I Really Am."

In high school, the sources of social identity expand because now various athletic and other clubs, as well as the school itself, are available as sources of identity. During this era, previous socialization of religion and nationality may be challenged and either rejected or accepted with greater intensity. *Patterns* or clusters of social identity have already been established in high school students. To cite one example, consider these clusters: (a) strong family and American identity but little religious identity; (b) strong family identity but low religious and ethnic identity; and (c) no family identity and otherwise little religious, family, or American identity (Yip, Klang, & Fuligni, 2008).

The development of identity continues well into adulthood as vocational and other social roles are added—for example, spouse and parent—and older adults become more acutely aware of the continuity of the self. Identity is one of the few aspects of personality that undergoes considerable change during adulthood.

Continuity Versus Distinctiveness

In one study, when children and adolescents were asked to describe themselves, all the 6-year-olds mentioned their lack of change over time

(Peevers, 1987). The percentage mentioning continuity dropped throughout childhood to about half in the 13-year-olds and rose only slightly in adolescents and young adults.

In another study, subjects were asked directly about continuity and distinctiveness (Hart, Maloney, & Damon, 1987). Young school-age children mentioned physical characteristics as examples of continuity (eye color) or distinctiveness (being taller than classmates). Older school children mentioned psychological features that remained the same (intelligence) or distinguished themselves (being the smartest). Early adolescents used social recognition (friends saw them as the same person as before) for continuity and personal identity (unique set of traits) for distinctiveness. Late adolescents mentioned only examples of personal identity for distinctiveness (private thoughts and feelings).

Perspective

Early Psychologists

William James (1890) wrote about the *spiritual self*, which consists of ideas about our origin, who we are, and our ultimate destiny—now-familiar aspects of personal identity. His *social self* consists of the social roles we play with family members, friends, and colleagues and is therefore a source of social identity. His *material self*, the possessions we are attached to, clearly is a source of vicarious identity.

Gordon Allport (1961) used James's ideas as a base from which to launch a more detailed analysis of the self, and two of his concepts are especially relevant here. His concept of the self as a *rational coper* centers on crucial questions about identity asked by many adolescents: "Precisely who am I?" and "Am I a child or an adult?" The other relevant concept is that of *propriate striving*, the search for a central purpose or meaning of life. Clearly, the writings of these early psychologists are still relevant today.

Identification and Identity

In the process of revising Freud's psychosexual stages, Erik Erikson (1950) added an adolescent stage called *identity versus role diffusion*, the endpoint of a developmental path. Children identify with parents, older siblings, and adult figures, including those seen on television and in videos or movies, and initially want to grow up to be like them. These tentative and changing childhood identifications give way in adolescence: "*Identity formation*, finally, begins when the usefulness of identification ends. It arises from the selective repudiation and mutual assimilation if childhood identifications and their absorption into a new configuration" (Erikson, 1968, p. 160). In some adolescents, the configuration has discordant elements, some holdovers from childhood and some from emerging adulthood, the result being the problem of *role diffusion*.

Role diffusion describes one of four adolescent identity statuses suggested by Marcia (1966, 1987). In the second, *foreclosure*, the childhood identifications are not examined but simply accepted. In the third identity status, *moratorium*, adolescents have suspended their search for identity and await further developments. The fourth status, *identity achievement*, is essentially the mature identity described by Erikson (1968). In three of the four statuses, then, there is an identity crisis, but is this crisis universal? Probably not: "In other cultures, the transition in social identity from child to adult is carried off without anything like the difficulties of identity crisis" (Baumeister, 1997, p. 196).

Meanwhile, researchers have continued to study identity status, and I cite only two longitudinal studies here. The identity status of a huge sample of Dutch adolescents in the age range of 12 to 20 years was examined in five waves (Meeus, van de Schoot, Keijsers, Schwartz, & Branje, 2010). Almost two thirds retained their identity status, but a minority either foreclosed or achieved an adult identity. Fadjukoff, Pullinen, and Kokko (2005) found that from their 20s to their 40s, adults typically were moving from diffusion to achievement status, although there was variability across such domains as occupation and relationships.

Individualist and Collectivist Cultures

I have been discussing personal and social identity, but a related distinction has been used in cross-cultural research: individualism and collectivism. Anthropologists alerted us decades ago that the concept of the self in America (individualist) is different from the concept of the self in Japan (collectivist; Barnlund, 1975). The difference hinges on the boundary between self and nonself:

> Although all cultures draw a line between a region defined as belonging intrinsically to the self and a region defined as extrinsic or outside the self and hence belonging to "the nonself other," where the line is drawn varies extensively. (Sampson, 1988, p. 15)

Americans tend to draw a tight line around the self, not much different from the boundary of the body.

At the other extreme, the Japanese boundary is looser, and "the self gains meaning by being firmly suspended and supported in a web of mutually binding relationships" (Heine, Lehman, Markus, & Kitayama, 1999, p. 5). Said another way, "Who I am is defined in and through my relations with others. I am completed by these relations and do not exist apart from them" (Sampson, 1988, p. 20).

all humans need to affiliate with others, and the function of self-esteem is to monitor being accepted or rejected by others. The theory was pursued further this way:

> Stated baldly, people do not have a need for self-esteem . . . Rather, people only appear to have need for self-esteem, because they typically try to behave in ways that maintain or increase their relational value to other people. . . . They appear to be seeking self-esteem, because self-esteem is the internal, subjective gauge that monitors their success in promoting relational value. (M. R. Leary, 2004, p. 376)

The theory was expanded by adding an informational component: whether feedback relating to self-esteem is consistent or inconsistent with one's level of self-esteem (Stinson et al., 2010). The theory suggests that when Lows receive positive feedback—information inconsistent with their self-view—this discrepancy makes them uncomfortable and that feeling good about oneself is wrong. The outcome would be confirmation of their low self-regard, which was documented earlier in the chapter.

Evolution

Lacking cognition, animals cannot have a sense of self-worth, but social animals can behave confidently, as has been observed repeatedly in alpha males. These observations are the starting point for a theory of how self-esteem evolved in our species:

> I am going to argue that natural selection has transformed our ancestors' general primate tendency to achieve high social rank into a need to maintain self-esteem. With the development of a sense of self, our ancestors' primate tendency would have been transformed. Having a sense of self means that self-evaluation is possible. The social dominance imperative would have taken the form of an imperative to evaluate the self as higher in rank than others: *To evaluate the self as higher than others is to maintain self-esteem.* (Barkow, 1975, p. 554)

Different Cultures

As these perspectives demonstrate, having good self-esteem is a positive attribute, which suggests a universal need for self-esteem. We must be careful, however, in generalizing from our individualist culture to collectivist countries. The outstanding example of a collectivist country is Japan, where children are taught humility and self-criticism, far different from what is taught in America. When asked, Japanese say they do not want to be self-confident:

> Conventional theories of self-esteem are based on a North American individualized view of the self that is motivated to achieve high self-esteem.

In contrast, the most characteristic view of the self in Japan (and else-where) is that it is crucial to developing a worthy and culturally appropri-ate self in Japan. (Heine, Lehman, Markus, & Kitayama, 1999, p. 785)

These authors also reported that as Japanese become exposed to North Amer-ican culture, their self-esteem rises. However, the findings for China, another East Asian culture, are different and more complex, self-esteem consisting of both self-competence and self-worth. The Chinese are too humble socially to admit to being self-competent, but their self-worth may not be different from that of Americans (Cai, Brown, Deng, & Oakes, 2007; Cai, Wu, & Brown, 2009). An earlier massive study of self-esteem in 53 countries found that gen-erally positive self-evaluations were universal, with American being most pos-itive and Japan least positive (Schmitt & Allik, 2005).

Another complication is the previously mentioned cultural trade-off, with self-competence being higher in Western cultures and self-worth being higher in East Asian cultures (Tafarodi & Swann, 1996). However, cultures vary in how power is distributed in the population, which turned out to be crucial: "Power disparities were most closely associated with national varia-tions in self-competence and self-liking, with greater power disparity associ-ated with more self-competence and less self-liking" (Schmitt & Allik, 2005, p. 637). This research is another reminder of (a) the importance of differen-tiating self-esteem into components and (b) cultural differences in personal-ity (Heine & Buchetel, 2009).

IDENTITY

Self-esteem and identity are linked in several ways. Both are ordinar-ily out of awareness but powerful determinants of behavior. Both have mul-tiple sources that may be divided into the categories of social and personal. These sources can elevate or diminish self-esteem and identity, and recall that social identity is a source of self-esteem. When threatened, both pro-voke strong cognitive and behavioral reactions. Whatever the links, how-ever, they are different in ways that help summarize what we know about identity.

Self-esteem involves how well we play such roles as family member and teacher, whereas identity involves how committed we are to these roles. Acceptance by the group makes us feel valued (self-esteem), but it also offers a stronger sense of belonging (identity). When our group is attacked, self-esteem is diminished, but group identity is strengthened. Loss of self-esteem usually involves lack of self-competence, but loss of social identity involves a feeling of rootlessness. For self-esteem, the basic question is "How worthwhile am I?" but for identity, the basic question is "Who am I?"

The pioneering psychologist on individualism–collectivism is Harry Triandis (1989, 2001). He placed individualism squarely within the personal self, the sources of identity being personal experiences, accomplishments, and possessions (vicarious identity). He placed collectivism squarely within the context of the social self, the sources of identity being family and residence. As his work became known, other North American psychologists became interested in the contrasts between the two kinds of self (see also Cohen, 2009).

Several decades of research have established that North Americans "are quite unique—even in comparison to western Europeans—let alone Asians—in the predominance of independence and individualism, as opposed to collectivism, in their cultural ethos" (Kitayama, Conway, Pietromonaco, Park, & Plaut, 2010, p. 560). This explanation assumes that it is adaptive to be independent and on your own in a frontier, and the American frontier is, historically, relatively recent. Kitayama et al. (2010) predicted and confirmed that more recently, frontier Western states such as Michigan and Montana would have more independent values than older Eastern states that were members of the original colonies, such as Massachusetts and Georgia.

The individualist–collectivist dichotomy may mask another way to construe the self, one that involves a sex difference (Markus & Kitayama, 1991). In this framework, the *independent self* is essentially the same as the individualist self and is typical of men. The *interdependent self*, which involves relationships and belonging—in my terms, social identity—is typical of women. A survey of the literature on Americans eventually confirmed this sex difference (Cross & Madson, 1997).

Meanwhile, individualism and collectivism were studied in America, Hawaii, Japan, and Korea (Kashima et al., 1995). In keeping with previous research, there were clear cultural differences in individualism, but now there was a gender difference in relational identity (interdependence). It appears, then, that there are three levels of self-construal, each more inclusive than the previous one: the personal self, the relational self, and the collective self (Brewer & Chen, 2007; Brewer & Gardner, 1996).

The idea of relational identity was taken a step further by the concept of *tribes*, which are socially constructed from three elements (Shapiro, 2010): (a) Members share one of the social sources of identity, such as religion or even a populist group like the Tea Party; (b) they share kinlike connections with others ("band of brothers"); and (c) they are emotionality invested and therefore committed to act in the service of the tribe. What are the implications for personality? It is that important aspects of personality are embedded in culture, especially those involving the self. Beyond that, variations across cultures even determine whether personality traits are of any importance. They are deemed important determiners of behavior in North America but not in East Asia (Heine & Buchtel, 2009).

Finally, let me review the dimensions used in these two chapters on the self, which for clarity are presented as dichotomies:

- *Private versus public*, as in the focus being on aspects of the self not open to observation versus aspects observable by others;
- *Personal versus social*, as in individual sources of identity versus sources that come from others;
- *Direct versus vicarious*, as in sources of self-esteem that derive from one's own accomplishments versus sources that derive from association with others;
- *Central versus peripheral*, as in sources of self-esteem that are crucial to it versus sources that are relatively unimportant;
- *Positive–negative*, as in a socially approved versus disapproved sources of identity; and
- *Unitary–multiple*, as in the debate about whether the self is one or the other.

Consider the following opposing positions. First,

a unitary "self" has philosophical charms but can hardly embrace all the modes of reflexive thought and conduct that we refer to by "self-" and "-self" terms. All that such compound terms have in common is reflexivity: instead of having someone else as a target, the thoughts and actions in question, in some way or other, turn back on the agent. The specific target of this "turning back" is not the same in all cases: it may be directed at any feature of an agent's habits or feelings, personality, body or skills. (Toulmin, 1986, p. 52)

Second,

The challenge of identity demands that the modern adult construct a narrative of the self . . . to suggest that (1) despite its many facets, the me is coherent and unified and (2) despite the many changes that attend the passage of time, the me of the past led up to or set the stage for the me of the present, which in turn will lead to or set the stage for the me of the future. (McAdams, 1997, p. 63)

This quotation introduces the next dichotomy.

- *Continuity–discontinuity*: "The apprehension of self that is continuous over time is thus not any illusion . . . but something that is essential to our existence" (Modell, 1993, p. 12).
- *Aware–unaware*, as in Aristotle's saying that an unexamined life was not worth living. Philosophers aside, there are people low in self-consciousness who lead entirely worthwhile lives and wonder why those high in self-consciousness are so self-centered.

IV

DIMENSIONS

8

PERSONALITY AND ABNORMALITY

In line with my conception of abnormality, the personality traits discussed in this book are relevant to certain aspects of abnormal behavior. Let us start with the diagnoses of abnormal behavior that appear to overlap personality traits so completely, we must wonder if there is any difference at all.

Social phobia is now called social *anxiety disorder* in psychiatric nomenclature, but the term *social anxiety* has been used by psychologists to include shame and guilt. To avoid confusion, I use the term *social phobia* here because it is distinct from shame and guilt.

The diagnosis of social phobia includes these elements: (a) persistent and intense fear in social situations or (b) anxiety about performing in public that might be embarrassing or humiliating (American Psychiatric Association, 2000). *Generalized* social phobia represents a combination of both elements. This diagnosis surely is familiar, for it is a description of the high end of the trait of shyness, including both anxious shyness and self-conscious shyness. When 2,200 people were interviewed and diagnosed, 49% of the high-shy people were diagnosed as social phobics (Chavira, Stein, & Malcarne, 2002)

The alternative approach is to regard social phobia as different from intense shyness. After admitting that social phobics and shy people have similar physiological responses and cognitions in distressing social contexts, Beidel and Turner (2007) wrote: "They differed, however, on social and occupational functioning, onset characteristics, course of the disorder, and overt behaviors. On each dimension, those with social anxiety disorder were more severe than those labeled shy" (p. 18). These differences are precisely the ones we would expect between milder and more intense shyness.

So why is the extreme end of the personality trait of shyness labeled abnormal? There are practical reasons for calling a personality trait a mental disorder. Statistics can then be accrued, health insurance will pay for diagnosis and treatment, and psychotherapy and drugs can be tried to alleviate it. There are also are good psychological reasons for preferring a personality perspective on shyness rather than a psychiatric perspective.

First, the psychiatric diagnosis of social phobia includes *circumscribed* or *specific* social phobia: anxiety about only one kind of performing. Anyone with a fear of public speaking or performing would be included, which may be the majority of the adult population, for whom avoiding public speaking or performing poses no interference with everyday life.

Second, the description of social phobia fails to distinguish between the milder *self-conscious* shyness and the more intense and serious *anxious* shyness. People who are embarrassed easily and often may be reluctant partygoers and shun being in the spotlight, but only anxiously shy people will avoid going on a job interview.

Third, this distinction between the two kinds of shyness is not a mere abstraction because it makes a difference in the psychotherapy of shyness. As mentioned in Chapter 3, anxious shyness calls for one of the familiar behavioral modification techniques such as counterconditioning. Self-consciousness shyness calls for teaching clients about conspicuousness and how to direct attention away from the self.

CONTINUITY

The overlap between the trait of shyness and social phobia is here regarded as the latter being just the extreme of the former. Said another way, there is continuity between the milder personality trait and the more serious abnormality, as a medical example illustrates.

According to American Heart Association guidelines, systolic blood pressure of 120 or less and diastolic blood pressure of 80 or less are normal. Systolic blood pressure of 120 to 139 or diastolic blood pressure of 80 to 89 are labeled as *high blood pressure—Stage 1*, sometimes called *prehypertensive*. Systolic blood pressure of 160 or above *or* diastolic blood pressure of 100 or above are called *high blood pressure—Stage 2*. This sequence proceeds from healthy to not healthy to seriously ill, marking a continuum from normal through abnormal. This continuum is analogous to the continuum that exists between certain personality traits and abnormal behavior.

Fear

Let me offer a hypothetical example of a fearful woman executive who must fly regularly to business destinations. If she cannot get on the airplane and therefore loses her job, her fear cripples her ability to function and is therefore abnormal behavior. If she gets on the plane and manages to fly even while feeling scared, her fear does not interfere with everyday life and thus is within the normal range as a personality trait. There is a presumed continuum of the personality trait—in this instance, fear—that runs from mild enough to allow a normal life to so intense that a normal life is not possible, which is abnormal behavior (anxiety disorder).

Most people with anxiety disorder do not have merely one intense fear but a multitude of fears. As the fears pile up, they shut down so many options that normal life is not possible. Even if any given fear is not extremely intense, the sheer number moves the personality trait in the direction of abnormal behavior. In brief, frequency and intensity usually translate into interference with everyday functioning, which makes the behavior abnormal.

In a study by Dixon, deMonchaux, and Sandler (1957), an inventory of fears was presented to clinic patients, and a factor analysis yielded two patterns:

Fear of separation
Being left alone
Crossing a bridge
Open spaces
Water, drowning
Train journey
Dark

Fear of harm
Surgery
Hospitals
Being hurt
Being in pain
Dentist

The first list consists mainly of the fear of isolation and would seem to be common in people who are dependent on others for nurture. Fears of the dark and being alone, for example, are notoriously common in children. The second list, consisting of aversive stimuli or the contexts in which they occur (hospitals, dentists), appear to be more rational, adult fears. Childish fears suggest more serious problems than adult fears, hence abnormality.

Attention-Deficit/Hyperactivity Disorder

Attention-deficit/hyperactivity disorder (ADHD) is another example of abnormal behavior that has considerable overlap with personality traits. The diagnosis of ADHD includes two subtypes. Consider first the subtype that involves only a deficit in attention, the symptoms of which are listed in the *Diagnostic and Statistical Manual of Mental Disorders* (4th ed., text revision; DSM–IV–TR; American Psychiatric Association, 2000): impulsive, inattentive, distractible, has difficulty waiting, lacking in planning or organizing.

As we saw in Chapter 4, these behaviors describe the temperament of impulsiveness, the differentiates of which appear in a developmental sequence. *Impulsive* refers to the inability to control emotions or motives, which appears early in the preschool era. *Inattentive, distractible,* and *has difficulty waiting* refer to lack of discipline, which appears at the start of the school era, and *lacking in planning or organizing* refers to two aspects of lack of reflection, which appears at the start of adolescence. This developmental sequence helps us to understand when children are diagnosed with attention-deficit disorder (ADD): when they are required to focus on the task at hand and wait in line (discipline). It has been suggested that boys are not a good fit for the typical school classroom and as a result are overdiagnosed with ADD. If schoolchildren display discipline, they will not be diagnosed with ADD, but they may later have problems due to lack of planning and organization (reflection). Thus, a personality perspective distinguishes among different components of impulsiveness and helps us understand their developmental sequence.

The other subtype of ADD includes all of the previously listed symptoms plus these: fidgets, squirms; cannot sit still; cannot engage in quiet play; overactive, just keeps moving. These behaviors describe a child at the high end of the temperament of activity who has trouble controlling a strong urge to expend energy, like a car with an engine too powerful to be controlled by its brakes. The ADHD child is thus at the high end of two temperaments: activity and impulsiveness. There is evidence consistent with this conclusion: two factors derived from the symptoms of ADHD, each with different genetic effects (Nikolas & Burt, 2010). One factor is called *inattention* and the other *hyperactivity*.

A low-active, high-impulsive child does not have the push to move around and be overactive. A high-active, low-impulsive child can control the urge to get moving, at least until there is recess or some other opportunity to expend energy. It is only the high-active, high-impulsive child who is likely to be diagnosed as ADHD (Pellegrini & Horvat, 1995). Furthermore, among a sample of children diagnosed as ADD, one subgroup was found to be within the normal range of high activity (Martel, Goth-Owens, Martinez-Torteya, & Nigg, 2010).

The crafters of the ADHD classification criteria were aware that children tend to be impulsive, so one of their criteria was that the impulsiveness has to be more severe than what would be expected in any given developmental era. However:

> Certain aspects of the new diagnostic criteria are problematic, particularly the operational definition of what constitutes developmental deviance. How this guideline is met is therefore open to interpretation, so clinicians and researchers are more likely to disagree about who does and who does not meet this criterion. (Anastopoulis & Shelton, 2001, p. 19)

This issue has assumed greater importance in recent years because of the impact of technology. Even children in elementary school have modern wireless phones that also allow text messaging, which splits attention so much that they are banned while driving in a number of states. Following adult models, modern children have been engaging in multitasking, which again involves splitting attention. Television advertisements have been compressed to 15 seconds or less, partly in response to the shortened attention span of viewers. As a result, the present generation of children and adolescents seem to have a shorter attention span than previous generations, which is likely to change the age norms of impulsiveness.

There is another complication. Children high in sensation seeking continually seek novelty and get bored easily, so they may appear inattentive and distractible. Any child suspected of having ADHD should be checked for the trait of sensation seeking. In addition to such possible co-occurrence, there is already real co-occurrence (comorbidity) between ADHD and the acting-out behavior that brings children to the attention of authorities (Martel et al., 2010).

What about the issue of drugs that can minimize ADHD? The fact that drugs work for some children suggests that the psychiatric approach to ADHD has its advantages but does not deny that the personality perspective is useful because the latter offers these insights: Only one component of impulsiveness, discipline, is crucial to a deficit in attention, and this explains why the problem is usually not recognized until school age; it also points out why the trait of activity by itself does not contribute to ADHD and suggests a role of sensation seeking.

Depression

The affective disorder of depression is another example of continuity because mild depression—studied as a personality trait—shades into debilitating, serious depression, which has these features: obsessive, dark thoughts; loss of pleasure; lack of energy or initiative; feelings of worthlessness.

People who are high in private self-consciousness, by definition, turn their focus inward, which lends itself to obsessive thinking, one feature of depression. Accordingly, a depression questionnaire has correlated in the .20s to .30s with private self-consciousness (Ingram & Smith, 1984; T. W. Smith & Greenberg, 1981).

Loss of pleasure has been conceived of as loss of *positive affect*, a personality factor defined by these adjectives: *active, alert, attentive, determined, enthusiastic, excited, inspired, interested, proud,* and *strong* (Watson, Clark, & Tellegen, 1988). A study of psychiatric inpatients and outpatients revealed that lack of positive affect correlates negatively with the diagnosis of depression (Watson, Clark, & Carey, 1988). Beyond that, temperament has been linked to the mood disorders (Clark, Watson, & Mineka, 1994).

Lack of energy is the hallmark of the trait of (low) activity, and it is worth noting that activity correlates .64 with the above-mentioned positive affect (Watson & Clark, 1997, p. 779). Lack of initiative is the opposite end of the trait of leadership. Feelings of worthlessness are prevalent in people low in self-esteem. Accordingly, low self-esteem in early adolescents predicted depression (scores on a depression questionnaire) in late adolescence and adulthood (Orth & Robins, 2008).

None of this is meant to suggest that personality traits account for all of depression, especially depression so intense that suicide is a possibility. However, as the evidence described here shows, we better understand depression when it is placed in the context of normal personality traits.

PERSONALITY DISORDERS

Personality disorders were added to psychiatric classification with the rationale that certain personality traits are inflexible and therefore maladaptive. However, inspection of the list of personality disorders raises questions about this rationale. To cite one example, the symptoms of schizotypal personality disorder are similar to the symptoms of schizophrenia but in milder form. The picture is of a person who is partway between good mental health and serious psychopathology. I see no role for personality traits here or in several others on the list of personality disorders, but this is no place for an extended critique of the classification system. Instead, the focus is on the personality disorders for which personality traits are relevant.

Avoidant

Avoidants display timidity in social situations, staying on the fringe and inhibiting conversation. They feel inadequate in social contexts and anticipate rejection in novel situations. They may even pass up job opportunities because they involve contact with others.

If these symptoms seem familiar, it is because they completely overlap the trait of shyness. Beyond that, avoidant personality disorder is hardly different from social phobia: "Efforts to distinguish between generalized social phobia and avoidant personality have been largely ineffective, indicating at best that avoidant personality disorder tends to be, on average, more dysfunctional than generalized social phobia" (Widiger & Samuel, 2005, p. 496). As has been pointed out, both social phobia and avoidant personality disorder are marked by "avoidance of occupational activities that require interpersonal contact, preoccupation with being criticized or rejected by others, and inhibition in new interpersonal situations because of feelings of inadequacy" (Beidel & Turner, 2007, p. 40).

I searched for differences between avoidant personality disorder and social phobia and found two candidates: (a) social anxiety may include embarrassment and avoidance of public speaking and performing, and (b) social anxiety, as its name suggests, emphasizes the fear component and is therefore more serious and debilitating. Are these reasons good enough to have a separate diagnostic category?

Recall that shyness overlaps social phobia, and now avoidant personality disorder overlaps social phobia, so there are three labels for much the same kind of behavior. Perhaps it would help to align them in order of increasing severity and dysfunction: shyness, avoidant personality disorder, social phobia.

Obsessive–Compulsive

The symptoms of obsessive–compulsive disorder are excessive orderliness, difficulty making decisions, and demands on the self to stick to rules and to make detailed plans. Before a decision is made, information is sought exhaustively, and there is excessive rumination about the risks, costs, and possible complications as well suggestions for other options. The best example of obsessiveness in literature is the conclusion of the Hamlet soliloquy that begins, "To be or not to be":

> And thus the native hue of resolution
> Is sicklied o'er with the pale cast of thought,
> And enterprises of great pitch and moment
> With this regard their currents turn awry,
> And lose the name of action.

The compulsive aspect of this disorder may be seen in the inflexible surrendering to rules and regulations and an unremitting focus on a problem to the exclusion of all else in life. These various symptoms are highly similar to two differentiates of the impulsiveness trait dimension described in Chapter 4. One is *discipline*, which in part involves maintaining focus on a task and the pursuit of it to the end. The other is *reflection*, as manifested in thought before action and well-laid-out plans. Clearly, obsessive–compulsive personality disorder may be understood as the abnormal extreme of the low end of the trait of impulsiveness.

Narcissistic

In the ancient Greek legend, Narcissus fell in love with his own image reflected in a pool of water, so this disorder is marked by an exaggerated sense of one's abilities; self-importance, grandiosity, arrogance; and even the idea that others are envious. However, all these features are included in the Narcissistic Personality Inventory (Raskin & Hall, 1979; see also Kubarych, Deary, & Austin, 2003), which assesses narcissism as a normal personality trait. Is narcissistic personality disorder just the high end of this personality trait?

Consider the high end of the trait of self-esteem. There is more here than just outrageous self-esteem because people with narcissism demand the admiration of others and are upset when they do not receive it. Thus, those with narcissistic personality disorder actually are likely to have fragile self-esteem (see Chapter 7).

Their intense self-focus suggests that two other self-related traits are relevant. Most people who are high in private self-consciousness are not high in public self-consciousness, but narcissists are high in both kinds of self-focus, the extreme of self-centeredness. These various linkages suggest that the answer to the above question is yes, narcissistic personality disorder is nothing more than the high end of the personality trait of narcissism.

Paranoid

As the term suggests, people with this disorder are extremely resentful, mistrustful of others, and suspect that others are out to demean or harm them. The overlap with the personality trait of hostility may be seen in four of the items of the Hostility scale of the Aggression Questionnaire (A. H. Buss & Perry, 1992):

> At times I feel I have gotten a raw deal out of life.
> I know that "friends" talk about me behind my back.
> I am suspicious of overly friendly strangers.
> When people are especially nice, I wonder what they want.

Recall the extreme degree of self-reference that marks paranoid ideation, as revealed in the correlation between public self-consciousness (awareness of oneself as a social object) and paranoid thinking (Fenigstein & Vanable, 1992). If we assume a personality trait perspective, then paranoid personality disorder is a combination of the high ends of the traits of hostility and public self-consciousness.

Passive–Aggressive

Passive–aggressive personality disorder, included in the *DSM–IV–TR* , may be removed in *DSM–V*, but it is worth discussing it here. The symptoms are sullenness, feelings of being controlled, and resistance to authority and complaints about it. People with this disorder do not openly oppose those in authority but engage in gossiping and backbiting, hence the name of the disorder.

The personality trait of submissiveness is relevant here; without it, such people would aggress openly. Instead, they engage in the more subtle aggressiveness called *negativism,* examples of which are on the Negativism scale of my original Aggression Questionnaire (A. H. Buss & Durkee, 1957):

> Unless somebody asks me in a nice way, I won't do what they want.
> When somebody makes a rule I don't like, I am tempted to break it.
> When someone is bossy, I do the opposite of what he asks.
> When people are bossy, I take my time just to show them.
> Occasionally, when I am mad at someone, I will give him the "silent treatment."

HARDINESS AND VULNERABILITY

In the face of unremitting danger, some of the soldiers and Marines fighting in Iraq and Afghanistan have developed posttraumatic stress disorder, but many others have adjusted to civilian life without apparent mental disorder. In everyday life, some people fall apart and never completely recover from divorce or widowhood, whereas others eventually get on with their lives. These are examples of the concepts of vulnerability and hardiness, which were originally applied to the impact of stress on disease (Kobasa, 1979), were extended to abnormal behavior (Maddi, Khoshaba, Harvey, Lu, & Persico, 2002) and have given rise to the concept of *stress tolerance* (Leyro, Zvolensky, & Bernstein, 2010). There is evidence of a U-shaped curve in the relationship between adversity and resilience: Low levels of adversity produced more resilience than high levels of no adversity at all (Seery, Holman, & Silver, 2010).

Consider how stress might affect blood pressure. One man on the floor of the New York Stock Exchange might remain calm in the face of flurries of trading, and his blood pressure would rise a little, if at all (*buffering*). Another man might get so upset as to cause a dangerous spike in his blood pressure (*vulnerability*). However, even a vulnerable man might learn to take breaks and ensure that he would leave his emotions on the stockroom floor, calming himself immediately after work (*coping*). In brief, there are three potential responses to stress, and when we consider their relevance to abnormal behavior, personality traits are involved.

Buffering

Several personality traits buffer us from the challenges of everyday life. When there is a threat to life and limb, those low in fear are less likely to react physiologically and more likely to remain calm enough to deal with the threat. Similarly, in a novel situation when there might be social evaluation, unshy people do not get rattled and can make the appropriate social responses.

Conflict between people tends to be stressful. When two people are trying to assert themselves, the more dominant one tends to be more relaxed and better able to maintain higher social status. Similarly, when there is a challenge to competence, people high in self-esteem have no problem in facing it, confident that they will succeed. Competitive people, faced with a loss, will not accept it and will try harder next time, and so will those high in self-esteem.

Vulnerability

Some personality traits make us more vulnerable to the challenges of everyday life. *Fearful* people have a strong physiological reaction when threatened, tend to panic, and are likely to escape from the situation rather than dealing with it. They condition to new fears easily and tend to generalize from one frightening situation to others that contain no threat, thereby widening their vulnerability. *Shy* people tend to become anxious or embarrassed in the face of novel social situations and may start avoiding them, which is maladaptive.

Angry people tend to turn others against them, making otherwise peaceful situations tense and sometimes threatening. *Hostile* people feel put upon and see threats from others that simply are not there. To live in such a seemingly threatening world is to be vulnerable.

A review of literature found that private self-consciousness is associated with depressive tendencies (Mor & Winquist, 2002), and the disposition to ruminate correlates with the Neuroticism factor of the Big Five (Trapnell & Campbell, 1999). Neuroticism is associated with low self-esteem (Robins, Tracy, Trzesniewski, Potter, & Gosling, 2001), and as documented in Chapter 7, low self-esteem correlates with loneliness, pessimism, and expectations of failures, all of which suggest vulnerability.

Coping

In the face of a challenge, *active* people are likely to move toward meeting the challenge rather than sitting by helplessly. *Sociable* people can turn to others for instrumental help and nurturance, as has been institutionalized in support groups for cancer survivors and others. People high in leadership, when dealing with a life crisis, are likely to be the ones who start a support group. Those high in self-esteem are typically optimistic, which is known to help deal with illness and psychological problems. As we saw in Chapter 7, *defensive pessimists*, despite their gloomy outlook, will try to meet challenges. *Incremental theorists* see challenges not as threats but as offering opportunities for improvement. If physical or psychological remediation is necessary, those at the deliberate end of the impulsiveness continuum have an advantage, specifically those who are planful and disciplined.

These various personality traits tilt people in the direction of coping with problems. Together with the traits that help people buffer against stress or threats, they comprise hardiness, in contrast to the traits that comprise vulnerability. Thus, personality plays an important role in whether people will adjust to the inevitable downturns in life or slide into abnormal behavior.

Perspective

Ever since the personality disorders were distinguished as a separate axis of mental disorder, psychologists have been searching for *personality dimensions* that would underlie the various disorders (Clark, 2007; Frick, 2004; Strack, 2006). The dimensions have been sought through factor analysis of the kind that yields a small number of superfactors or through the (usually) two axes that define an interpersonal circumplex.

Five-Factor Model

The dominant conception of personality trait structure consists of five superfactors (McCrae & Costa, 1985, 1987): Neuroticism, Extraversion, Agreeableness, Conscientious, and Openness. Normal subjects were administered the appropriate questionnaire items, as well as items assessing the various symptoms of the personality disorders (Costa & McCrae, 1990; Wiggins & Pincus, 1989). I converted the factor loadings into the five factors, examined the correlations of personality disorders, and combined the two studies to yield these associations with the personality disorders discussed earlier:

- avoidant: neurotic, introverted
- obsessive–compulsive: neurotic, conscientious

- dependent: neurotic, introverted
- narcissistic: extraverted, not neurotic
- paranoid: neurotic, not agreeable
- passive–aggressive: neurotic, not conscientious

Notice that with the exception of narcissism, all these disorders are marked by neuroticism. The introversion of those with avoidance reflects their shyness, the extraversion of those with narcissism reflects their enormous self-esteem, and the opposite of agreeableness reflects the hostility of those with paranoia. The relation of the five factors to abnormal behavior has been updated (McCrae, 2006).

Interpersonal Circumplex

The first model started as a circumplex in which social behaviors were arranged around a circle so that similar behaviors were located nearby and dissimilar behaviors were located farther away (M. B. Freedman, Leary, Ossorio, & Coffee, 1951). Using this model, T. F. Leary (1957) arranged adjectives around a circle that had two orthogonal dimensions, love–hate and dominance–submission. These two axes allowed for blends such as loving and submissive.

Wiggins (1979), on the basis of analyzing personality adjectives, empirically assigned 16 personality traits along a circle with these two axes: status (power, domination) and love (solidarity, affiliation). The personality traits around the circle were regarded as continuous with abnormal behavior:

> The Interpersonal Circle is a conceptual representation of the domain of interpersonal behavior that depicts interpersonal variables as vectors in a two-dimensional circular space formed by the coordinates of dominance and love. Within that circular space, the vectors that emanate from the center of the circle are interpreted as continua of intensity ranging from the moderate and generally adaptive to the extreme and often maladaptive. (Wiggins, Phillips, & Trapnell, 1989, p. 303)

Wiggins et al. (1989) found correlations between vector length and self-reported mental health problems ranging from .41 to .69. Further research linked interpersonal traits to diagnoses of personality disorders (Pincus & Wiggins, 1990; Wiggins & Pincus, 1989). In the following, I have arranged these interpersonal traits so as to compare them with my descriptions, which are in parentheses:

- avoidant: aloof-introverted, unassured-submissive (anxiously shy)
- narcissistic: arrogant-calculating (fragile, high self-esteem, strong self-focus)

- paranoid: coldhearted, arrogant-calculating (hostility, high in public self-consciousness)
- dependent: unassured-submissive, unassuming-ingenuous (submissive, low in self-esteem)

The interpersonal circumplex, with its axes of dominance and love, was later applied more broadly to the personality disorders (Pincus, 2005).

Three-Factor Model

A three-factor model has been derived from the Differential Personality Questionnaire (Tellegen, 1985). The factors of Positive Emotionality, Negative Emotionality, and Constraint contain elements of several of my temperaments. Positive emotionality has elements of activity and sociability, Negative Emotionality has elements of emotionality, and Constraint appears close to the deliberate end of impulsiveness. These three superfactors have been used as a model for the personality disorders:

> The framework explicitly embraces a two-affect systems model of positive and negative affectivity—emotionality—activation, which are manifested as general biobehavioral systems of approach–withdrawal, respectively, and which are regulated, in large part by a third system that itself is nonaffective but plays a fundamental "gatekeeping" role in the degree to which incoming stimuli are subject to inhibitory influence. (Clark, 2005, p. 511)

This model is more general in attempting to offer dimensions (superfactors) for both personality disorders (Axis II) and the more serious psychiatric disorders (Axis I), and it and the previous two adopt a personality approach to mental disorders. Are there advantages to this approach? Let me answer with one more quotation:

> Dimensional models have the advantage of providing more flexible, specific, and comprehensive information, whereas categorical systems tend to be procrustean, lose information, and result in many classificatory dilemmas when patients fall at the boundaries of the categories. . . . In the absence of any clear boundaries between a normal, adaptive personality trait and a maladaptive, inflexible trait, or between the different constellations of maladaptive traits, a dimensional model is more consistent with the current research than a categorical model. (Widiger & Frances, 1985, p. 619)

Psychiatric Classification

The current psychiatric classification as described in the *DSM–IV* is being revised, and the new edition, *DSM–V*, will appear in 2013. Meanwhile, the panel working on the revision has sent word of the changes to take place, and of particular relevance here will be the deletion of narcissistic and paranoid personality disorders. However, it is reasonable to expect further revisions in the classification system, and it would not be surprising if these two personality disorders made their way back into the *DSM*, although perhaps in another part of the classification. Whether they do or not, these two personality disorders represent the extremes of personality dimensions.

Although there will still be categories of abnormal personality, they will be leavened by insistence that these are also dimensions that vary from mild to serious symptoms—that is, there is an emphasis on dimensionality with the addition of personality traits (Widiger & Trull, 2007). There is another addition as well: Clinicians will be asked as part of the diagnosis to assess the risk of later abnormality, and this assessment can be checked by follow-up research in the service of amending the classification.

However, there seem to be problems inherent in any categorical classification, problems that date back to the original classification. As I once wrote, that classification

> wanders back and forth between syndrome and type concepts. A syndrome is a group of symptoms that occur together, whereas a type is a group of *persons* with certain common characteristics. . . . The classification also employs a mixture of class and trait concepts. A *class* consists of objects, events, or people that meet the criteria of class membership. Both types and syndromes are class concepts, which are discontinuous. A *trait is* a continuous variable, some aspect of behavior which varies from one person to the next. (A. H. Buss, 1966, p. 43)

What was true then seems just as true now, which reinforces the need to emphasize the use of personality traits and dimensions in our attempt to understand abnormal behavior.

9

STYLE

The ways people walk, use gestures, and even peel an orange can reflect their motives, needs, and important dimensions of personality. Just as there is linguistic content, there is also linguistic style—how people put their words together to create a message . . . . We can begin to detect linguistic style by paying attention to "junk words"—those words that do not convey much in the way of content. (Chung & Pennebaker, 2007, p. 345)

Chung and Pennebaker (2007) reviewed how much what they termed *junk words*—prepositions, articles, and conjunctions—tell us about social behavior and allow inferences about personality. Like them, I focus not on content but on style, the domain being the kind of movements described in the first sentence of this quotation.

The *content* of behavior may be regarded as the answer to the question, "What?" Examples are emotionality, sensation seeking, shyness, and so on. The *style* of behavior may be regarded as the answer to the question, "How?" Style is not the vocabulary and grammar of conversation but how the talk is delivered: loudness, pitch, timbre, and inflections. Our regional speech accent (style) is more enduring and more constant than what we say (content) because the accent is a background variable that ordinarily exists below the level of awareness, as is true for style in general. Thus, as stated by DePaulo (1992), "Nonverbal behavior is less accessible to actors than to observers. . . . People never see their own facial expressions exactly as others do" (p. 206). The author added that posture (style) is much harder to control than verbal behavior (content). Similarly, although we control what we say, we have little control over qualities of our voice—for example, breathy, thin, full, tense, relaxed, or nasal (Scherer, 1986).

Look for style in these behaviors:

1. Gestures and paralinguistics that accompany speech, including vocal characteristics (e.g., loudness, pitch);
2. Nonverbal gestures that substitute for speech (e.g., pointing);
3. Vocal, facial, hand, and body behavior that accompanies emotional displays (e.g., laughing);
4. Posture and movement, especially in the absence of social behavior or emotional display (e.g., sitting or walking); and
5. The stylistic component of trait behavior (e.g., head held high in dominance)

These examples are a small segment of a multitude of behaviors that need to be organized. I have assembled them into a short list of the dimensions of movement, emphasizing extreme examples for the sake of exposition.

DIMENSIONS OF MOVEMENT

The physical dimensions of observable behavior are time, frequency, force, and space. Concerning time, we may measure *latency*, how long it takes for a response to be initiated or, alternatively, how long a single response lasts. Frequency and time may be combined to yield the rate of responding, the typical measure of operant conditioning. Force involves the energy expended in movement. Space is measured by how much is taken up in posture or movement, the variation ranging from constricted to spread out. These physical dimensions of behavior yield five dimensions of movement, the basic ingredients of style.

Pace

The rate of responding is called *pace* or the more familiar *tempo*, one differentiate of the personality trait of activity. The behavior in question is a series of movements, and the time element is typically measured in seconds or minutes Examples are the following:

- Speech (rapid–drawled), gestures, blinking
- Walk briskly, skip, jump, climb fast versus slow
- Wash fast versus slow, gulp down food versus chew slowly, guzzle or sip drink

- Sweep, slice, whisk through versus dawdle; cut bread fast or slow
- Gallop up stairs, scamper down versus stately descent; creep up, inch up
- Dash for door, cab, elevator versus stroll, saunter, linger
- Brush hair, teeth fast or slow; comb, wash, apply makeup, shave, dress quickly versus unhurriedly; button or zip fast or slow
- Scribble away or write slowly

Duration

Duration appears at first glance to be nothing more than pace because if a word is spoken slowly, for example, speech must necessarily be slow, but this equivalence holds only for a series of responses. When there is a single response, obviously there can be no rate of behavior, but we can measure how long it takes to complete the response: abruptly or in a stretched-out fashion. Examples are the following:

- Gaze: fixed versus shifting; a look held too long
- Gestures: short versus long time held in place, drawn-out versus abrupt
- A drawn-out sigh
- Single word, clipped or drawn out
- The quick "aha" of success, the "oh" of surprise: brief or extended

Suddenness

This dimension involves the time it takes to start a response. The behavior may be a response to another person, that is, how long it takes to react: promptly or with a pause. Otherwise, it may be nonsocial, merely the time it takes to start any action: as fast as a startle reflex or with all due deliberation.

Presumably, people who respond suddenly also have a fast pace. Similarly, people whose responses are of short duration also tend to respond suddenly, and people who respond suddenly probably have a fast tempo. The link among these dimensions is, of course, time, which undoubtedly accounts for their being related. That they are related, however, does not deny the value of keeping the concepts separate and measuring them independently. Indeed, we might be especially interested in people for whom the three dimensions are not related, for example, someone with a slow pace and short-lived responses who nevertheless responds suddenly. Examples of suddenness are the following:

- Bound out of a chair or rise slowly
- Respond to other person quickly or slowly (smile, laugh)
- Rapid versus slow change of expression, as in smiling

Vigor

Vigor is, of course, the other differentiate of the trait of activity. It involves the degree of physical strength being applied, so that expressive and other movements vary from strong to weak. Examples are the following:

- Gestures: forceful, vigorous, chopping motion, fist clenched, punch air
- Handshake: firm versus feeble, hard versus soft
- Pound on table, knock on door
- Open and close door, jump, stamp, push button, hammer, saw, slice, peel, sweep, chop, shovel, brush hair, all strenuously or weakly
- Loudness of voice and laughter: booming versus weak or feeble

Displacement

Displacement consists of the space taken up by facial expressions, gestures, or the body. The appropriate dichotomy is expansive versus constricted, as the following examples demonstrate:

- Expansive versus constricted (tight, enclosed)
- Amount of space taken up while at rest: sprawled versus scrunched; legs, arms extended or held in
- Length of stride: loping versus small stride, the latter typical of shy people (Sakaguchi & Hasegawam, 2006)
- Width of smile, length of stride and arm swing, diameter of hand rotation, nods, dilation of nostrils versus pinched
- Eyes: wide open versus hooded, squinting
- Extent of shrug
- Lateral displacement of head at rest or during nodding the head (yes) or shaking it (no).

In addition to lateral displacement, there is vertical displacement. Examples are the following:

- Standing and walking straight up versus leaning forward or backward

- Walking up on the balls of the feet versus walking flatfooted
- Holding the head straight or tilted to one side, or forward or backward

PSYCHOLOGICAL DIMENSIONS (STYLISTIC TRAITS)

The physical elements of movement are fairly easy to record objectively (watch, tape measure), but these physical elements are just the start of our understanding of style because there are also psychological dimensions of style, involving behaviors more difficult to record objectively. Judgments by observers are required, for example, distinguishing among the Duchenne smile of enjoyment, the smile when admiring infants, and the smile of anticipation (Ekman, 2003; Ekman, Davidson, & Friesen, 1990). The physical elements may be the objective underpinnings of style, but the psychological dimensions must be the focus of any attempt to understand style as an aspect of personality. I offer abundant examples of each dimension, mainly through the use of adjectives. In this respect, I follow the lead of Goldberg and his colleagues (Ashton, Lee, & Goldberg, 2004; Goldberg, 1990): "*Important phenotypic attributes become encoded in the natural language*. . . . As a result personality concepts in everyday language inevitably form a substantial part of the subject matter of personality psychology" (Saucier & Goldberg, 2001, p. 848). For the purpose of exposition, I describe here the extremes of each dimension.

Animated–Lethargic

These extremes bracket a dimension that includes four physical dimensions of style: pace, suddenness, vigor, and displacement. Animated people tend to be described as brisk and vivacious. They are likely to gallop up stairs, answer questions immediately, and use broad and forceful gestures. Lethargic people tend to be described as sluggish and languid. They are likely to ascend stairs at a leisurely pace, take their time replying to questions, speak slowly and deliberately, and have limp gestures. However, there is more to this psychological dimension than a combination of physical dimensions of style. Consider these additions:

- An alertness component with the extremes of vigilant versus drowsy
- A lightness component with the extremes of sprightly–ponderous (as when sitting or rising from a chair), bouncy–leaden, and springy–shuffling (as when walking)

- A fresh–weary component: eyes bright versus hooded, an alert look versus a sleepy look, a bright smile versus a bare grin, and shoulders square versus drooping; a springy step versus trudging along

Emphatic–Mild

This dimension is essentially the same as the physical dimensions of vigor and displacement, so the examples given under those headings are appropriate here and need not be repeated. Those examples involve locomotion or posture, but the emphatic–mild dimension also refers to the style that shows up in interpersonal contexts, in which communication and emotional reactions come into play. The emphatic style is one of intensity: a penetrating stare, a wider expanse of gritted teeth, a broader smile, or a heartier hug.

Dramatic–Bland

Certain adjectives convey the flavor of this dimension: showy, flashy, ostentatious, theatrical, histrionic, embellishing, florid, and extravagant versus wishy-washy, dull, subdued, flat, dim, and tame. Although the dramatic and emphatic styles overlap, both involving vigor and displacement, the dramatic style is one of exaggeration, especially with respect to displacement, whereas the emphatic style is one of intensity, especially with respect to vigor. So we find actions that are emphatic without being dramatic, such as the ones in the previous paragraph, and we find actions that are dramatic but not emphatic:

- Dazzling, flashing, radiant smile versus a minimal smile
- Flamboyant versus a deadpan facial greeting
- Inflected speech versus monotone
- Mobile versus unchanging facial expressions
- Striking a pose with arms akimbo versus arms at the side
- A drawn-out pause or a slowed spacing of words to mark their importance
- A swaggering walk versus an erect walk
- Heavy versus light sigh
- Elaborate versus barely perceptible shrug

Notice that the first four examples involve qualities of the expressions, whereas the rest involve displacement or vigor.

Playful–Serious

We characterize some people as playful and others as sober in mien and movement. Play has been given sufficient attention in the social science literature, especially by developmental psychologists, but playfulness as an aspect of personality has largely been ignored. Strangely enough, playfulness emerged as a factor in two massive studies of personality traits in dogs (Svartberg, 2005; Svartberg & Forkman, 2002).

I see playfulness in our species as a content personality trait, exemplified by teasing, ridiculing, or parodying others; playing practical jokes; acting drunk; delivering outrageous puns and making a game out of work; and being jolly, facetious, flippant, winking, and even clownish. One of the needs suggested by the pioneering personality psychologist Henry Murray was play: "To relax, amuse oneself, seek diversion and entertainment. To 'have fun,' to play games. To laugh, joke, and be merry" (H. Murray, 1938, p. 83). These examples illustrate one pole of the content of trait of playfulness, the opposite end of which is serious, as described by the adjectives *earnest* and *staid*.

There is a related set of behaviors involving not the *what* of responses but the *how*. The style of playful people is frisky and frolicsome but not necessarily dramatic. The style of serious people is restrained and subdued, which makes it clear that serious overlaps bland. However, the opposite of bland is dramatic, whereas the opposite of serious is playful, for example, play face versus poker face; hop, skip, prance versus plain walk; and wink versus a straight look. Other examples of playful style are the following:

- Mock surprise
- Roll eyes, cross eyes, mischievous sidelong glances
- Waggle eyebrows versus straight eyebrows
- Flutter eyelashes in a mock serious way
- Mischievous smile versus poker face
- Movement: hop, skip, jump, prance, spin, whirl
- Gestures: exaggerated, caricatured
- Raucous laugh, giggle, snicker

Precise–Loose

This dimension of movement and bearing may be pinned down by adjectives that mark the extremes: *careful, neat,* and *meticulous* versus *careless, sloppy,* and *slapdash*. Consider the following behavior: erect versus slumping posture, fastidious versus messy eating, and articulated versus mumbled speech.

Both alone and with others, those with a precise style are disciplined, orderly, and focused; an extreme example would be the crisp behavior of a well-trained Marine. Those with a loose style tend to be undisciplined and unfocused; an extreme example would be a 1960s hippie. Other examples are the following:

- Exact versus vague gestures
- Gaze: stare versus wandering; steady versus fluctuating

- Mouth firm versus slack
- Disciplined versus casual demeanor, posture erect versus flaccid or slumping
- Distinct versus indistinct in speech
- Neat versus sloppy eating and drinking

Tense–Relaxed

This dimension is not about transient anxiety but rather an enduring style marked by the extremes of movements that are rigid versus flexible: body movements being stiff versus supple and shoulders being hunched versus squared. Other examples are the following:

- Voice strained, hoarse; pinched nose, eyes squinting
- Loose fist versus clenched, limp handshake
- Jaw (clenched), brows knitted
- Neck strained, grimace
- Forehead furrowed

Graceful–Clumsy

This is the most evaluative dimension of style. Consider the adjectives *agile*, *nimble*, and *surefooted* versus *uncoordinated*, *gawky*, and *floundering*. Is this dimension different from precise–loose? Precision implies care, and looseness implies lack of care, whereas grace implies motor ability and clumsiness implies lack of it. Thus, a person may be precise without necessarily being graceful, and looseness does not automatically translate into clumsiness, so we are best served by keeping the dimensions separate. The need for two dimensions is further demonstrated by these dichotomies of particular actions involving skill but not precision: fluid versus stumbling walk and smooth versus awkward gestures.

Consider these examples of body movements, gestures, instrumental movements of hands, sitting, standing, carrying, minor carpentry, reaching, and walking:

- Adroit versus maladroit
- Dexterous versus fumbling
- Lithe, graceful, versus bumbling, awkward, uncoordinated, lurching
- Smooth versus jerky, balanced versus lurching
- Nimble, coordinated versus uncoordinated
- Gliding versus stumbling

THE DIMENSIONS

The psychological dimensions of style are summarized in Exhibit 9.1. The dimensions in the top part of this exhibit are based on physical elements of style, and it is worth noting that vigor is common to all four of these styles. Beyond the physical elements, part of animated shades into emphatic, which itself has some commonality with dramatic, which in turn partly overlaps playful.

The bottom three styles in Exhibit 9.1 are not based on the aforementioned physical dimensions. Instead, these three styles have features not easily quantified, features that make these styles evaluative: Who would argue that it is better to be precise, relaxed, and graceful? These three styles also overlap. Playful–serious is close to precise–loose, but the link is between playful and loose, not between serious and precise because a person can be serious without being precise, but a playful person is likely to be loose, not precise. This reminder of the importance of examining the top and bottom halves of trait dimensions leads to the issue of unipolarity versus bipolarity.

Four of the stylistic dimensions—animated, emphatic, dramatic, and tense—are unipolar, but the other three appear to be bipolar. Playful moves down to an absence of frivolity and then up toward being more and more serious. Precision moves down to an absence of precision and then up toward being increasingly slapdash. Graceful moves down to an absence of agility and then up toward increasing clumsiness.

The overlap among dimensions is the result of a strategy of attempting a detailed map of personality style, on the assumption that finer distinctions offer a more complete picture, while knowing in advance that the more detail offered, the more likely the occurrence of overlap. This strategy reflects knowledge that many content personality traits are also correlated. Presumably, the

---

EXHIBIT 9.1
Psychological Dimensions of Style

Styles Based on Elements of Movement

- Animated–lethargic: pace, suddenness, vigor, displacement
- Emphatic–mild: vigor, displacement
- Dramatic–bland: duration, vigor, displacement
- Playful–serious: pace, suddenness, vigor

Qualitative Styles

- Precise–loose
- Tense–relaxed
- Graceful–clumsy

---

correlations among personality traits reflect the way people are, not an artifact of the way we measure personality. Regardless of these correlations, it is still worthwhile to distinguish between personality traits. Recall that shyness and sociability are significantly, negatively correlated (Chapter 4), but treating them as separate trait dimensions revealed that shy–sociable people behave differently from shy–unsociable people. Similarly, even though several stylistic dimensions overlap, we might be interested, for example, in people who are playful but not loose, emphatic but not dramatic, and precise but not graceful.

STYLE AND CONTENT

Most of the personal styles are related to content traits, as shown in Table 9.1. There is an obvious connection between animated–lethargic and the content trait of activity, but there is more to animated style than sheer energy, specifically, alertness, lightness, and freshness. Thus, there are people with abundant energy who are not necessarily animated, although animated people are always energetic.

Emphatic–mild is related to dominance in that dominant people tend talk louder and interrupt more (J. A. Hall, Coats, & Lebeau, 2005). Louder talk is more vigorous and interruptions are necessarily louder, both being emphatic. Dominant people also gaze more at the other person when talking (Koch et al, 2010), suggesting greater intensity, which, as mentioned earlier, is part of emphatic style.

Dramatic–bland is related to the trait of exhibitionism. It has been assessed by Jackson (1974) but otherwise has been ignored, which is unfortunate because there are people who never mature beyond show-and-tell. They are dramatic, perhaps in an effort to obtain attention, but some dramatic people do not necessarily seek attention because their being dramatic may be explained by their having been reared in a family or a culture that expresses emotions openly and intensely.

TABLE 9.1
Style and Content Traits

Style	Content trait
Animated	Activity
Emphatic	Dominance
Dramatic	Exhibitionism
Playful	Playfulness
Precise	Order
Tense	Emotionality
Sudden	Impulsiveness
Expressive	Extraversion

Playful–serious is the stylistic component of the content trait of playfulness, described earlier. It has not been studied as a personality trait in humans, but doing so would help us to seek the developmental antecedents of adults who kid others, spin puns, create nonhostile pranks, and dress up in wild costumes.

Precise–loose is related to the *order* facet of the Big Five superfactor called Conscientiousness (McCrae & Costa, 1985). Consider the adjectives that are markers for conscientiousness: *organized, neat, orderly, prompt, meticulous,* and *practical* versus *disorganized, disorderly, careless, sloppy,* and *impractical* (Goldberg, 1990). Except for the last two, these adjectives define the style trait of precise–loose.

The content trait of emotionality shows up stylistically in our muscles. Those of the face, neck, and body are strained in high-emotional people and relaxed in low-emotional people.

The last two items in Table 9.1 require comment. Although suddenness is not a psychological dimension of style but a physical dimension of movement, it is worth noting that impulsive people are likely to make sudden movements.

Extraversion, well represented as a personality supertrait, represents a combination of sociability, activity, dominance, and perhaps impulsiveness. Extraverts tend to be expressive, a broad concept that consists of three styles: animated, emphatic, and dramatic.

I have made no attempt to trace the developmental trajectory of style because of a dearth of information, although informal observations of children shed some light. As young children develop, they move from playful, animated, and clumsy toward the opposite end of these dimensions.

What we know about content traits may be of service here. It is reasonable to suppose that the development of style is influenced by physique, gender, and culture. Thus, as travelers visit different countries, they are confronted with variations in the loudness of speech (vigor), enunciation (precision), and the eloquence of gestures (displacement). However, within each culture, there are striking individual differences in style. Unlike the content of behavior, the style of behavior is rarely shaped by reinforcement contingencies, and like speech accents, style may be acquired through imitation. The movements involved in style are made many thousands of time during the course of development so that by adulthood, they are overlearned and therefore automatic and habitual, which is why style is the most consistent part of personality.

PERSPECTIVE

I owe a debt to a pioneering and classic book on style by Allport and Vernon (1933). After observing individual differences in handshaking, they boiled them down to dimensions of vigor (pumping), strength, duration, and kind of grip. In the laboratory, they also observed their subjects' finger tapping, walking, running, and handwriting. Two of the three factors they extracted may be seen in my construction of style. I adopted their *broad–constricted* factor as displacement, an element of movement, and their *forceful–weak* factor as part of amplitude and therefore of emphatic–mild, a psychological dimension of style.

Allport and Vernon's (1933) research stimulated others in the 1930s. P. Eisenberg (1937) found that dominant people drew and wrote faster, put more pressure on pens and pencils, and had more expansive handwriting. Estes (1938) reported that accuracy in assessing style depended largely on the raters who were observing it, a finding that is related to the more general problem of accuracy of observation (Funder, 1995).

The 1940s saw a book, *The Expression of Personality* (Wolf, 1943), that described results indicating that observers inferred such personality traits as introversion and optimism from the way people walked. Maslow (1949) contrasted coping behavior with expressive behavior (style) as follows:

- Means to an end versus an end in itself
- Aim is to change environment versus no particular aim
- Determined by the task versus by temperament personality traits
- Controllable versus less so and hard to change
- Conscious versus usually not conscious

There was some interest in style by psychologists in the 1950s. For example, Rimoldi (1951) had 59 measures of tempo and extracted these second-order factors: motor activity, perception, cognition, and reaction time. Style was still discussed in a few personality texts; for example,

> We might note that different persons' movements are vigorous, expansive, dainty, crude, clumsy, heavy, sluggish, or vivacious. Different persons' performance of tasks might be described as rapid, precise, orderly, or hurried. Some of these qualities, of course, can be objectively scored. Some are best rated for lack of objectively measurable variables. (Guilford, 1959, p. 272)

Instead, *expressive style* has been studied as an aspect of emotion (Ekman, 1965; 2003; Goetz, Keltner, & Simon-Thomas, 2010; Scherer, 1986; Tracy & Robins, 2008) or as communication via nonverbal behavior generally (Argyle, 1975; Scherer & Ekman, 1982). Alternatively, nonverbal aspects of behavior have been studied as part of self-presentation (DePaulo, 1992) or to examine how we judge others, for example, dominant status (Mast & Hall, 2004). When style is observed, it can be contaminated by a person's face and body appearance, One solution is to video people so that observers can see only points of light in the subjects' movement, a procedure that identified hip sway, knee movement, displacement of arms, and a bouncy rhythm as qualities of youthfulness both in Americans (Montepare & Zebrowitz-McArthur, 1988) and Koreans (Montepare & Zebrowitz, 1993).

The book *Nonverbal Sex Differences* (J. A. Hall, 1984) is relevant here, specifically the chapter that summarized the literature on observed body movement and posture during dyadic interaction. These were organized into categories in a manner analogous to my ordering of style along several dimensions:

- Restlessness
- Relaxation—leaning, reclining
- Expansiveness—legs open, arms not at sides
- Involvement—nodding, forward lean
- Expressiveness—hand gestures, head movement
- Self-consciousness—stroking the hair, self-touching

Of particular relevance here is a doctoral dissertation by a student of mine, which was subsequently published (Gallaher, 1992). The raters, roommates or close friends of the subjects, rated the subjects on a list of behaviors involving style. A correlation matrix yielded four factors. *Expressiveness* included such items as "fast talker" and "broad gestures," which makes this factor equivalent to animated–lethargic. *Animated* included such items as "climbs stairs quickly" and "erect shoulders," which makes it equivalent to a combination of animated–lethargic and precise–loose. *Expansiveness* included such items as "takes large steps" and "hands away from body," which makes it equivalent to the movement element I call displacement. *Coordination* includes such items as "fluid walk" and "fluid gestures," which is equivalent to graceful–clumsy. Two caveats need to be added. First, some of the items loaded on more than one factor, and second, the raters were undergraduates who were not trained and therefore perhaps not the best observers.

Notice that several of my psychological dimensions of style did not show up as factors. The major reason is that few items tapping these dimensions were included in the list to be rated, and the minor reason is that the few included items tended to load on Gallaher's (1992) expressiveness and animated factors. So for now it is reasonable to retain seven dimensions of personal style as a way to organize this aspect of personality.

EPILOGUE

The Introduction in this volume laid out the plan of this book. Now that the plan has been filled in with specific ideas and their empirical basis, it is time for a summary and a few comments.

THEORY

Evolution

In using evolution as an overview for understanding personality traits, I diverge from mainstream evolutionary psychologists, who, with a few exceptions, seek general laws of behavior, not explanations of personality traits. In their edited volume, D. M. Buss and Hawley (2011) stated,

> Instead, evolutionary psychology has been most successful in providing theories about, and evidence for, human universals. . . . These theoretical and empirical successes, however, have been achieved at the level of illuminating *species-typical* (characteristics of most or all humans) or *sex-differentiated* adaptations. Individual differences within each sex—profound

and integral to all human functioning—have been almost entirely ignored. (D. M. Buss & Hawley, 2011, p. xi)

Buss and Hawley's work should help remedy this situation, but my approach remains different from theirs.

I see three related evolutionary perspectives on personality, the first of which consists of dispositions we share with other animals. These include the traits of emotionality, activity, sociability, impulsiveness, aggressiveness, and dominance.

The second evolutionary perspective consists of features unique to our species. Our cognitions are sufficiently advanced over those of others animals to be considered unique. We are able to make attributions and to focus on the self beyond mirror-image recognition. Individual differences in self-focus are found in the trait of private self-consciousness, and the combination of self-focus and attributions establishes the basis of the trait of self-esteem.

Our advanced cognitive ability leads to elaborations of the personality traits we share with other animals, such that direct physical aggression elaborates into indirect aggression and verbal aggression, indirect aggression elaborates further into relational aggression, and anger elaborates into hostility.

Our culture is also advanced enough to be considered unique. Just as we are born into a physical world, we are born into a cultural world and therefore have a social identity. The particular culture may lead us to emphasize how different we are from each other or, alternatively, how completely connected we are to each other. Such cultural immersion, together with our advanced cognitions, produces the personality trait of public self-consciousness and its extremes of self-conscious shyness and self-presentation.

The third evolutionary perspective consists of two trends in the evolutionary line that led to our species, trends crucial to understanding behavior in general and, specifically, personality. One trend is the elongation of childhood, culminating in our species having the longest childhood in relation to life span of any species. The other trend is the weakening, but certainly not the disappearance, of the impact of innate tendencies, together with the strengthening of the impact of experience. The two trends clearly are connected: less built in means more to be acquired, especially cultural learning, and hence a longer childhood.

Development

I have borrowed two key concepts from biological development and, in applying them to personality, necessarily use them differently than they are used in biology. One key concept is *differentiation*: An initially broad tendency branches into more specific tendencies during the course of development.

The other key concept is *canalization:* An initial disposition becomes more strongly entrenched during the course of development.

That person and environment interact is so well accepted as to be a cliché, but I have pursued this interaction in the more complex sequence of person to environment to person. We make the very environment that affects us, and there are three such feedback systems. First, on the basis of an initial personality trait, we *choose* situations or contexts that are congruent with the trait, say, sensation seeking, and by obtaining the sought after arousal from such activities, strengthen the trait. Second, we *set the tone* of a social interaction with a trait such as animated style, enlivening the situation for others, their pleasure being rewarding for the animated person. Third, we *react to the situation* positively; for example, the trait of sociability typically includes warmth, and a warm response to others elicits a similar response from them, strengthening the motivation to be with others.

Even when the direction of effects is from environment to person, a *match* between them in a particular personality trait serves to strengthen the trait. Start with a child who has some dominant tendencies; her parents introduce her to competitive athletics, which she finds so rewarding that she becomes increasingly competitive. Even if her competitive drive was initially moderate, the keen edge of competing and a fair number of wins will push her toward the top of the trait of competitiveness.

This example illustrates the concept of a *cascade,* in which a small initial tendency is multiplied by a reinforcing environment. All that may be needed is a *tilt* to set the cascade in motion. So, for example, a larger muscular physique might tilt an adolescent toward dominance. A tilt may also determine differentiation of trait-related behavior, for example, gender. Aggressive boys tend to be more physically aggressive, and aggressive girls tend to be more verbally aggressive. The tilt may be another personality trait, so, for example, when sensation seekers are sociable, they are likely to seek arousal in the presence of others.

TEMPERAMENT AND LATER DEVELOPING TRAITS

Temperament

I distinguish temperaments from other personality traits with genetic input by these features: part of our evolutionary legacy, first occur in infancy, and observable in adults. I specify how the temperaments differentiate over the course of development, such differentiation having implications for consistency of personality over time. For example, impulsiveness starts in infancy with lack of control over emotions and motives; in the school era, it shows up as a lack of discipline; and in adolescence, it appears as a lack of reflection. Once it is realized that impulsiveness has facets that appear during different eras of development, we can understand why research on this trait is likely to show less consistency: Psychologists are measuring different behaviors during different developmental eras.

Of course, it could be argued that impulsiveness is not one trait but three. The same argument might be used for intelligence because the items used on IQ tests of adults differ markedly from those used on preschool children. However, virtually no one uses this argument, on the assumption that there is a disposition underlying the observed ability in both childhood and adulthood. I suggest that the same is true for impulsiveness, the underlying disposition being a lack of inhibition: over emotions, over distractions, and over rash behavior. Recall that the ability to inhibit is part of a species-wide trend during development, spurred by both neural maturation and socialization pressure. It is a small step to suggest individual differences in the ability to inhibit throughout development.

I postulate differentiation of the other three temperaments: emotionality into fear and anger, each with their own differentiates, including anxious shyness, and sociability into gregariousness and warmth. The temperament of activity involves energetic behavior, but how is energy expended? The answer is through rapid pace (tempo) or strength (vigor).

Later Developing Traits

The term *later developing* refers to the fact that these traits do not appear until the preschool era, so they are not part of infant personality. The first evidence of sensation seeking in preschool children is seen in their motivation to obtain body sensations by leaping, spinning, or being tossed. Theorizing about the development of sensation seeking requires abandoning the factors that emerged from Zuckerman's (1971, 2007) adult questionnaire because young children obviously do not engage in such adult activities as parachute jumping or trying illicit drugs. In addition to seeking bodily sensations, however, children high in the trait of sensation seeking also want novelty, suspense, and vicarious excitement, and they take physical risks. These are differentiates of sensation seeking, and by adding them to Zuckerman's factors of thrill and adventure seeking, experience seeking, disinhibition, and boredom susceptibility, we arrive at a more complete understanding of the trait.

As for aggressiveness, it is so broad a concept that it almost demands a search for more components. Aggressive behavior, which has a victim, needs to be distinguished from anger, which is not instrumental (e.g., scowling) or may involve only inanimate objects (e.g., throwing the remote at the TV). This distinction leads to separating angry aggression (the goal is solely to hurt another) from instrumental aggression (the goal is to acquire *any* reward). The emotional, transient emotion of anger is distinguished from the more enduring negative cognition of hostility, but there is more: separating hostility into the components of resentment and suspiciousness, which acknowledges that resentful people may not be suspicious.

The strategy of analyzing traits into differentiates continues by inquiring about the paths to dominance. In animals, there is only one path: aggression; in our species, there are two others: leadership and competitiveness. Another difference unique to our species is that we are not stuck in a single social group but occupy a place in multiple groups, so when another person attempts to dominate, we have an option beyond rebelling or submitting; we can choose autonomy.

THE SELF

The traits of private and public self-consciousness were mentioned earlier as part of our human uniqueness. So was self-conscious shyness, but the distinction between this trait and anxious shyness is worth pointing out because it highlights the value of the evolutionary and developmental perspectives used in this book. Anxious shyness appears in infancy in both our species and other animals, whereas self-conscious shyness appears later in childhood but only in our species.

As for the two other realms of the self discussed in this book, self-esteem and identity, the distinction between the personal and the social aspects of the self is crucial to understanding them. The personal aspects are emphasized in individualist cultures, and the social aspects are emphasized in collectivist cultures, a reminder that with respect to personality, so much of the behavior falling under the heading of self is culturally constructed during the process of human socialization.

DIMENSIONS

Abnormal Behavior

The concepts of vulnerability and hardiness were borrowed from others, my contribution being to specify relevant personality traits. Thus, the trait of emotionality contributes to being vulnerable to stress and therefore to dysfunctional behavior, and the trait of (high) self-esteem contributes to being hardy.

The relationship between personality traits and abnormal behavior has been evident at least since the mid-20th century. The addition of personality disorders to psychiatric classification spurred clinicians and personality psychologists to suggest the dimensions of the overlap between personality and abnormal behavior. I have suggested particular traits as such dimensions—for example, paranoid personality as the extreme end of the trait dimension of hostility (resentment and suspicion). Beyond personality disorders, I suggested other dimensions—for example, social phobia—as the extreme of the trait dimension of anxious shyness.

Style

The chapter on style is an attempt to bring back this concept as part of personality. The communication and emotionally expressive aspects of style have been well studied, but individual differences in style have not. It might be argued that style is merely a superficial aspect of personality, but that would confuse observability with superficiality. Style is important, first, as one of the most basic parts of our individuality—the way we sit, walk, or laugh; second, as the other face of a number of content traits—for example, the trait of dominance; and third, as the aspect of personality that has an immediate impact on others (Chaplin, Phillips, Brown, Clanton, & Stein, 2000).

My contribution is first to describe the physical elements of style and then to postulate its psychological dimensions, some based on the physical elements and the rest qualitative in nature. It is entirely fitting that style is the last chapter of this book and that this discussion of style is the last paragraph of the book because it completes the circle that started in the Introduction: the issue of personality trait dimensions.

REFERENCES

Ahlgren, A., & Johnson, D. W. (1979). Sex differences in cooperative and competitive attitudes from the 2nd through the 12th grades. *Developmental Psychology, 15,* 45–49. doi:10.1037/h0078076

Ahmad, Y., & Smith, P. K. (1994). Bullying in schools and the issue of sex differences. In J. Archer (Ed.), *Male violence* (pp. 70–83). London, England: Routledge.

Ainsworth, M. D. S., Blehar, M. C., Waters, E., & Wall, S. (1978). *Patterns of attachment: A psychological study of the strange situation.* Hillsdale, NJ: Erlbaum.

Alicke, M. D., LoSchiavo, F. M., Zerbst, J., & Zhang, S. (1997). The person who outperforms me is a genius: Maintaining perceived competence in upward social comparison. *Journal of Personality and Social Psychology, 73,* 781–789. doi:10.1037/0022-3514.73.4.781

Allport, G. W. (1961). *Pattern and growth in personality.* New York, NY: Holt, Rinehart & Winston.

Allport, G. W., & Vernon, P. E. (1933). *Studies in expressive movement.* New York, NY: MacMillan. doi:10.1037/11566-000

American Association of University Women. (2001). *Hostile hallways: Bullying, teasing, and sexual harassment in school.* Washington, DC: American Association of University Women Educational Foundation.

American Psychiatric Association. (2000). *Diagnostic and statistical manual of mental disorders* (4th ed., text revision). Washington, DC: Author.

Amsterdam, B. (1972). Mirror self-reactions before the age of two. *Developmental Psychology, 5,* 297–305.

Anastopoulis, A. D., & Shelton, T. L. (2001). *Assessing attention-deficit/hyperactivity disorder.* New York, NY: Kluwer Academic/Plenum.

Andersen, J. A. (2006). Leadership, personality and effectiveness. *The Journal of Socio-Economics, 35,* 1078–1091. doi:10.1016/j.socec.2005.11.066

Anderson, C. A., & Anderson, K. B. (2008). Men who target women: Specificity of target, generality of aggressive behavior. *Aggressive Behavior, 34,* 605–622. doi:10.1002/ab.20274

Anderson, C. A., & Bushman, B. J. (2002). Human aggression. *Annual Review of Psychology, 53,* 27–51. doi:10.1146/annurev.psych.53.100901.135231

Anderson, C. A., Sakamoto, A., Gentile, D. A., Ihori, N., Shibuya, A., Yukawa, S., & Hobayashi, M. (2008). Longitudinal effects of violent video games on aggression in Japan and the United States. *Pediatrics, 122,* e1067–e1072. doi:10.1542/peds.2008-1425

Angyal, A. (1951). A theoretical model for personality study. *Journal of Personality, 20,* 131–142. doi:10.1111/j.1467-6494.1951.tb01517.x

Archer, J. (2006). Testosterone and human aggression: An evaluation of the challenge hypothesis. *Neuroscience and Biobehavioral Reviews, 30*, 319–345. doi:10.1016/j.neubiorev.2004.12.007

Archer, J., Kilpatrick, G., & Bramwell, R. (1995). Comparison of two aggression inventories. *Aggressive Behavior, 21*, 371–380. doi:10.1002/1098-2337(1995)21:5<371::AID-AB2480210506>3.0.CO;2-P

Ardrey, R. (1961). *African genesis.* New York, NY: Atheneum.

Argyle, M. (1969). *Social interaction.* New York, NY: Atherton.

Argyle, M. (1975). *Bodily communication.* London, England: Methuen.

Argyle, M. (1990). *Bodily communication* (2nd ed.). Madison, CT: International Universities Press.

Argyle, M., & Williams, M. (1969). Observer or observed? A reversible perspective in person perception. *Sociometry, 32*, 396–412. doi:10.2307/2786543

Arnett, J. (1994). Sensation seeking: A new conceptualization and a new scale. *Personality and Individual Differences, 16*, 289–296. doi:10.1016/0191-8869(94)90165-1

Asendorpf, J. B. (2000). Shyness and adaptation to the social world of university. In W. R. Crozier (Ed.), *Shyness: Development, consolidation and change* (pp. 103–120). New York, NY: Routledge.

Asendorpf, J. B., & Meier, G. H. (1993). Personality effects on children's speech in everyday life: Sociability-mediated exposure and shyness-mediated reactivity to social situations. *Journal of Personality and Social Psychology, 64*, 1072–1083. doi:10.1037/0022-3514.64.6.1072

Ashton, M. C., Lee, K., & Goldberg, L. R. (2004). A hierarchical analysis of 1,710 English personality-descriptive adjectives. *Journal of Personality and Social Psychology, 87*, 707–721. doi:10.1037/0022-3514.87.5.707

Ashton, M. C., Lee, K., Peruginia, M., Szarota, P., deVries, R. E., DiBlas, L. D., . . . deRaad, B. (2004). A six-factor structure of personality-descriptive adjectives: Solutions from psycholexical studies in seven languages. *Journal of Personality and Social Psychology, 86*, 356–366. doi:10.1037/0022-3514.86.2.356

Baker, L., & McNulty, J. K. (2010). Shyness and marriage: Does shyness shape even established relationships? *Personality and Social Psychology Bulletin, 36*, 665–676. doi:10.1177/0146167210367489

Bandura, A. (1977). Self-efficacy: Toward a unifying theory of behavioral change. *Psychological Review, 84*, 191–215. doi:10.1037/0033-295X.84.2.191

Bandura, A. (1994). Self-efficacy. In V. S. Ramachaudran (Ed.), *Encyclopedia of human behavior* (Vol. 4, pp. 71–81). New York, NY: Academic Press.

Barkow, J. H. (1975). Prestige and culture: A biosocial interpretation. *Current Anthropology, 16*, 553–572. doi:10.1086/201619

Barnlund, D. C. (1975). *Public and private self in Japan and the United States.* Tokyo, Japan: Simul Press.

Baron, R. A., & Richardson, D. R. (1994). *Human aggression* (2nd ed.). New York, NY: Plenum Press.

Barratt, E. S. (1959). Anxiety and impulsiveness related to psychomotor efficiency. *Perceptual and Motor Skills, 9,* 191–198. doi:10.2466/PMS.9.3.191-198

Barratt, E. S. (1983). The biological basis of impulsiveness: The significance of timing and rhythm disorders. *Personality and Individual Differences, 4,* 387–391. doi:10.1016/0191-8869(83)90004-1

Bates, J. E., Maslin, C. A., & Frankel, K. A. (1985). Attachment, security, mother–infant interaction and temperament as predictors of behavior problems at age three years. *Monographs of the Society for Research in Child Development, 50,* 167–193.

Bauer, H. R. (1980). Chimpanzee society and social dominance in evolutionary perspective. In D. R. Omark, E. F. Strayer, & D. G. Freedman (Eds.), *Dominance relations: An ethological view of human conflict and social interaction* (pp. 97–119). New York, NY: Garland.

Baumeister, R. F. (1997). The self and society. In R. D. Ashmore & L. Jussim (Eds.), *Self and identity* (pp. 191–217). New York, NY: Oxford University Press.

Baumeister, R. F., Heatherton, T. F., & Tice, D. M. (1993). When ego threats lead to self-regulation failure: Negative consequences of high self-esteem. *Journal of Personality and Social Psychology, 64,* 141–156.

Baumgardner, A. H. (1990). To know oneself is to like oneself. *Journal of Personality and Social Psychology, 58,* 1062–1072. doi:10.1037/0022-3514.58.6.1062

Baumrind, D. (1971). Current patterns of parental authority. *Developmental Psychology Monographs, 4*(1, part 2).

Beauregard, K. S., & Dunning, D. (2001). Defining self-worth: Trait self-esteem moderates the use of self-serving trait definitions in social judgment. *Motivation and Emotion, 25,* 135–161. doi:10.1023/A:1010665926045

Becker, E. (1962). *The birth and death of meaning.* New York, NY: Free Press.

Beidel, D. C., & Turner, S. M. (2007). *Shy children, phobic adults* (2nd ed.). Washington, DC: American Psychological Association.

Bell, R. Q. (1968a). Adaptation of small wrist watches for mechanical recording of activity In infants and children. *Journal of Experimental Child Psychology, 6,* 302–305. doi:10.1016/0022-0965(68)90093-3

Bell, R. Q. (1968b). A reinterpretation of the direction of effects in studies of socialization. *Psychological Review, 75,* 81–95. doi:10.1037/h0025583

Benenson, J. F., Markowitz, H., Fitzgerald, C., Geoffrey, D., Flemming, J., Kahlenberg, S. M., & Wrangham, R. W. (2009). Males' greater tolerance of same-sex peers. *Psychological Science, 20,* 184–190. doi:10.1111/j.1467-9280.2009.02269.x

Benet-Martínez, V., & Haritatos, J. (2005). Bicultural identity integration (BII): Components and psychological antecedents. *Journal of Personality, 73,* 1015–1050. doi:10.1111/j.1467-6494.2005.00337.x

Bennett, M. (1989). Children's self-attribution of embarrassment. *British Journal of Developmental Psychology, 7*, 207–217.

Bernstein, L., Teng, G., & Garbin, C. (1986). A confirmatory factoring of the self-consciousness scale. *Multivariate Personality Research, 21*, 459–475. doi:10.1207/s15327906mbr2104_6

Berscheid, E., & Walster, E. (1978). *Interpersonal attraction* (2nd ed.). Reading, MA: Addison-Wesley.

Bertenthal, B. I., & Fischer, K. W. (1978). Development of self-recognition in the infant. *Developmental Psychology, 14*, 44–50.

Bjorklund, D. F., & Pellegrini, A. D. (2002). *The origins of human nature. Evolutionary developmental psychology.* Washington, DC: American Psychological Association. doi:10.1037/10425-000

Block, J., & Robins, R. W. (1993). A longitudinal study of consistency and change in self- esteem from early adolescence to early adulthood. *Child Development, 64*, 909–923. doi:10.2307/1131226

Blyth, D. A., & Foster-Clarke, F. S. (1987). Gender differences in perceived intimacy with different members of adolescents' social networks. *Sex Roles, 17*, 689–718. doi:10.1007/BF00287683

Boldizar, J. P., Perry, D. G., & Perry, L. C. (1989). Outcome values and aggression. *Child Development, 60*, 571–579. doi:10.2307/1130723

Bond, C. F., & Titus, L. J. (1983). Social facilitation: A meta-analysis of 241 studies. *Psychological Bulletin, 94*, 265–292. doi:10.1037/0033-2909.94.2.265

Bowlby, J. (1967). Foreword. In M. D. S. Ainsworth, *Infancy in Uganda.* Baltimore, MD: Johns Hopkins University Press.

Brame, B., Nagin, D. S., & Tremblay, R. E. (2001). Developmental trajectories of physical aggression from school entry to late adolescence. *Journal of Child Psychology and Psychiatry, 42*, 503–512. doi:10.1111/1469-7610.00744

Brewer, M. B., & Chen, Y-R. (2007). Where (who) are collectives in collectivism? Toward conceptual clarification of individualism and collectivism. *Psychological Review, 114*, 133–151.

Brewer, M. B., & Gardner, W. (1996). Who is this "we"? Levels of collective identity and self representations. *Journal of Personality and Social Psychology, 71*, 83–93. doi:10.1037/0022-3514.71.1.83

Bridges, K. M. B. (1932). Emotional development in early infancy. *Child Development, 3*, 324–341.

Brockner, J., Derr, W. R., & Laing, W. N. (1987). Self-esteem and reactions to negative feedback: Toward greater generality. *Journal of Research in Personality, 21*, 318–333. doi:10.1016/0092-6566(87)90014-6

Brockner, J., & Lloyd, K. (1986). Self-esteem and likability: Separating fact from fantasy. *Journal of Research in Personality, 20*, 496–508. doi:10.1016/0092-6566(86)90128-5

Bronson, G. W., & Pankey, W. B. (1977). On the distinction between fear and wariness. *Child Development, 48,* 1167–1183. doi:10.2307/1128474

Brown, J. D. (1993). Motivational conflict and the self: The double bind of low self-esteem. In R. F. Baumeister (Ed.), *Self-esteem: The puzzle of low self-regard* (pp. 117–130). New York, NY: Plenum Press.

Brown, J. D., & Smart, S. A. (1991). The self and social conduct: Linking self-presentations to social conduct. *Journal of Personality and Social Psychology, 60,* 368–375. doi:10.1037/0022-3514.60.3.368

Bruch, M. A., Giordano, S., & Pearl, L. (1986). Differences between fearful and self-conscious shy subtypes in background and adjustment. *Journal of Research in Personality, 20,* 172–186. doi:10.1016/0092-6566(86)90116-9

Bruch, M. A., Gorsky, J. M., Collins, T. M., & Berger, P. A. (1989). Shyness and sociability reexamined: A multicomponent analysis. *Journal of Personality and Social Psychology, 57,* 904–915. doi:10.1037/0022-3514.57.5.904

Burger, J., & Cosby, M. (1999). Do women prefer dominant men? The case of the missing control condition. *Journal of Research in Personality, 33,* 358–368. doi:10.1006/jrpe.1999.2252

Burnkrant, R. E., & Page, T. (1984). A modification of the Fenigstein, Scheier, and Buss Self-Consciousness Scale. *Journal of Personality Assessment, 48,* 629–637. doi:10.1207/s15327752jpa4806_10

Buss, A. H. (1961). *The psychology of aggression.* New York, NY: Wiley. doi:10.1037/11160-000

Buss, A. H. (1966). *Psychopathology.* New York, NY: Wiley.

Buss, A. H. (1971). Aggression pays. In J. L. Singer (Ed.), *The control of aggression and violence* (pp. 7–18). New York, NY: Academic Press.

Buss, A. H. (1988). *Personality: Evolutionary heritage and human distinctiveness.* Hillsdale, NJ: Erlbaum.

Buss, A. H. (1989). Personality as traits. *American Psychologist, 44,* 1378–1388. doi:10.1037/0003-066X.44.11.1378

Buss, A. H. (1992). [Rankings of group identification.] Unpublished data, University of Texas, Austin.

Buss, A. H., & Durkee, A. (1957). An inventory to assess different kinds of hostility. *Journal of Consulting Psychology, 21,* 343–349. doi:10.1037/h0046900

Buss, A. H., Iscoe, I., & Buss, E. H. (1979). The development of embarrassment. *Journal of Psychology: Interdisciplinary and Applied, 103,* 227–230.

Buss, A. H., & Perry, M. (1991). [Sources of esteem in men and women.] Unpublished data, University of Texas, Austin

Buss, A. H., & Perry, M. (1992). The Aggression Questionnaire. *Journal of Personality and Social Psychology, 63,* 452–459. doi:10.1037/0022-3514.63.3.452

Buss, A. H., & Plomin, R. (1975). *A temperament theory of personality development.* New York, NY: Wiley-Interscience.

Buss, A. H., & Plomin, R. (1984). *Temperament: Early developing personality traits*. Hillsdale, NJ: Erlbaum.

Buss, A. H., & Portnoy, N. W. (1967). Pain tolerance and group identification. *Journal of Personality and Social Psychology, 6*, 106–108. doi:10.1037/h0024525

Buss, A. H., & Warren, W. L. (2000). *Aggression Questionnaire manual*. Los Angeles, CA: Western Psychological Services.

Buss, D. M. (1981). Sex differences in the evaluation and performance of dominant acts. *Journal of Personality and Social Psychology, 40*, 147–154. doi:10.1037/0022-3514.40.1.147

Buss, D. M. (1989). Sex differences in human mate preferences: Evolutionary hypothesis testing in 37 cultures. *Behavioral and Brain Sciences, 12*, 1–49. doi:10.1017/S0140525X00023992

Buss, D. M. (2003). *The evolution of desire: Strategies of human mating* (rev. ed.). New York, NY: Free Press.

Buss, D. M. (2008). *Evolutionary psychology: The new science of the mind* (3rd ed.). Needham, MA: Allyn & Bacon.

Buss, D. M., & Hawley, P. H. (Eds.). (2011). *The evolution of personality and individual differences*. New York, NY: Oxford University Press.

Buss, L. (1978). *Does overpraise cause embarrassment?* Unpublished research. Austin: University of Texas.

Cai, H., Brown, J. D., Deng, C., & Oakes, M. A. (2007). Self-esteem and culture: Differences in cognitive evaluations or affective self-regard? *Asian Journal of Social Psychology, 10*, 162–170. doi:10.1111/j.1467-839X.2007.00222.x

Cai, H., Wu, Q., & Brown, J. D. (2009). Is self-esteem a universal need? Evidence from the People's Republic of China. *Asian Journal of Social Psychology, 12*, 104–120. doi:10.1111/j.1467-839X.2009.01278.x

Cairns, R. B., Cairns, B. D., Neckerman, H. J., Ferguson, L. L., & Gariepy, J.-L. (1989). Growth and aggression: I. Childhood to early adolescence. *Developmental Psychology, 25*, 320–330. doi:10.1037/0012-1649.25.2.320

Campbell, A. (1993). *Men, women, and aggression*. New York, NY: Basic Books.

Campbell, D. W., & Eaton, W. O. (1999). Sex differences in the activity level of infants. *Infant and Child Development, 8*, 1–17. doi:10.1002/(SICI)1522-7219(199903)8:1<1::AID-ICD186>3.0.CO;2-O

Campbell, J. D., & Fairey, P. J. (1985). Effects of self-esteem, hypothetical explanations, and verbalizations of future performance. *Journal of Personality and Social Psychology, 48*, 1097–1111. doi:10.1037/0022-3514.48.5.1097

Campbell, J. D., & Fehr, B. (1990). Self-esteem and perceptions of conveyed impressions. Is negative affectivity associated with greater realism? *Journal of Personality and Social Psychology, 58*, 122–133. doi:10.1037/0022-3514.58.1.122

Caprara, G. V., Steca, P., Cervone, D., & Artistico, D. (2003). The contribution of self-efficacy beliefs to dispositional shyness: On social cognitive systems and the development of personality dispositions. *Journal of Personality, 71,* 943–970. doi:10.1111/1467-6494.7106003

Card, N. A., Stucky, B. D., Sawalami, G. M., & Little, T. D. (2008). Direct and indirect aggression during childhood and adolescence: A meta-analytic review of gender differences, intercorrelations, and relations to maladjustment. *Child Development, 79,* 1185–1229. doi:10.1111/j.1467-8624.2008.01184.x

Carey, W. B. (1970). A simplified method for measuring infant temperament. *The Journal of Pediatrics, 77,* 188–194. doi:10.1016/S0022-3476(70)80322-5

Carey, W. B., & McDevitt, S. C. (1978). Revision of the infant temperament questionnaire. *Pediatrics, 61,* 735–739.

Carver, C. S., & Scheier, M. F. (1981). *Attention and self-regulation: A control theory approach to human behavior.* New York, NY: Springer-Verlag.

Carver, C. S., & Scheier, M. F. (1998). *On the self-regulation of behavior.* New York, NY: Cambridge University Press.

Cash, T. F. (1989). The psychosocial effects of male pattern balding. *Patient Care, 1,* 18–23.

Cash, T. F., & Szymanski, M. L. (1995). The development and validation of the Body-Image Ideals Questionnaire. *Journal of Personality Assessment, 64,* 466–477. doi:10.1207/s15327752jpa6403_6

Caspi, A., Elder, G. H., Jr., & Bem, D. J. (1988). Moving away from the world: Life course patterns of shy children. *Developmental Psychology, 24,* 824–831. doi:10.1037/0012-1649.24.6.824

Castelfranchi, C., & Poggi, I. (1990). Blushing as discourse: Was Darwin wrong? In W. R. Crozier (Ed.), *Shyness and embarrassment: Perspectives from social psychology* (pp. 230–252). Cambridge, England: Cambridge University Press. doi:10.1017/CBO9780511571183.009

Chamove, A. S., Eysenck, H. J., & Harlow, H. (1972). Personality in monkeys: Factor analysis of rhesus social behavior. *The Quarterly Journal of Experimental Psychology, 24,* 496–504. doi:10.1080/14640747208400309

Chaplin, W. F., Phillips, J. B., Brown, J. D., Clanton, N. R., & Stein, J. L. (2000). Handshaking: Gender, personality, and first impressions. *Journal of Personality and Social Psychology, 79,* 110–117. doi:10.1037/0022-3514.79.1.110

Chavira, D. A., Stein, M. B., & Malcarne, V. L. (2002). Scrutinizing the relationship between shyness and social phobia. *Journal of Anxiety Disorders, 16,* 585–598. doi:10.1016/S0887-6185(02)00124-X

Cheek, J. M., & Buss, A. H. (1981). Shyness and sociability. *Journal of Personality and Social Psychology, 41,* 330–339. doi:10.1037/0022-3514.41.2.330

Cheek, J. M., Carpentieri, A. M., Smith, T. G., Rierdan, J., & Koff, E. (1986). Adolescent shyness. In W. H. Jones, J. M. Cheek, & S. R. Briggs (Eds.), *Shyness* (pp. 105–115). New York, NY: Plenum Press.

Cheek, J. M., & Melchior, L. A. (1990). Shyness, self-esteem, and self-consciousness. In H. Leitenberg (Ed.), *Handbook of social and evaluation anxiety* (pp. 47–82). New York, NY: Plenum Press.

Chen, X. (2010). Shyness-inhibition in childhood and adolescence: A cross-cultural perspective. In K. H. Rubin & R. J. Coplan (Eds.), *The development of shyness and social withdrawal* (pp. 213–235). New York, NY: Guilford Press.

Chen, X., Chen, H., Li, D., & Wang, L. (2009). Early childhood behavioral inhibition and social and school adjustment in Chinese children: A 5-year longitudinal study. *Child Development, 80,* 1692–1704. doi:10.1111/j.1467-8624.2009.01362.x

Chen, X., & Tse, H. C. (2008). Social functioning and adjustment in Canadian-born children with Chinese and European backgrounds. *Developmental Psychology, 44,* 1184–1189. doi:10.1037/0012-1649.44.4.1184

Chung, C., & Pennebaker, J. (2007). The psychological functions of function words. In K. Fiedler (Ed.), *Social communication* (pp. 343–359). New York, NY: Psychology Press.

Cialdini, R. B., Borden, R. J., Thorne, A., Walker, M. R., Freeman, S., & Sloan, L. R. (1976). Basking in reflected glory: Three (football) field studies. *Journal of Personality and Social Psychology, 34,* 366–375. doi:10.1037/0022-3514.34.3.366

Cicone, M. V., & Ruble, D. M. (1978). Beliefs about males. *Journal of Social Issues, 34,* 5–16. doi:10.1111/j.1540-4560.1978.tb02537.x

Clark, L. A. (2005). Temperament as a unifying basis for personality and psychopathology. *Journal of Abnormal Psychology, 114,* 505–521. doi:10.1037/0021-843X.114.4.505

Clark, L. A. (2007). Assessment and diagnosis of personality disorder: Perennial issues and an emerging reconceptualization. *Annual Review of Psychology, 58,* 227–257. doi:10.1146/annurev.psych.57.102904.190200

Clark, L. A., Watson, D., & Mineka, S. (1994). Temperament, personality, and the mood disorders. *Journal of Abnormal Psychology, 103,* 103–116. doi:10.1037/0021-843X.103.1.103

Clarke-Stewart, K. A., Umeh, B. J., Snow, M. E., & Peterson, J. A. (1980). Development and prediction of children's sociability from 1 to 2½ years. *Developmental Psychology, 16,* 290–302. doi:10.1037/0012-1649.16.4.290

Cline, V. B., Croft, R. G., & Courrier, S. (1973). Desensitization of children to television violence. *Journal of Personality and Social Psychology, 27,* 360–365.

Cohen, A. B. (2009). Many forms of culture. *American Psychologist, 64,* 194–204. doi:10.1037/a0015308

Collaer, M. L., & Hines, M. (1995). Human behavioral sex differences: A role for gonadal hormones during early development. *Psychological Bulletin, 118,* 55–107. doi:10.1037/0033-2909.118.1.55

Collins, R. L. (1996). For better or worse: The impact of upward comparison on self-evaluations. *Psychological Bulletin, 119,* 51–69. doi:10.1037/0033-2909.119.1.51

Compas, B. E. (1987). Coping with stress during childhood and adolescence. *Psychological Bulletin, 101*, 393–403.

Cook, M., Mineka, S., Wolkenstein, B., & Laitsch, K. (1985). Observational conditioning of snake fear in unrelated rhesus monkeys. *Journal of Abnormal Psychology, 94*, 591–610. doi:10.1037/0021-843X.94.4.591

Coopersmith, S. (1967). *The antecedents of self-esteem.* San Francisco, CA: Freeman.

Coplan, R. J., & Weeks, M. (2010). Unsociability and preference for solitude in childhood. In K. H. Rubin & R. J. Coplan (Eds.), *The development of shyness and social withdrawal* (pp. 64–83). New York, NY: Guilford Press.

Costa, P. T., & McCrae, R. R. (1990). Personality disorders and the five-factor model of personality. *Journal of Personality Disorders, 4*, 362–371.

Costa, P. T., Jr., McCrae, R. R., & Dye, D. A. (1991). Facet scales for Agreeableness and Conscientiousness: A revision of the NEO Personality Inventory. *Personality and Individual Differences, 12*, 887–898. doi:10.1016/0191-8869(91)90177-D

Creed, A. T., & Funder, D. C. (1998). The two faces of private self-consciousness. *European Journal of Personality, 12*, 411–431. doi: 10.1002/(SICI)1099-0984(199811/12)12:6<411::AID-PER317>3.0.CO;2-C

Crick, N. R. (1995). Relational aggression: The role of intent attributions, feelings of distress, and provocation type. *Development and Psychopathology, 7*, 313–322. doi:10.1017/S0954579400006520

Crick, N. R., Grotpeter, J. K., & Bigbee, M. A. (2002). Relationally and physically aggressive children's intent attributions and feelings of distress for relational and instrumental peer provocations. *Child Development, 73*, 1134–1142. doi:10.1111/1467-8624.00462

Crick, N. R., Ostrov, J. M., & Werner, N. E. (2006). A longitudinal study of relational aggression physical aggression, and children's social-psychological adjustment. *Journal of Abnormal Child Psychology, 34*, 131–142. doi:10.1007/s10802-005-9009-4

Crocker, J., & Gallo, L. (1995, August). The self-enhancing effect of downward comparison. Paper presented at the 93rd Annual Convention of the American Psychological Association, Los Angeles, CA.

Crocker, J., Karpinski, A., Quinn, D. M., & Chase, S. (2003). When grades determine self-worth: Consequence of contingent self-worth for male and female engineering students and psychology majors. *Journal of Personality and Social Psychology, 85*, 507–516. doi:10.1037/0022-3514.85.3.507

Crocker, J., Luhtanen, R. K., Cooper, M. L., & Bouvrette, S. (2003). Contingencies of self-worth in college students. *Journal of Personality and Social Psychology, 85*, 894–908. doi:10.1037/0022-3514.85.5.894

Crocker, J., & Wolfe, C. T. (2001). Contingencies of self-worth. *Psychological Review, 108*, 593–623. doi:10.1037/0033-295X.108.3.593

Cronbach, L. J. (1957). The two disciplines of scientific psychology. *American Psychologist, 12*, 671–684. doi:10.1037/h0043943

Cross, S. E., & Madson, L. (1997). Models of the self: Self-construals and gender. *Psychological Bulletin, 122,* 5–37. doi:10.1037/0033-2909.122.1.5

Cunningham, N. J., Taylor, M., Whitten, M. E., Hardesty, P. H., Eder, K., & DeLaney, N. (2010). The relationship between self-perception of physical attractiveness and sexual bullying in early adolescence. *Aggressive Behavior, 36,* 271–281.

Dabbs, J. M., & Dabbs, M. G. (2000). *Heroes, rogues, and lovers: Testosterone and behavior.* New York, NY: McGraw-Hill.

Dabbs, J. M., Frady, R. L., Carr, T. S., & Besch, N. F. (1987). Saliva testosterone and criminal violence in young prison inmates. *Psychosomatic Medicine, 49,* 174–182.

Darwin, C. R. (1955). *The expression of the emotions in man and animals.* New York, NY: Philosophical Library. (Original work published 1883)

Davis-Kean, P. E., & Sandler, H. M. (2001). A meta-analysis of measures of self-esteem for young children: A framework for future measures. *Child Development, 72,* 887–906.

Deci, E. L., & Ryan, R. M. (1995). Human agency: The basis for true self-esteem. In M. Kernis (Ed.), *Efficacy, agency, and self-esteem* (pp. 31–50). New York, NY: Plenum Press.

DePaulo, B. M. (1992). Nonverbal behavior and self-presentation. *Psychological Bulletin, 111,* 203–243.

Derryberry, D., & Rothbart, M. K. (1988). Arousal, affective and attentional components of adult temperament. *Journal of Personality and Social Psychology, 55,* 958–966. doi:10.1037/0022-3514.55.6.958

Derryberry, D., & Rothbart, M. K. (1997). Reactive and effortful processes in the organization of temperament. *Development and Psychopathology, 9,* 633–652. doi:10.1017/S0954579497001375

de Waal, F. (1982). *Chimpanzee politics: Power and sex among apes.* New York, NY: Harper & Row.

Diamond, S. (1957). *Personality and temperament.* New York, NY: Harper.

Dickens, W. T., & Flynn, J. R. (2001). Heritability estimates versus large environmental effects: The IQ paradox resolved. *Psychological Review, 108,* 346–369. doi:10.1037/0033-295X.108.2.346

Diener, E., & Larson, R. J. (1984). Temporal stability and cross-situational consistency of affective, behavioral, and cognitive responses. *Journal of Personality and Social Psychology, 47,* 871–883. doi:10.1037/0022-3514.47.4.871

DiPietro, J. A. (1981). Rough and tumble play: A function of gender. *Developmental Psychology, 17,* 50–58. doi:10.1037/0012-1649.17.1.50

Dixon, J. J., deMonchaux, C., & Sandler, J. (1957). Patterns of anxiety: The phobias. *British Journal of Medical Psychology, 30,* 34–40.

Dodge, K. A. (1983). Behavioral antecedents of peer social status. *Child Development, 54,* 1386–1399.

Dodge, K. A. (1991). The structure and function of reactive and proactive aggression. In D. Pepler & K. Rubin (Eds.), *The development and treatment of childhood aggression* (pp. 201–218). Hillsdale, NJ: Erlbaum.

Dodge, K. A., Bates, J. E., & Pettit, G. S. (1990). Mechanisms in the cycle of violence. *Science, 250,* 1678–1683. doi:10.1126/science.2270481

Dodge, K. A., & Coie, J. D. (1987). Social information-processing factors in reactive and proactive aggression in children's peer groups. *Journal of Personality and Social Psychology, 53,* 1146–1158. doi:10.1037/0022-3514.53.6.1146

Dodge, K. A., Lansford, J. E., Burks, V. S., Bates, J. E., Pettit, G. S., Fontaine, R., & Price, J. M. (2003). Peer rejection and social information-processing factors in the development of aggressive behavior problems in children. *Child Development, 74,* 374–393. doi:10.1111/1467-8624.7402004

Dodge, K. A., & Somberg, D. R. (1987). Hostile attributional biases are exacerbated under conditions of threats to the self. *Child Development, 58,* 213–224. doi:10.2307/1130303

Dollard, J., Doob, L., Miller, N., Mowrer, O. H., & Sears, R. R. (1939). *Frustration and aggression.* New Haven, CT: Yale University Press. doi:10.1037/10022-000

Drummond, P. D., Camacho, L., Formentin, N., Heffernan, T. D., Williams, F., & Zekas, T. E. (2003). The impact of verbal feedback about blushing on social discomfort and facial blood flow during embarrassing tasks. *Behaviour Research and Therapy, 41,* 413–425. doi:10.1016/S0005-7967(02)00021-9

DuBois, D. L., Bull, C. A., Sherman, M. D., & Roberts, M. (1998). Self-esteem and adjustment in early adolescence. *Journal of Youth and Adolescence, 27,* 557–583. doi:10.1023/A:1022831006887

Dunning, D. (1999). A newer look: Motivated social cognition and the schematic representation of social concepts. *Psychological Inquiry, 10,* 1–11. doi:10.1207/s15327965pli1001_1

Duval, S., & Wicklund, R. A. (1972). *A theory of objective self-awareness.* New York, NY: Academic Press.

Dweck, C. S. (2006). *Mindset: The new psychology of success.* New York, NY: Random House.

Dweck, C. S., Davidson, W., Nelson, S., & Enna, B. (1978). Sex differences in learned helplessness: II. The contingencies of evaluative feedback in the classroom; and III. An experimental analysis. *Developmental Psychology, 14,* 268–276. doi:10.1037/0012-1649.14.3.268

Dweck, C. S., & Leggett, E. L. (1988). A social–cognitive approach to motivation and personality. *Psychological Review, 95,* 256–273. doi:10.1037/0033-295X.95.2.256

Eagly, A. H., & Karau, S. J. (1991). Gender and the emergence of leaders: A meta-analysis. *Journal of Personality and Social Psychology, 60,* 685–710. doi:10.1037/0022-3514.60.5.685

Eagly, A. H., & Steffen, V. J. (1986). Gender and aggressive behavior: A meta-analytic review of social psychological literature. *Psychological Bulletin, 100*, 309–330. doi: 10.1037/0033-2909.100.3.309

Eaton, W. O., & Enns, L. R. (1986). Sex differences in human motor activity level. *Psychological Bulletin, 100*, 19–28. doi:10.1037/0033-2909.100.1.19

Eaton, W. O., McKeen, N. A., & Campbell, D. W. (2001). The waxing and waning of movement: Implications for psychological development. *Developmental Review, 21*, 205–223. doi:10.1006/drev.2000.0519

Eccles, J., Wigfield, A., Harold, R. D., & Blumenfield, P. (1993). Age and gender differences in children's self- and task perceptions during elementary school. *Child Development*, 830–847.

Edelmann, R. J. (1987). *The psychology of embarrassment.* Chichester, England: Wiley.

Eisenberg, N., Fabes, R. A., & Murphy, B. C. (1995). Relations of shyness and low sociability to regulation and emotionality. *Journal of Personality and Social Psychology, 68*, 505–517. doi:10.1037/0022-3514.68.3.505

Eisenberg, N., Spinrad, T. L., Fabes, R. A., Reiser, M., Cumberland, A., Shepard, S. A., . . . Thompson, M. (2004). The relation of effortful control and impulsivity to children's resiliency and adjustment. *Child Development, 75*, 25–46. doi:10. 1111/j.1467-8624.2004.00652.x

Eisenberg, P. (1937). Expressive movements related to feeling of dominance [whole volume]. *Archives of Psychology, 211.*

Ekman, P. (1965). The differential communication of affect by head and body cues. *Journal of Personality and Social Psychology, 2*, 726–735. doi:10.1037/h0022736

Ekman, P. (2003). *Emotions revealed.* New York, NY: Holt.

Ekman, P., Davidson, R. J., & Friesen, W. V. (1990). The Duchenne smile: Emotional expression and brain physiology II. *Journal of Personality and Social Psychology, 58*, 342–353. doi:10.1037/0022-3514.58.2.342

Elliott, E. S., & Dweck, C. S. (1988). Goals: An approach to motivation and achievement. *Journal of Personality and Social Psychology, 54*, 5–12. doi:10.1037/0022-3514.54.1.5

Ellis, L. (1986). Evidence of neuroandrogenic etiology of sex roles from a combined analysis of human, nonhuman primates, and nonprimate mammalian studies. *Personality and Individual Differences, 7*, 519–552. doi:10.1016/0191-8869(86)90131-5

Ember, C. R. (1973). Feminine task assignment and the social behavior of boys. *Ethos, 1*, 424–439. doi:10.1525/eth.1973.1.4.02a00050

Epstein, S., & O'Brien, E. J. (1985). The person–situation debate in historical and current perspective. *Psychological Bulletin, 98*, 513–537. doi:10.1037/0033-2909.98.3.513

Erikson, E. (1950). *Childhood and society.* New York, NY: Norton.

Erikson, E. (1968). *Identity: Youth and crisis.* New York, NY: Norton.

Eron, L. D. (1982). Parent–child interaction, television violence, and aggression of children. *American Psychologist, 37,* 197–211. doi:10.1037/0003-066X.37.2.197

Eron, L. D. (1987). The development of aggressive behavior from the perspective of a developing behaviorism. *American Psychologist, 42,* 435–442. doi:10.1037/0003-066X.42.5.435

Eron, L. D., Gentry, P., & Schlegel, P. (Eds.). (1994). *Reason to hope: A psychosocial perspective on violence and youth.* Washington, DC: American Psychological Association.

Eron, L. D., Walder, L. O., & Lefkowitz, M. M. (1971). *Learning of aggression in children.* Boston, MA: Little, Brown.

Estes, S. G. (1938). Judging personality from expressive behavior. *The Journal of Abnormal and Social Behavior, 33,* 217–236.

Eysenck, H. J. (1947). *Dimensions of personality.* London, England: Routledge & Kegan Paul.

Eysenck, S. B. G., & Eysenck, H. J. (1963). On the dual nature of extraversion. *British Journal of Social and Clinical Psychology, 2,* 46–55.

Fabes, R. A., & Eisenberg, N. (1992). Young children's coping with interpersonal anger. *Child Development, 63,* 116–128. doi:10.2307/1130906

Fadjukoff, P., Pullinen, L., & Kokko, K. (2005). Identity process in adulthood: Diverging domains. *Identity: An International Journal of Theory and Research, 5,* 1–20. doi:10.1207/s1532706xid0501_1

Feingold, A. (1992). Good-looking people are not what we think. *Psychological Bulletin, 111,* 304–341. doi:10.1037/0033-2909.111.2.304

Feingold, A. (1994). Gender differences in personality: A meta-analysis. *Psychological Bulletin, 116,* 429–456. doi:10.1037/0033-2909.116.3.429

Fenigstein, A. (1979). Self-consciousness, self-attention, and social interaction. *Journal of Personality and Social Psychology, 37,* 75–86.

Fenigstein, A. (1984). Self-consciousness and the overperception of the self as a target. *Journal of Personality and Social Psychology, 47,* 860–870. doi:10.1037/0022-3514.47.4.860

Fenigstein, A., Scheier, M. F., & Buss, A. H. (1975). Public and private self-consciousness: Assessment and theory. *Journal of Consulting and Clinical Psychology, 43,* 522–527. doi:10.1037/h0076760

Fenigstein, A., & Vanable, P. A. (1992). Paranoia and self-consciousness. *Journal of Personality and Social Psychology, 62,* 129–138. doi:10.1037/0022-3514.62.1.129

Feshbach, S. (1964). The function of aggression and the regulation of aggressive drive. *Psychological Review, 71,* 257–272. doi:10.1037/h0043041

Figuerredo, A. J., Wolf, P. S. A., Gladden, P. R., Olderbak, S., Andrzejczak, D. J., & Hacobs, W. J. (2011). Ecological approaches to personality. In D. M. Buss & P. H. Hawley (Eds.), *The evolution of personality and individual differences* (pp. 210–239). New York, NY: Oxford University Press.

Fiske, D. W. (1979). Two worlds of psychological phenomena. *American Psychologist, 34*, 733–739. doi:10.1037/0003-066X.34.9.733

Flavell, J. H. (1968). *The development of role-taking and communication skills in children.* New York, NY: Wiley.

Flavell, J. H. (1992). Perspectives on perspective taking. In H. Beilin & P. B. Pufall (Eds.), *Piaget's theory: Prospects and possibilities* (pp. 107–139). Hillsdale, NJ: Erlbaum.

Flavell, J. H. (1999). Cognitive development: Children's knowledge about the mind. *Annual Review of Psychology, 50*, 21–45. doi:10.1146/annurev.psych.50.1.21

Fleeson, W. (2004). Moving personality beyond the person-situation debate. *Current Directions in Psychological Science, 13*, 83–87. doi:10.1111/j.0963-7214.2004.00280.x

Flory, J. D., Raikkonen, K., Matthews, K. A., & Owens, J. F. (2000). Self-focused attention and mood during everyday social interactions. *Personality and Social Psychology Bulletin, 26*, 875–883. doi:10.1177/0146167200269012

Ford, M. B., & Collins, N. L. (2010). Self-esteem moderates neuroendocrine and psychological responses to interpersonal rejection. *Journal of Personality and Social Psychology, 98*, 405–419. doi:10.1037/a0017345

Forkman, B., Furuhaug, I. L., & Jensen, P. (1995). Personality coping patterns in piglets. *Applied Animal Behaviour Science, 45*, 31–42. doi:10.1016/0168-1591(95)00601-N

Franzoi, S. L., Anderson, J., & Frommelt, S. (1990). Individual differences in men's perception of and reactions to thinning hair. *The Journal of Social Psychology, 130*, 209–218. doi:10.1080/00224545.1990.9924571

Freedman, D. G. (1971). An evolutionary approach to research on the life cycle. *Human Development, 14*, 87–99. doi:10.1159/000271204

Freedman, M. B., Leary, T. F., Ossorio, A., & Coffee, H. S. (1951). The interpersonal dimension of personality. *Journal of Personality, 20*, 143–161. doi:10.1111/j.1467-6494.1951.tb01518.x

Frick, P. J. (2004). Special Section: Temperament and childhood psychopathology. *Journal of Clinical Child and Adolescent Psychology, 33*, 2–7. doi:10.1207/S1537 4424JCCP3301_1

Frischeisen-Köhler, I. (1933). The personal tempo and its inheritance. *Character & Personality; A Quarterly for Psychodiagnostic and Allied Sciences, 1*, 301–313.

Fromm, E. (1941). *Escape from freedom.* New York, NY: Rinehart.

Frone, M. R., & McFarlin, D. B. (1989). Chronic occupational stressors, self-focused attention, and well-being: Testing a cybernetic model. *Journal of Applied Psychology, 74*, 876–883. doi:10.1037/0021-9010.74.6.876

Funder, D. C. (1995). On the accuracy of personality judgment: A realistic approach. *Psychological Review, 102*, 652–670.

Funder, D. C., & Ozer, D. J. (1983). Behavior as a function of the situation. *Journal of Personality and Social Psychology, 44*, 107–112. doi:10.1037/0022-3514.44.1.107

Gallaher, P. (1991). *Self-consciousness and nonverbal behavior*. Unpublished manuscript, University of Texas at Austin.

Gallaher, P. (1992). Individual differences in nonverbal behavior: Dimensions of style. *Journal of Personality and Social Psychology, 63,* 133–145. doi:10.1037/0022-3514.63.1.133

Gallaher, P., & Buss, A. H. (1987). *Components of dominance*. Unpublished manuscript, University of Texas, Austin.

Gallup, G. G., Jr. (1970). Chimpanzees: Self-recognition. *Science, 167,* 86–87. doi:10.1126/science.167.3914.86

Gallup, G. G., Jr. (1977). Self-recognition in primates: A comparative approach to the bidirectional properties of consciousness. *American Psychologist, 32,* 329–338. doi:10.1037/0003-066X.32.5.329

Gallup, G. G., Jr., Povinelli, D. J., Suarez, S. D., Anderson, J. R., Lethmate, J., & Menzel, E. W. (1995). Further reflections on self-recognition in primates. *Animal Behaviour, 50,* 1525–1532. doi:10.1016/0003-3472(95)80008-5

Gardner, R. A., & Gardner, B. T. (1969). Teaching sign language to a chimpanzee. *Science, 165,* 664–672. doi:10.1126/science.165.3894.664

Gazelle, H., & Rudolph, K. (2004). Moving toward and away from the world: Social approach and avoidance trajectories in anxious solitary youth. *Child Development, 75,* 829–849. doi:10.1111/j.1467-8624.2004.00709.x

Geen, R. G. (1981). Behavioral and physiological reactions to observed violence: Effects of prior exposure to aggressive stimuli. *Journal of Personality and Social Psychology, 40,* 868–875. doi:10.1037/0022-3514.40.5.868

Gellert, E. (1961). Stability and fluctuation in the power relationships of young children. *The Journal of Abnormal and Social Psychology, 62,* 8–15. doi:10.1037/h0040436

Gifford, R. (1991). Mapping nonverbal behavior on the interpersonal circle. *Journal of Personality and Social Psychology, 61,* 279–288. doi:10.1037/0022-3514.61.2.279

Goetz, J. L., Keltner, D., & Simon-Thomas, E. (2010). Compassion: An evolutionary analysis and empirical review. *Psychological Bulletin, 136,* 351–374. doi:10.1037/a0018807

Goffman, E. (1959). *The presentation of self in everyday life*. Garden City, NY: Doubleday.

Goldberg, L. R. (1990). An alternative "description of personality": The big-five factor structure. *Journal of Personality and Social Psychology, 59,* 1216–1229. doi:10.1037/0022-3514.59.6.1216

Goodall, J. (1986). *The chimpanzees of Gombe*. Cambridge, MA: Harvard University Press.

Gormly, J. (1983). Predicting behavior from personality trait scores. *Personality and Social Psychology Bulletin, 9,* 267–270.

Gormly, J., & Champagne, B. (1974). *Validity in personality trait ratings: A multicriteria approach.* Paper presented at the Eastern Psychological Association Meeting, New York, NY.

Gosling, S. D. (1998). Personality dimensions in spotted hyenas (*Crocuta crocuta*). *Journal of Comparative Psychology, 112,* 107–118. doi:10.1037/0735-7036.112.2.107

Gosling, S. D. (2001). From mice to men: What can we learn about personality from animal research? *Psychological Bulletin, 127,* 45–86. doi:10.1037/0033-2909.127.1.45

Gosling, S. D., Kwan, V. S. Y., & John, O. P. (2003). A dog's got personality: A cross-species comparative approach to personality judgments in dogs and humans. *Journal of Personality and Social Psychology, 85,* 1161–1169. doi:10.1037/0022-3514.85.6.1161

Goy, R. W., & McEwen, B. S. (1980). *Sex differentiation of the brain.* Cambridge, MA: MIT Press.

Greenberg, J., Pyszczynski, T., & Solomon, S. (1986). The causes and consequences of a need for self-esteem: A terror management theory. In R. F. Baumeister (Ed.), *Public self and private self* (pp. 189–207). New York, NY: Springer-Verlag.

Greenberg, M. T., & Marvin, R. S. (1982). Reactions of preschool children to an adult stranger: A behavioral systems approach. *Child Development, 53,* 481–490. doi:10.2307/1128991

Greenier, K. D., Kernis, M. H., McNamara, C. W., Waschull, S. B., Berry, A. J., Herlocker, C. E., & Abend, T. A. (1999). Individual differences in reactivity to daily events: Examining the roles of stability and level of self-esteem. *Journal of Personality, 67,* 187–208. doi:10.1111/1467-6494.00052

Grossman, K. E., Grossman, K., & Waters, E. (Eds.). (2005). *Attachment from infancy to adulthood: The major longitudinal studies.* New York, NY: Guilford Press.

Guerin, D. W., Gottfried, A. W., Oliver, P. H., & Thomas, C. W. (2003). *Temperament: Infancy through adolescence.* New York, NY: Kluwer Academic/Plenum.

Guilford, J. P. (1959). *Personality.* New York, NY: McGraw-Hill.

Guilford, J. P., & Zimmerman, W. S. (1956). Fourteen dimensional temperament factors. *Psychological Monographs, 70,* 1–26.

Haimes, E. (1987). "Now I know who I really am." Identity change and redefinitions of the self in adoption. In T. Honess & K. Yardley (Eds.), *Self and identity* (pp. 359–371). London, England: Routledge & Kegan Paul.

Hall, E. T. (1966). *The hidden dimension.* Garden City, NY: Doubleday.

Hall, J. A. (1984). *Nonverbal sex differences: Communication accuracy and expressive style.* Baltimore, MD: Johns Hopkins University Press.

Hall, J. A., Coats, E. J., & Lebeau, L. S. (2005). Nonverbal behavior and the vertical dimension of social relations: A meta-analysis. *Psychological Bulletin, 131,* 898–924. doi:10.1037/0033-2909.131.6.898

Hardy, L., & Leone, C. (2008). Real evidence for the failure of the Jamesian perspective or more evidence in support of it. *Journal of Personality, 76,* 1123–1136. doi:10.1111/j.1467-6494.2008.00515.x

Harlow, H. F., & Harlow, M. (1962). Social deprivation in monkeys. *Scientific American, 207,* 136–146. doi:10.1038/scientificamerican1162-136

Harrison, R. (1941). Personal tempo and the interrelationship between voluntary and maximal rates of movement. *Journal of General Psychology, 24,* 343–379.

Harrist, A. W., Zaia, A. F., Bates, J. E., Dodge, K. A., & Pettit, G. S. (1997). Subtypes of social withdrawal in early childhood: Sociometric status and social-cognitive differences across four years. *Child Development, 68,* 278–294. doi:10.2307/1131850

Hart, D., Maloney, J., & Damon, W. (1987). The meaning and development of identity. In T. Honess & K. Yardley (Eds.), *Self and identity* (pp. 121–133). London, England: Routledge & Kegan Paul.

Harter, S. (1982). The Perceived Competence Scale for Children. *Child Development, 53,* 87–97. doi:10.2307/1129640

Harter, S. (1986). Processes underlying the construction, maintenance, and enhancement of the self-concept in children. In J. Suls & A. G. Greenwald (Eds.), *Psychological perspectives on the self* (pp. 136–181). Hillsdale, NJ: Erlbaum.

Harter, S. (1999). *The construction of the self.* New York, NY: Guilford Press.

Harter, S., & Pike, R. (1984). The pictorial scale of perceived competence and social acceptance for young children. *Child Development, 55,* 1969–1982. doi:10.2307/1129772

Heaven, P., & Ciarrochi, J. (2008). Parental styles, gender, and the development of hope. *European Journal of Personality, 22,* 707–724. doi:10.1002/per.699

Heerey, E. A., & Kring, A. M. (2007). Interpersonal consequences of social anxiety. *Journal of Abnormal Psychology, 116,* 125–134. doi:10.1037/0021-843X.116.1.125

Heine, S. J., & Buchtel, E. E. (2009). Personality: The universal and the cultural. *Annual Review of Psychology, 60,* 369–394. doi:10.1146/annurev.psych.60.110707.163655

Heine, S. J., Kitayama, S., Lehman, D. R., Takata, T., Ide, E., Leung, C., & Matsumoto, H. (2001). Divergent consequences of success and failure in Japan and North America. *Journal of Personality and Social Psychology, 81,* 599–615. doi:10.1037/0022-3514.81.4.599

Heine, S. J., Lehman, D. R., Markus, H. R., & Kitayama, S. (1999). Is there a universal need for self-regard? *Psychological Review, 106,* 766–794. doi:10.1037/0033-295X.106.4.766

Henderson, H. A., Marshal, P. J., Fox, N. A., & Rubin, K. H. (2004). Psychophysiological and behavioral evidence for varying forms and functions of nonsocial behavior in preschoolers. *Child Development, 75,* 251–263. doi:10.1111/j.1467-8624.2004.00667.x

Henrich, J., & Gil-White, F. J. (2001). The evolution of prestige: Freely conferred deference as a mechanism for enhancing the benefits of cultural transmission. *Evolution and Human Behavior, 22*, 165–196. doi:10.1016/S1090-5138(00)00071-4

Henry, B., Caspi, A., Moffitt, B. T., & Silva, P. A. (1996). Temperamental and familial predictors of violent and nonviolent criminal convictions. *Developmental Psychology, 32*, 614–623. doi:10.1037/0012-1649.32.4.614

Herman, C. P., Roth, D. A., & Polivy, J. (2003). Effects of presence of others on food intake: A normative interpretation. *Psychological Bulletin, 129*, 873–886. doi:10.1037/0033-2909.129.6.873

Heyes, C. M. (1998). Theory of mind in nonhuman primates. *Behavioral and Brain Sciences, 21*, 101–114. doi:10.1017/S0140525X98000703

Hirt, E. R., Zillman, D., Erickson, G. A., & Kennedy, C. (1992). Costs and benefits of allegiance: Changes in fans' self-ascribed competencies and team victory versus defeat. *Journal of Personality and Social Psychology, 63*, 724–738. doi:10.1037/0022-3514.63.5.724

Hodgson, R., & Rachman, S. (1974). Desynchrony in measures of fear. *Behaviour Research and Therapy, 12*, 319–326. doi:10.1016/0005-7967(74)90006-0

Hogan, R., & Kaiser, R. B. (2005). What we know about leadership. *Review of General Psychology, 9*, 169–180. doi:10.1037/1089-2680.9.2.169

Horowitz, E. (1962). Reported embarrassment memories of elementary school, high school, and college students. *The Journal of Social Psychology, 56*, 317–325. doi:10.1080/00224545.1962.9919400

Hubbard, J. A., Morrow, M. T., Romano, L. J., & McAuliffe, M. D. (2010). The role of anger in children's reactive versus proactive aggression: Review of findings, issues of measurement, and implications for intervention. In W. Arsenio & E. Lemerise (Eds.), *Emotions, aggression, and morality in children: Bridging development and psychopathology* (pp. 201–217). Washington, DC: American Psychological Association.

Huesmann, L. R., Dubow, E. R., & Boxer, P. (2009). Continuity of aggression from childhood as a predictor of life outcomes for the adolescent-limited and life-course-persistent models. *Aggressive Behavior, 35*, 136–149. doi:10.1002/ab.20300

Huesmann, L. R., Eron, L. D., Leflowitz, M. M., & Walder, L. O. (1984). The stability of aggression over time and generations. *Child Development, 55*, 746–775.

Huesmann, L. R., Moise-Titus, J., Podolski, C.-L., & Eron, L. D. (2003). Longitudinal relationships between children's exposure to TV violence and their aggressive and violent behavior in young adulthood, 1997–1992. *Developmental Psychology, 39*, 201–221. doi:10.1037/0012-1649.39.2.201

Huo, Y. J., Binning, K. R., & Molina, L. E. (2010). Testing an integrative model of respect: Implications for social engagement and well-being. *Personality and Social Psychology Bulletin, 36*, 200–212. doi:10.1177/0146167209356787

Ickes, W., Snyder, M., & Garcia, S. (1997). Personality influences on the choice of situations. In R. Hogan, J. Johnson, & S. Briggs (Eds.), *Handbook of personality psychology* (pp. 165–195). San Diego, CA: Academic Press.

Ingram, R., & Smith, T. W. (1984). Depression and internal versus external focus of attention. *Cognitive Therapy and Research, 8,* 139–151. doi:10.1007/BF01 173040

Jackson, D. N. (1974). *Personality research form manual* (rev. ed.). Port Huron, MI: Research Psychologists Press.

James, W. (1890). *Principles of psychology* (Vol. I). New York, NY: Holt, Rinehart & Winston. doi:10.1037/10538-000

Jensvold, M. L., & Gardner, R. A. (2000). Interactive use of sign language by cross-fostered chimpanzees (*Pan troglodytes*). *Journal of Comparative Psychology, 114,* 335–346. doi:10.1037/0735-7036.114.4.335

Johnson, R. T., Burk, J. A., & Kirkpatrick, L. A. (2007). Dominance and prestige as differential predictors of aggression and testosterone levels in men. *Evolution and Human Behavior, 28,* 345–351. doi:10.1016/j.evolhumbehav.2007.04.003

Jones, A. C., & Gosling, S. D. (2005). Temperament and personality in dogs (*Canis familiaris*): A review and evaluation of past research. *Applied Animal Behaviour Science, 95,* 1–53. doi:10.1016/j.applanim.2005.04.008

Jones, E. E., & Berglas, S. C. (1978). Control of attributions about the self through self-handicapping strategies: The appeal of alcohol and the role of underachievement. *Personality and Social Psychology Bulletin, 4,* 200–206. doi:10.1177/0146167278 00400205

Josephs, R. A., Bosson, J. K., & Jacobs, C. G. (2003). Self-esteem maintenance processes: Why Low self-esteem may be resistant to change. *Journal of Personality and Social Psychology, 29,* 920–933.

Josephs, R. A., Larrick, R. P., Steele, C. M., & Nisbett, R. E. (1992). Protecting the self from the negative consequences of risky decisions. *Journal of Personality and Social Psychology, 62,* 26–37. doi:10.1037/0022-3514.62.1.26

Josephs, R. A., Markus, H. R., & Tafarodi, R. W. (1992). Gender and self-esteem. *Journal of Personality and Social Psychology, 63,* 391–402. doi:10.1037/0022-3514.63.3.391

Kagan, J. (2000). Inhibited and uninhibited temperaments. In W. R. Crozier (Ed.), *Shyness. Development, consolidation and change* (pp. 22–29). New York, NY: Routledge.

Kagan, J., Reznick, J. S., Clarke, C., Snidman, N., & Garcia-Coll, C. (1984). Behavioral inhibition to the unfamiliar. *Child Development, 55,* 2212–2225. doi:10.2307/ 1129793

Kagan, J., Reznick, J. S., & Snidman, N. (1987). The physiology and psychology of behavioral inhibition in children. *Child Development, 58,* 1459–1473. doi:10. 2307/1130685

Kamide, H., & Daibo, I. (2009). Application of a self-evaluation maintenance model to psychological health in interpersonal contexts. *The Journal of Positive Psychology, 4*, 557–565. doi:10.1080/17439760903157158

Kashima, Y., Yamaguchi, S., Kim, U., Choi, S.-G., Gelfand, M. J., & Yuki, M. (1995). Culture, gender, and the self: A perspective from individualism–collectivism research. *Journal of Personality and Social Psychology, 69*, 925–937. doi:10.1037/0022-3514.69.5.925

Keenan, K., & Wakschlag, L. S. (2004). Are oppositional defiant and conduct disorder symptoms normative behaviors in preschoolers? A comparison of referred and nonreferred children. *The American Journal of Psychiatry, 161*, 356–358. doi:10.1176/appi.ajp.161.2.356

Keltner, D. (1995). The signs of appeasement: Evidence for the distinct displays of embarrassment, amusement, and shame. *Journal of Personality and Social Psychology, 68*, 441–454.

Keltner, D., & Buswell, B. N. (1997). Embarrassment: Its distinct form and appeasement functions. *Psychological Bulletin, 122*, 250–270.

Keltner, D., Capps, L., King, A. M., Young, R. C., & Heery, E. A. (2001). Just teasing: A conceptual analysis and empirical review. *Psychological Bulletin, 127*, 229–248. doi:10.1037/0033-2909.127.2.229

Keltner, D., Young, R. C., & Buswell, B. N. (1997). Appeasement in human emotion, social practice, and personality. *Aggressive Behavior, 23*, 359–374.

Kendall, P. C., & Brophy, C. (1981). Activity and attentional correlates of teacher ratings of hyperactivity. *Journal of Pediatric Psychology, 6*, 451–458. doi:10.1093/jpepsy/6.4.451

Kenrick, D. T., & Funder, D. C. (1988). Profiting from controversy: Lessons from the person- situation debate. *American Psychologist, 43*, 23–34. doi:10.1037/0003-066X.43.1.23

Kern, M. L., Reynolds, C. A., & Friedman, H. S. (2010). Predictors of physical activity patterns across adulthood: A growth curve analysis. *Personality and Social Psychology Bulletin, 36*, 1058–1072.

Kernis, M. H., Brockner, J., & Frankel, B. S. (1989). Self-esteem and reactions to failure: The mediating role of overgeneralization. *Journal of Personality and Social Psychology, 57*, 707–714. doi:10.1037/0022-3514.57.4.707

Kernis, M. H., Granneman, B. D., & Barclay, L. C. (1989). Stability and level of self-esteem as predictors of anger arousal and hostility. *Journal of Personality and Social Psychology, 56*, 1013–1023.

Kernis, M. H., and Lakey, C. E. (2009). Fragile versus secure high self-esteem: Implications for defensiveness and insecurity. In R. M. Arkin, K. C. Oleson, & P. J. Carroll (Eds.), *Handbook of the uncertain self* (pp. 360–378). New York, NY: Psychology Press.

Kernis, M. H., Lakey, C. E., & Heppner, W. L. (2008). Secure versus fragile self-esteem as a predictor of verbal defensiveness: Converging findings across three different markers. *Journal of Personality, 76,* 477–512. doi:10.1111/j.1467-6494.2008.00493.x

Kerr, M. (2000). Childhood and adolescent shyness in long term perspective. In W. R. Crozier (Ed.), *Shyness: Development, consolidation and change* (pp. 64–87). New York, NY: Routledge.

Kitayama, S., Conway, L. C., III, Pietromonaco, P. R., Park, H., & Plaut, V. C. (2010). Ethos of independence across regions in the United States. *American Psychologist, 65,* 559–574. doi:10.1037/a0020277

Kitzinger, C. (1992). The individuated self-concept: A critical analysis of social-constructionist writing on individualism. In G. M. Breakwell (Ed.), *Social psychology of identity and the self-concept* (pp. 221–250). Guildford, England: Surrey University Press.

Kobasa, S. C. (1979). Stressful life events, personality, and hardiness: An inquiry into hardiness. *Journal of Personality and Social Psychology, 37,* 1–11. doi:10.1037/0022-3514.37.1.1

Koch, S. C., Baehne, C. G., Kruse, L., Zimmerman, F., & Zumbach, J. (2010). Visual dominance and visual egalitarianism: Individual and group-level influences of sex and status in group interactions. *Journal of Nonverbal Behavior, 34,* 137–153. doi:10.1007/s10919-010-0088-8

Kochanska, G. (1991). Patterns of inhibition to the unfamiliar in children of normal and affectively ill mothers. *Child Development, 62,* 250–263. doi:10.2307/1131001

Kochanska, G., Murray, K. T., & Harlan, E. T. (2000). Effortful control in early childhood: Continuity and change, antecedents, and implications for social development. *Developmental Psychology, 36,* 220–232. doi:10.1037/0012-1649.36.2.220

Kochanska, G., Murray, K., Jacques, T. Y., Koening, L., & Vandegeest, K. (1996). Inhibitory control and its role in emerging internalization. *Child Development, 67,* 490–507. doi:10.2307/1131828

Kochanska, G., & Radke-Yarrow, M. (1992). Inhibition in toddlerhood and the dynamics of the child's interaction with an unfamiliar peer at age five. *Child Development, 63,* 325–335. doi:10.2307/1131482

Kohlberg, L. (1969). Stage and sequence: The cognitive–developmental approach to socialization. In D. A. Goslin (Ed.), *Handbook of socialization theory and research* (pp. 247–380). Chicago, IL: Rand-McNally.

Kohlberg, L. (1981). *The philosophy of moral development: The nature and development of moral stages.* New York, NY: HarperCollins.

Kristal, J. (2005). *The temperament perspective.* New York, NY: Brookes.

Kubarych, T. S., Deary, I. J., & Austin, E. J. (2003). The Narcissistic Personality Inventory: Factor structure in a non-clinical sample. *Personality and Individual Differences, 36,* 857–872. doi:10.1016/S0191-8869(03)00158-2

LaBrie, J., Pederen, E. R., Neighbors, C., & Hummer, J. F. (2008). The role of self-consciousness in the experience of alcohol-related consequences among college students. *Addictive Behaviors, 33,* 812–820. doi:10.1016/j.addbeh.2008.01.002

Lagerspetz, K. M., Bjorkquist, K., & Peitonen, T. (1988). Is indirect aggression typical of females? Gender differences in 11- to 12-year-old children. *Aggressive Behavior, 14,* 403–414. doi:10.1002/1098-2337(1988)14:6<403::AID-AB2480140602>3.0.CO;2-D

Lalwani, A. K., Shrum, L. J., & Chiu, C. (2009). Motivated response styles: The role of cultural values, regulatory focus, and self-consciousness in socially desirable responding. *Journal of Personality and Social Psychology, 96,* 870–882. doi:10.1037/a0014622

Lamiell, J. T. (1981). Toward an idiothetic psychology of personality. *American Psychologist, 36,* 276–289. doi:10.1037/0003-066X.36.3.276

Lamiell, J. T. (1997). Individuals and the differences between them. In R. Hogan, J. Johnson, & S. Briggs (Eds.), *Handbook of personality psychology* (pp. 117–141). San Diego, CA: Academic Press. doi:10.1016/B978-012134645-4/50006-8

Lancaster, J. B. (1975). *Primate behavior and the emergence of human culture.* New York, NY: Holt, Rinehart & Winston.

Langlois, J. H., Roggman, L. A., Casey, R. J., Rieser-Danner, L. A., & Jenkins, V. Y. (1987). Infant preferences for attractive faces: Remnants of a stereotype. *Developmental Psychology, 23,* 363–369. doi:10.1037/0012-1649.23.3.363

Larson, R. W. (2000). Toward a psychology of positive youth development. *American Psychologist, 55,* 170–183. doi:10.1037/0003-066X.55.1.170

Lazarus, P. J. (1982). Correlation of shyness and self-esteem in elementary school children. *Perceptual and Motor Skills, 55,* 8–10.

Leary, M. R. (2004). The sociometer, self-esteem, and the regulation of interpersonal behavior. In R. K. Baumeister & K. D. Vohs (Eds.), *Handbook of self-regulation* (pp. 373–391). New York, NY: Guilford Press.

Leary, M. R., Britt, T. W., Cutlip, W. D., & Templeton, J. L. (1992). Social blushing. *Psychological Bulletin, 112,* 446–460. doi:10.1037/0033-2909.112.3.446

Leary, M. R., & Buckley, K. E. (2000). Shyness and the pursuit of social acceptance. In W. R. Crozier (Ed.), *Shyness: Development, consolidation and change* (pp. 139–153). New York, NY: Routledge.

Leary, M. R., Cottrell, C. A., & Phillips, M. (2001). Deconfounding the effects of dominance and social acceptance on self-esteem. *Journal of Personality and Social Psychology, 81,* 898–909. doi:10.1037/0022-3514.81.5.898

Leary, M. R., & Kowalski, R. M. (1995). *Social anxiety.* New York, NY: Guilford Press.

Leary, M. R., Tambor, E. S., Terdal, S. K., & Downs, D. L. (1995). Self-esteem as an interpersonal monitor: The sociometer hypothesis. *Journal of Personality and Social Psychology, 68,* 518–530. doi:10.1037/0022-3514.68.3.518

Leary, T. F. (1957). *The interpersonal diagnosis of personality.* New York, NY: Ronald.

Lefkowitz, M. M., Eron, L. D., Walder, L. O., & Huesmann, L. R. (1977). *Growing up to be violent*. New York, NY: Pergamon Press.

Lennox, R. D., & Wolfe, R. N. (1984). Revision of the Self-Monitoring Scale. *Journal of Personality and Social Psychology, 46,* 1349–1364. doi:10.1037/0022-3514.46.6.1349

Lerner, J. V., Nitz, K., Talwar, R., & Lerner, R. V. (1989). On the functional significance of temperamental individuality: A developmental contextual view of the concept of goodness of fit. In G. A. Kohnstamm, J. E. Bates, & M. K. Rothbart (Eds.), *Temperament in childhood* (pp. 509–522). New York, NY: Wiley.

Lewis, C. C. (1981). The effect of firm parental control: A reinterpretation of findings. *Psychological Bulletin, 90,* 547–563. doi:10.1037/0033-2909.90.3.547

Lewis, M. (1995). Self-conscious emotions. *American Scientist, 83,* 68–78.

Lewis, M. (2007). Self-conscious emotional development. In J. L. Tracy, R. W. Robins, & J. P. Tangney (Eds.), *The self-conscious emotions: Theory and research* (pp. 134–152). New York, NY: Guilford Press.

Lewis, M. (2010). Loss, protest, and emotional development. In S. Hart & M. Legerstee (Eds.), *Handbook of jealousy* (pp. 27–39). Chichester, England: Wiley. doi:10.1002/9781444323542.ch2

Lewis, M., & Ramsey, D. (2002). Cortisol responses to embarrassment and shame. *Child Development, 73,* 1034–1045. doi:10.1111/1467-8624.00455

Lewis, M., Sullivan, M. W., Stanger, C., & Weiss, M. (1989). Self-development and self-conscious emotions. *Child Development, 60,* 146–156. doi:10.2307/1131080

Leyro, T. M., Zvolensky, M. J., & Bernstein, A. (2010). Distress tolerance and psychopathological symptoms and disorders: A review of the empirical literature among adults. *Psychological Bulletin, 136,* 576–600. doi:10.1037/a0019712

Li, R., O'Connor, L., Buckley, D., & Specker, B. (1995). Relation of activity levels to body fat in infants 6 to 12 months of age. *The Journal of Pediatrics, 126,* 353–357. doi:10.1016/S0022-3476(95)70447-7

Li-Grining, C. P. (2007). Effortful control among low-income preschoolers in three cities: Stability, change, and individual differences. *Developmental Psychology, 43,* 208–221. doi:10.1037/0012-1649.43.1.208

Lorenz, K. (1966). *Evolution and modification of behavior.* Chicago, IL: University of Chicago Press.

Lorr, M., & Moore, W. W. (1980). Four dimensions of assertiveness. *Multivariate Behavioral Research, 15,* 127–138. doi:10.1207/s15327906mbr1502_1

Luengo, M. A., Carill-de-la-Peña, M. T., Otero, J. M., & Romero, E. (1994). A short-term longitudinal study of impulsivity and antisocial behavior. *Journal of Personality and Social Psychology, 66,* 542–548. doi:10.1037/0022-3514.66.3.542

Lyman, R. (2006, October 26). How he found America. *New York Times,* p. B26.

Maccoby, E. E. (1990). Gender and relationships: A developmental account. *American Psychologist, 45,* 513–520. doi:10.1037/0003-066X.45.4.513

MacDonald, K. B. (2008). Effortful control, explicit processing, and the regulation of evolved predispositions. *Psychological Review, 115,* 1012–1031. doi:10.1037/a0013327

MacDonald, K. B., & Hershberger, S. L. (2005). Theoretical issues in the study of evolution and development. In R. L. Burgess & K. Macdonald (Eds.), *Evolutionary perspectives on human development* (pp. 21–72). Thousand Oaks, CA: Sage.

Maddi, S. R. (1961). Exploratory behavior and variation seeking in man. In D. W. Fiske & S. R. Maddi (Eds.), *Functions of varied experience* (pp. 253–277). Homewood, IL: Dorsey.

Maddi, S. R., Khoshaba, D. M., Harvey, R., Lu, J., & Persico, M. (2002). The personality construct of hardiness. Relationships with comprehensive tests of personality and psychopathology. *Journal of Research in Personality, 36,* 72–85. doi:10.1006/jrpe.2001.2337

Magnusson, D., & Hefler, B. (1969). The generality of behavioral data. III. Generalization potential as a function of the number of observation instances. *Multivariate Behavioral Research, 4,* 29–41. doi:10.1207/s15327906mbr0401_3

Marcia, J. E. (1966). Development and validation of ego-identity status. *Journal of Personality and Social Psychology, 3,* 551–558. doi:10.1037/h0023281

Marcia, J. E. (1987). The identity status approach to the study of ego development. In T. Honess & K. Yardley (Eds.), *Self and identity* (pp. 161–171). London, England: Routledge & Kegan Paul.

Markus, H. R., & Kitayama, S. (1991). Culture and the self: Implications for cognition, emotion, and motivation. *Psychological Review, 98,* 224–253. doi:10.1037/0033-295X.98.2.224

Marsh, H. W. (1986). Global self-esteem: Its relations to the specific facets of the self-concept and their importance. *Journal of Personality and Social Psychology, 51,* 1224–1236. doi:10.1037/0022-3514.51.6.1224

Marsh, H. W. (2008). The elusive importance effect or failure for the Jamesian perspective on the importance of importance in shaping self-esteem. *Journal of Personality, 76,* 1081–1122. doi:10.1111/j.1467-6494.2008.00514.x

Martel, M. M., Goth-Owens, T., Martinez-Torteya, C. M., & Nigg, J. T. (2010). A person-centered personality approach to heterogeneity in attention-deficit/hyperactivity disorder (ADHD). *Journal of Abnormal Psychology, 119,* 186–196. doi:10.1037/a0017511

Martin, R., Watson, D., & Wan, C. K. (2000). A three-factor model of trait anger: Dimensions of affect, behavior, and cognition. *Journal of Personality, 68,* 869–897. doi:10.1111/1467-6494.00119

Maslow, A. H. (1937). Dominance, feeling, behavior and status. *Psychological Review, 44,* 404–429. doi:10.1037/h0056714

Maslow, A. H. (1949). The expressive component of behavior. *Psychological Review, 56,* 261–272. doi:10.1037/h0053630

Mason, W. A. (1970). Motivational factors in psychosocial development. In U. J. Arnold & M. M. Page (Eds.), *Nebraska Symposium on Motivation* (Vol. 18, pp. 35–67). Lincoln: University of Nebraska Press.

Mast, M. S., & Hall, J. A. (2004). Who is the boss and who is not? Accuracy of judging status. *Journal of Nonverbal Behavior, 28,* 145–165. doi:10.1023/B:JONB.0000039647.94190.21

Matthews, K. A., Gump, B. B., Harris, K. F., Haney, T. L., & Barefoot, T. C. (2004). Hostile behaviors predict cardiac mortality among men enrolled in the Multiple Risk Factor Intervention Trial. *Circulation, 109,* 66–70. doi:10.1161/01.CIR.0000105766.33142.13

Mavissakalian, M., & Michelson, L. (1982). Psychophysiological pattern of change in the treatment of agoraphobia. *Behaviour Research and Therapy, 20,* 347–356. doi:10.1016/0005-7967(82)90094-8

Mazur, A., & Booth, A. (1998). Testosterone and dominance in men. *Behavioral and Brain Sciences, 21,* 353–363. doi:10.1017/S0140525X98001228

McAdams, D. P. (1997). The case for unity in the (post)modern self. In R. D. Ashmore & L. Jussim (Eds.), *Self and identity* (pp. 46–78). New York, NY: Oxford University Press.

McCrae, R. R. (2006). Psychopathology from the perspective of the five-factor model. In S. Strack (Ed.), *Differentiating normal from abnormal personality* (2nd ed., pp. 51–64). New York, NY: Springer Publishing Company.

McCrae, R. R., & Costa, P. T., Jr. (1985). Updating Norman's "Adequate Taxonomy": Intelligence and personality dimensions in natural language and in questionnaires. *Journal of Personality and Social Psychology, 49,* 710–721. doi:10.1037/0022-3514.49.3.710

McCrae, R. R., & Costa, P. T., Jr. (1987). Validation of the five-factor model across instruments and observers. *Journal of Personality and Social Psychology, 52,* 81–90. doi:10.1037/0022-3514.52.1.81

McCrae, R. R., Martin, T. A., Hrebikova, M., Urbanek, T., Boomsman, D. I., Willemsen, G., & Costa, P. T., Jr. (2008). Personality trait similarity between spouses in four cultures. *Journal of Personality, 76,* 1137–1164. doi:10.1111/j.1467-6494.2008.00517.x

McGowan, J., & Gormly, J. (1976). Validity of personality traits: A multicriteria approach. *Journal of Personality and Social Psychology, 4034,* 791–795. doi:10.1037/0022-3514.34.5.791

Meeus, W., van de Schoot, R., Keijsers, L., Schwartz, S. J., & Branje, S. (2010). On the progression and stability of adolescent identity formation: A five-wave longitudinal study in early-to-middle and middle-to-late adolescence. *Child Development, 81,* 1565–1581. doi:10.1111/j.1467-8624.2010.01492.x

Megargee, E. I. (1969). The influence of sex roles in the manifestation of leadership. *Journal of Applied Psychology, 53,* 377–382. doi:10.1037/h0028093

Meleshko, K. G. A., & Alden, L. E. (1993). Anxiety and self-disclosure: Toward a motivational model. *Journal of Personality and Social Psychology, 64,* 1000–1009. doi:10.1037/0022-3514.64.6.1000

Miller, G., Galanter. E., & Pribram, K. H. (1960). *Plans and the structure of behavior.* New York, NY: Holt, Rinehart, & Winston.

Miller, L. C., & Cox, C. L. (1982). For appearances' sake: Public self-consciousness and makeup use. *Personality and Social Psychology Bulletin, 8,* 748–751. doi:10.1177/0146167282084023

Miller, R. S. (1996). *Embarrassment.* New York, NY: Guilford Press.

Miller, R. S. (2007). Is embarrassment a blessing or a curse? In J. L. Tracy, R. W. Robins, & J. P. Tangney (Eds.), *The self-conscious emotions: Theory and research* (pp. 245–262). New York, NY: Guilford Press.

Mineka, S., Davidson, M., Cook, M., & Keir, R. (1984). Observational conditioning of snake fear in rhesus monkeys. *Journal of Abnormal Psychology, 93,* 355–372. doi:10.1037/0021-843X.93.4.355

Mischel, W. (1968). *Personality and assessment.* New York, NY: Wiley.

Mischel, W. (1974). Processes in delay of gratification. In L. Berkowitz (Ed.), *Advances in experimental social psychology* (pp. 249–292). New York, NY: Academic Press.

Mischel, W., & Metzner, R. (1962). Preferences for delayed reward as a function of age, intelligence, and length of delay interval. *The Journal of Abnormal and Social Psychology, 64,* 425–431. doi:10.1037/h0045046

Mischel, W., & Shoda, Y. (1995). A cognitive–affective system of personality: Reconceptualizing situations, dispositions, dynamics, and invariance in personality structure. *Psychological Review, 102,* 246–268. doi:10.1037/0033-295X.102.2.246

Mitchell, R. W. (1994). Multiplicities of self. In S. T. Parker, R. W. Mitchell, & M. L. Boccia (Eds.), *Self-awareness in animals and humans* (pp. 81–107). New York, NY: Cambridge University Press. doi:10.1017/CBO9780511565526.008

Modell, A. H. (1993). *The private self.* Cambridge, MA: Harvard University Press.

Montepare, J. M., & Zebrowitz, L. A. (1993). A cross-cultural comparison of impressions created by age-related variations in gait. *Journal of Nonverbal Behavior, 17,* 55–68. doi:10.1007/BF00987008

Montepare, J. M., & Zebrowitz-McArthur, L. (1988). Impressions of people created by age- related qualities of their gaits. *Journal of Personality and Social Psychology, 55,* 547–556. doi:10.1037/0022-3514.55.4.547

Mor, N., & Winquist, J. (2002). Self-focused attention and negative affect. *Psychological Bulletin, 128,* 638–662. doi:10.1037/0033-2909.128.4.638

Moskowitz, D. S. (2010). Quarrelsomeness in everyday life. *Journal of Personality, 78,* 39–66. doi:10.1111/j.1467-6494.2009.00608.x

Moskowitz, D. S., & Schwarz, J. C. (1982). Validity comparison of behavior counts and ratings by knowledgeable informants. *Journal of Personality and Social Psychology, 42,* 518–528. doi:10.1037/0022-3514.42.3.518

Murray, H. A. (1938). *Explorations in personality.* New York, NY: Oxford University Press.

Murray, S. L., Holmes, J. G., & Griffin, D. W. (2000). Self-esteem and the quest for security: How perceived self-regard regulates the attachment process. *Journal of Personality and Social Psychology, 64,* 1000–1009.

Murray-Close, D., & Ostrov, J. M. (2009). A longitudinal study of forms and functions of aggressive behavior in early childhood. *Child Development, 80,* 828–842. doi:10.1111/j.1467-8624.2009.01300.x

Niederle, M., & Vesterlund, L. (2007). Do women shy away from competition? Do men compete too much? *The Quarterly Journal of Economics, 122,* 1067–1101.

Nikolas, M. A., & Burt, S. A. (2010). Genetic and environmental influences on ADHD symptom dimensions of inattention and hyperactivity: A meta-analysis. *Journal of Abnormal Psychology, 119,* 1–17. doi:10.1037/a0018010

Norem, J. K. (2001) *The power of negative thinking: Using defensive pessimism to harness anxiety and perform at your peak.* New York, NY: Basic Books.

Nussbaum, A. D., & Dweck, C. S. (2008). Defensiveness versus remediation: Self-theories and modes of self-esteem maintenance. *Personality and Social Psychology Bulletin, 34,* 599–612. doi:10.1177/0146167207312960

Öhman, A. (1986). Face the beast and fear the face: Animal and social fears as prototypes for evolutionary analyses of emotion. *Psychophysiology, 23,* 123–145.

Öhman, A., & Mineka, S. (2001). Fears, phobias, and preparedness: Toward an evolved module of fear and fear learning. *Psychological Review, 108,* 483–522. doi:10.1037/0033-295X.108.3.483

Olweus, D. (1979). Stability of aggressive reaction patterns in males: A review. *Psychological Bulletin, 86,* 852–875. doi:10.1037/0033-2909.86.4.852

Olweus, D. (1984). Aggressors and their victims: Bullying at school. In N. Frude & H. Gault (Eds.), *Disruptive behavior in the schools* (pp. 57–75). Washington, DC: Hemisphere.

Olweus, D. (1993). *Bullying in schools.* Cambridge, MA: Blackwell.

Orth, U., & Robins, W. W. (2008). Low self-esteem prospectively predicts depression in adolescence and young adulthood. *Journal of Personality and Social Psychology, 95,* 695–708. doi:10.1037/0022-3514.95.3.695

Oyserman, D., & Markus, H. R. (1993). The sociocultural self. In J. Suls (Ed.), *Psychological perspectives on the self: Vol. 4. The self in social perspective* (pp. 187–219). Hillsdale, NJ: Erlbaum.

Paikoff, R. L., & Savin-Williams, R. C. (1983). An exploratory study of dominance interactions among adolescent females at a summer camp. *Journal of Youth and Adolescence, 12,* 419–433. doi:10.1007/BF02088724

Park, L. E., Crocker, J., & Kiefer, A. K. (2007). Contingencies of self-worth, academic failure, and goal pursuit. *Personality and Social Psychology Bulletin, 33,* 1503–1517. doi:10.1177/0146167207305538

Parker, S., & deVries, B. (1993). Patterns of friendship for women and men is same and cross- sex relationships. *Journal of Social and Personal Relationships, 10*, 617–626. doi:10.1177/0265407593104010

Parker, S. T., Mitchell, R. W., & Boccia, M. L. (Eds.). (1994). *Self-awareness in animals and humans.* New York, NY: Cambridge University Press. doi:10.1017/CBO97 80511565526

Parten, M. B. (1933). Leadership among preschool children. *The Journal of Abnormal and Social Psychology, 27*, 430–440. doi:10.1037/h0073032

Pasterski, V. L., Geffner, M. E., Brain, C., Hindmarch, P., Brook, C., & Hines, M. (2005). Prenatal hormones and postnatal socialization by parents as determinants of male-typical play in girls with congenital adrenal hyperplasia. *Child Development, 76*, 264–278. doi:10.1111/j.1467-8624.2005.00843.x

Patterson, F., & Gordon, W. (1993). The case for personhood of gorillas. In P. Cavalieri & P. Singer (Eds.), *The great ape project* (pp. 58–77). New York, NY: St. Martin's Griffin.

Patterson, G. R., Littman, R. A., & Bricker, W. (1967). Assertive behavior in children. *Monographs of the Society for Research in Child Development, 32*(5, No. 113).

Patton, J. H., Stanford, M. S., & Barratt, E. S. (1995). Factor structure of the Barratt Impulsiveness Scale. *Journal of Clinical Psychology, 51*, 768–774. doi:10.1002/ 1097-4679(199511)51:6<768::AID-JCLP2270510607>3.0.CO;2-1

Paunonen, S. V. (1989). Consensus in personality judgments: Moderating effects of target–rater acquaintanceship and behavior observability. *Journal of Personality and Social Psychology, 56*, 823–833. doi:10.1037/0022-3514.56.5.823

Pavlov, I. P. (1927). *Conditioned reflexes: An investigation of the physiological activity of the cerebral cortex* (G. V. Anrep, Trans.). Oxford, England: Oxford University Press.

Peevers, B. H. (1987). The self as observer of the self: A developmental analysis of the subjective self. In T. Honess & K. Yardley (Eds.), *Self and identity* (pp. 147–158). London, England: Routledge & Kegan Paul.

Pelham, B. W., & Swann, W. B., Jr. (1989). From self-conceptions to self-worth: On the sources and structure of global self-esteem. *Journal of Personality and Social Psychology, 57*, 672–680. doi:10.1037/0022-3514.57.4.672

Pellegrini, A. D., & Horvat, M. (1995). A developmental contextual critique of attention deficit hyperactivity disorder. *Educational Researcher, 24*, 13–20.

Perry, D. G., Kusel, S. J., & Perry, L. C. (1988). Victims of peer aggression. *Developmental Psychology, 24*, 807–814. doi:10.1037/0012-1649.24.6.807

Perry, D. G., Perry, L. C., & Rasmussen, P. (1986). Cognitive social learning mediators of aggression. *Child Development, 57*, 700–711. doi:10.2307/1130347

Perry, D. G., Perry, L. C., & Weiss, R. J. (1989). Sex differences in the consequences that children anticipate for aggression. *Developmental Psychology, 25*, 312–319. doi:10.1037/0012-1649.25.2.312

Peskin, J., & Ardino, V. (2003). Representing the mental world in children's social behavior: Playing hide-and-seek and keeping a secret. *Social Development, 12*, 496–512. doi:10.1111/1467-9507.00245

Pettit, G. S., Bakshi, A., Dodge, K. A., & Coie, J. D. (1990). The emergence of social dominance in young boys play groups: Developmental differences and behavioral correlates. *Developmental Psychology, 26*, 1017–1025. doi:10.1037/0012-1649.26.6.1017

Pincus, A. L. (2005). A contemporary integrative interpersonal theory of personality disorders. In M. F. Lenzenweger & J. F. Clarkin (Eds.), *Major theories of personality disorder* (pp. 282–331). New York, NY: Guilford Press.

Pincus, A. L., & Wiggins, J. S. (1990). Interpersonal problems and conceptions of personality disorder. *Journal of Personality Disorders, 4*, 342–352.

Plomin, R., & Daniels, D. (1987). Why are children in the same family so different from one another? *Behavioral and Brain Sciences, 10*, 1–16. doi:10.1017/S0140525X00055941

Plomin, R., & Defries, J. C., McClearn, G. E., & McGuffin, P. (2001). *Behavior genetics* (4th ed.). New York, NY: Worth.

Plotnik, J. M., de Waal, F. B. M., & Reiss, D. (2006). Self-recognition in an Asian elephant. *Proceedings of the National Academy of Sciences of the United States of America, 103*, 17053–17057. doi:10.1073/pnas.0608062103

Premack, D., & Woodruff, G. (1978). Does the chimpanzee have a theory of mind? *Behavioral and Brain Sciences, 1*, 515–526. doi:10.1017/S0140525X00076512

Pulkkinen, L. (1987). Offensive and defensive aggression in humans: A longitudinal perspective. *Aggressive Behavior, 13*, 197–212.

Pulkkinen, L., & Pitkanen, T. (1993). Continuities in aggressive behavior from childhood to adulthood. *Aggressive Behavior, 19*, 249–263. doi:10.1002/1098-2337(1993)19:4<249::AID-AB2480190402>3.0.CO;2-I

Pulkkinen, L., & Tremblay, R. E. (1992). Patterns of boys' social adjustment in two cultures and at different ages: A longitudinal perspective. *International Journal of Behavioral Development, 15*, 527–553.

Putnam, S. P. (1998). *Sensation seeking in five year old boys.* Masters' thesis, University of Pennsylvania, Philadelphia.

Pyszczynski, T., Greenberg, J., Solomon, S., Arndt, J., & Schimel, J. (2004). Why do people need self-esteem? A theoretical and empirical review. *Psychological Bulletin, 130*, 435–468. doi:10.1037/0033-2909.130.3.435

Raevuori, A., Dick, D. M., Keski-Rahonen, A., Pukkinen, L., Rose, R., Rissanen, A., ... Silventoinen, K. (2007). Genetic and environmental factors affecting self-esteem from age 14 to 17: A longitudinal study of Finnish twins. *Psychological Medicine, 37*, 1625–1633. doi:10.1017/S0033291707000840

Raine, A., Reynolds, C., Venables, P. H., Mednick, S. A., & Faringon, D. P. (1998). Fearlessness, stimulus-seeking, and large body size at 3 years as early predispositions to childhood aggression at age 11 years. *Archives of General Psychiatry, 55,* 745–751. doi:10.1001/archpsyc.55.8.745

Ramsdal, G. H. (2008). Differential relations between two dimensions of self-esteem and the Big Five? *Scandinavian Journal of Psychology, 49,* 333–338. doi:10.1111/j.1467-9450.2008.00657.x

Rankin, J. L., Lane, D. J., Gibbons, F. X., & Gerrard, M. (2004). Adolescent self-consciousness: Longitudinal differences in two cohorts. *Journal of Research on Adolescence, 14,* 1–21. doi:10.1111/j.1532-7795.2004.01401001.x

Raskauskas, J., & Stoltz, A. D. (2007). Involvement in traditional and electronic bullying among adolescents. *Developmental Psychology, 43,* 564–575.

Raskin, R. N., & Hall, C. S. (1979). A narcissistic personality inventory. *Psychological Reports, 45,* 590.

Ray, J. J. (1981). Authoritarianism, dominance, and assertiveness. *Journal of Personality Assessment, 45,* 390–397. doi:10.1207/s15327752jpa4504_8

Reale, D., & Dingemanse, N. J. (2011). Selection and evolutionary, explanations for the maintenance of personality differences. In D. M. Buss & P. H. Hawley (Eds.), *The evolution of personality and individual differences* (pp. 400–424). New York, NY: Oxford University Press.

Reiss, D., & Marino, L. (2001). Mirror self-recognition in the bottlenose dolphin: A case of cognitive convergence. *Proceedings of the National Academy of Sciences of the United States of America, 98,* 5937–5942.

Rimoldi, H. J. (1951). Personal tempo. *The Journal of Abnormal and Social Psychology, 46,* 283–303. doi:10.1037/h0057479

Robins, R. W., Tracy, J. L., Trzesniewski, L., Potter, J., & Gosling, S. D. (2001). Personality correlates of self-esteem. *Journal of Research in Personality, 35,* 463–482. doi:10.1006/jrpe.2001.2324

Robins, R. W., & Trzesniewski, K. H. (2005). Self-esteem across the life span. *Psychological Inquiry, 14,* 158–160.

Rogers, C. R. (1951). *Client-centered therapy.* Boston, MA: Houghton-Mifflin.

Rogoff, B., Sellers, J., Perrota, S., Fox, N., & White, S. (1975). Age of assignment of roles and responsibilities in children. *Human Development, 18,* 353–369. doi:10.1159/000271496

Rose, R. J., Miller, J. Z., Pogue-Geile, M.F., & Cardwell, G. F. (1981). Twin-family studies of common fears and phobias. In L. Gedda, P. Parisi, & W. E. Nance (Eds.), *Twin research 3: Intelligence, personality, and development* (pp. 169–174). New York, NY: Liss.

Rothbart, M. K. (1989). Temperament in childhood. In G. A. Kohnstamm, J. E. Bates, & M. K. Rothbart (Eds.), *Temperament in childhood* (pp. 59–73). New York, NY: Wiley.

Rothbart, M. K. (2004). Temperament and the pursuit of integrated developmental psychology. *Merrill-Palmer Quarterly, 50,* 492–505.

Rothbart, M. K., & Derryberry, D. (1981). Development of individual differences in temperament. In M. E. Lamb & A. L. Brown (Eds.), *Advances in developmental psychology* (Vol. 1, pp. 37–86). Hillsdale, NJ: Erlbaum.

Rothbart, M. K., & Rueda, M. R. (2005). The development of effortful control. In U. Mayr, E. Awh, & S. Keele (Eds.), *Developing individuality in the human brain: A tribute to Michael I. Posner* (pp. 167–188). Washington, DC: American Psychological Association.

Rubin, K. H. (1993). The Waterloo longitudinal project: Correlates and consequences of social withdrawal from childhood to adolescence. In K. H. Rubin & J. B. Asendorpf (Eds.), *Social withdrawal, inhibition, and shyness* (pp. 291–314). Hillsdale, NJ: Erlbaum.

Rubin, K. H. (1982). Nonsocial play in children: Necessary evil? *Child Development, 53,* 651–657. doi:10.2307/1129376

Rubin, K. H., & Asendorpf, J. B. (1993). Social withdrawal, inhibition and shyness: Conceptual and definitional issues. In K. H. Rubin & J. B. Asendorpf (Eds.), *Social withdrawal, inhibition, and shyness* (pp. 3–17). Hillsdale, NJ: Erlbaum.

Rutter, M. (1989). Temperament: Conceptual issues and clinical implications. In G. A. Kohnstamm, J. E. Bates, & M. K. Rothbart (Eds.), *Temperament in childhood* (pp. 463–479). New York, NY: Wiley.

Sadalla, E. K., Kenrick, D. T., & Vershure, B. (1987). Dominance and heterosexual attraction. *Journal of Personality and Social Psychology, 52,* 730–738. doi:10.1037/0022-3514.52.4.730

Sakaguchi, K., & Hasegawam, T. (2006). Personal perception through gait information and target choice for sexual advances: Comparison of likely targets in experiments and real life. *Journal of Nonverbal Behavior, 30,* 63–85. doi:10.1007/s10919-006-0006-2

Sampson, E. E. (1988). The debate on individualism: Indigenous psychologies of the individual and their role in personal and social functioning. *American Psychologist, 43,* 15–22. doi:10.1037/0003-066X.43.1.15

Sánchez-Martin, J. R., Fano, E., Ahedo, J., Cardas, P. F., Brain, P. F., & Azpiroz, A. (2000). Relating testosterone levels and free play behavior in male and female preschool children. *Psychoneuroendocrinology, 25,* 773–783. doi:10.1016/S0306-4530(00)00025-1

Saucier, G., & Goldberg, L. R. (2001). Lexical studies of indigenous personality factors: Premises, products, and prospects. *Journal of Personality, 69,* 847–879. doi:10.1111/1467-6494.696167

Savage-Rumbaugh, S., McDonald, K., Sevcik, R. A., Hopkins, W. D., & Rubert, E. (1986). Spontaneous symbol acquisition and communicative use by pygmy chimpanzees (*Pan paniscus*). *Journal of Experimental Psychology: General, 115,* 211–235. doi:10.1037/0096-3445.115.3.211

Savin-Williams, R. C. (1976). An ethological study of dominance formation and maintenance. *Child Development, 47,* 972–979. doi:10.2307/1128433

Savin-Williams, R. C. (1979). Dominance hierarchies in groups of early adolescents. *Child Development, 50,* 923–935. doi:10.2307/1129316

Savin-Williams, R. C. (2005). *The new gay teenager.* Cambridge, MA: Harvard University Press.

Schachter, S. (1959). *The psychology of affiliation.* Stanford, CA: Stanford University Press.

Scheibel, M. E., & Scheibel, A. B. (1964). Some neural substrates of postnatal development. In M. L. Hoffman (Ed.), *Review of child development research* (pp. 481–519). New York, NY: Russell Sage Foundation.

Scheier, M. F., Buss, A. H., & Buss, D. M. (1978). Self-consciousness, self-report of aggressiveness, and aggression. *Journal of Research in Personality, 12,* 133–140. doi:10.1016/0092-6566(78)90089-2

Scheier, M. F., & Carver, C. S. (1985). Optimism, coping, and health: Assessment and implications of generalized outcome expectancies. *Health Psychology, 4,* 219–247. doi:10.1037/0278-6133.4.3.219

Scheier, M. F., Carver, C. S., & Bridges, M. W. (1994). Distinguishing optimism from neuroticism (and trait anxiety, self-mastery, and self-esteem): A re-evaluation of the Life Orientation Test. *Journal of Personality and Social Psychology, 67,* 1063–1078. doi:10.1037/0022-3514.67.6.1063

Scherer, K. R. (1986). Vocal affect expression: A review and a model for future research. *Psychological Bulletin, 99,* 143–165. doi:10.1037/0033-2909.99.2.143

Scherer, K. R., & Ekman, P. (Eds.). (1982). *Handbook of methods in nonverbal behavior research.* New York, NY: Cambridge University Press.

Schlenker, B. R., & Leary, M. R. (1982). Social anxiety and self-presentation. *Psychological Bulletin, 92,* 641–669. doi:10.1037/0033-2909.92.3.641

Schlenker, B. R., Weigold, M. F., & Hallam, J. R. (1990). Self-serving attributions in social contexts: Effects of self-esteem and social pressure. *Journal of Personality and Social Psychology, 58,* 855–863. doi:10.1037/0022-3514.58.5.855

Schmidt, L. A., & Buss, A. H. (2010). Understanding shyness: Four questions and four decades of research. In K. H. Rubin & R. J. Coplan (Eds.), *The development of shyness and social withdrawal* (pp. 23–41). New York, NY: Guilford Press.

Schmidt, L. A., & Fox, N. A (1994). Patterns of electrophysiology and autonomic activity in adults' shyness and sociability. *Biological Psychology, 38,* 183–198.

Schmidt, L. A., & Fox, N. A. (1998). Fear-potentiated startle responses in temperamentally different human infants. *Developmental Psychobiology, 32,* 113–120.

Schmidt, L. A., & Robinson, T. R. (1992). Low self-esteem in differentiating fearful and self-conscious forms of shyness. *Psychological Reports, 70,* 255–257. doi:10.2466/PR0.70.1.255-257

Schmidt, L. A., & Tasker, S. L. (2000). Childhood shyness: Development and "depathology." In W. R. Crozier (Ed.), *Shyness: Development, consolidation and change* (pp. 30–46). New York, NY: Routledge.

Schmitt, D. P., & Allik, J. (2005). Simultaneous administration of the Rosenberg Self-Esteem Scale in 53 nations: Exploring the universal and culture-specific features of global self-esteem. *Journal of Personality and Social Psychology, 89,* 623–642. doi:10.1037/0022-3514.89.4.623

Schulman, J. L., & Reisman, J. (1959). An objective measure of hyperactivity. *American Journal of Mental Deficiency, 64,* 455–456.

Scott, J. P. (1958). *Aggression.* Chicago, IL: University of Chicago Press.

Seery, M. D., Holman, E. A., & Silver, R. C. (2010). Whatever does not kill us: Cumulative lifetime adversity, vulnerability, and resilience. *Journal of Personality and Social Psychology, 99,* 1025–1041.

Segerdahl, P., Fields, W., & Savage-Rumbaugh, S. (2005). *Kanzi's primal language: Cultural initiation of primates into language.* New York, NY: Palgrave MacMillan.

Shapiro, D. L. (2010). Relational identity theory: A systematic approach for transforming the emotional dimension of conflict. *American Psychologist, 65,* 634–645. doi:10.1037/a0020004

Shearn, D., Bergman, E., Hill, K., Abel, A., & Hinds, L. (1992). Blushing as a function of audience size. *Psychophysiology, 29,* 431–436. doi:10.1111/j.1469-8986.1992.tb01716.x

Shearn, D., & Spellman, L. (1993). [Empathic blushing in friends and strangers.] Unpublished research, Colorado College, Colorado Springs, CO.

Sheppard, S. C., Malatras, J. W., & Israel, A. C. (2010). The impact of deployment on U.S. military families. *American Psychologist, 65,* 599–609. doi:10.1037/a0020332

Shields, S. A., Mallory, M. E., & Simon, A. (1989). The Body Awareness Questionnaire: Reliability and validity. *Journal of Personality Assessment, 53,* 802–815. doi:10.1207/s15327752jpa5304_16

Shoda, Y., Mischel, W., & Wright, J. C. (1994). Intraindividual stability in the organization and patterning of behavior: Incorporating psychological situations into the idiographic analysis of behavior. *Journal of Personality and Social Psychology, 67,* 674–687. doi:10.1037/0022-3514.67.4.674

Simmons, R. G. (1987). Self-esteem in adolescence. In T. Honess & K. Yardley (Eds.), *Self and Identity* (pp. 172–192). London, England: Routledge & Kegan Paul.

Smith, J. D., & Shaffer, D. R. (1986). Self-consciousness, self-reported altruism, and helping behavior. *Social Behavior and Personality, 14,* 215–220. doi:10.2224/sbp.1986.14.2.215

Smith, P. K., Madsen, K. C., & Moody, J. C. (1999). What causes age decline in reports of being bullied at school? Towards a developmental analysis of risks of being bullied. *Educational Research, 41,* 267–285.

Smith, T. W. (1984). The polls: Gender attitudes toward violence. *Public Opinion Quarterly, 48,* 384–396. doi:10.1093/poq/48.1B.384

Smith, T. W., Glazer, K., Ruiz, J. M., & Gallo, L. C. (2004). Hostility, anger, aggressiveness, and coronary heart disease: An interpersonal perspective on personal-

ity, emotion, and health. *Journal of Personality, 72,* 1217–1270. doi:10.1111/j.
1467-6494.2004.00296.x

Smith, T. W., & Greenberg, J. (1981). Depression and self-focused attention. *Motivation and Emotion, 5,* 323–331. doi:10.1007/BF00992551

Snodgrass, S. E., & Rosenthal, R. (1984). Females in charge: Effect of sex of subordinate and romantic attachment status upon self-ratings of dominance. *Journal of Personality, 52,* 355–371. doi:10.1111/j.1467-6494.1984.tb00357.x

Snyder, C. R., & Fromkin, H. L. (1980). *Uniqueness. The pursuit of human difference.* New York, NY: Plenum Press.

Snyder, M. (1974). The self-monitoring of expressive behavior. *Journal of Personality and Social Psychology, 30,* 526–537. doi:10.1037/h0037039

Snyder, M., Berscheid, E., & Glick, P. (1985). Focusing on the exterior and the interior: Two investigations of the initiation of personal relationships. *Journal of Personality and Social Psychology, 48,* 1427–1439. doi:10.1037/0022-3514.48.6.1427

Snyder, M., Gangestad, S., & Simpson, J. A. (1983). Choosing friends and activity partners. *Journal of Personality and Social Psychology, 45,* 1061–1072. doi:10.1037/0022-3514.45.5.1061

Solomon, R. L. (1957). *Temperament and personality.* New York, NY: Harper.

Solomon, R. L., & Wynne, L. (1954). Traumatic avoidance learning: The principles of anxiety conservation and partial irreversibility. *Psychological Review, 61,* 353–385. doi:10.1037/h0054540

Sorrentino, R., & Short, J. C. (1977). The case of the mysterious moderates: Why motives sometimes fail to predict behavior. *Journal of Personality and Social Psychology, 35,* 478–484. doi:10.1037/0022-3514.35.7.478

Spence, J. T., & Helmreich, R. L. (1983). Achievement-related motives and behavior. In J. T. Spence (Ed.), *Achievement and achievement motives: Psychological and sociological approaches* (pp. 10–74). New York, NY: Freeman.

Spere, K. A., Schmidt, L. A., Rinolo, T. C., & Fox, N. A. (2005). Is a lack of cerebral hemisphere dominance a risk factor for social "conflictedness"? Mixed-handedness in shyness and sociability. *Personality and Individual Differences, 39,* 271–281. doi:10.1016/j.paid.2005.01.005

Spielberger, C. D. (1988). *Manual for the State–Trait Anger Inventory.* Odessa, FL: PAR.

Stagner, R. (1948). *Psychology of personality* (rev. ed.). New York, NY: McGraw-Hill.

Stinson, D. A., Logel, C., Holmes, J. G., Wood, J. V., Forest, A., Gaucher, D., . . . & Kath, J. (2010). The regulatory, function of self-esteem: Testing the epistemic and signaling systems. *Journal of Personality and Social Psychology, 99,* 993–1013.

Strack, S. (Ed.). (2006). *Differentiating normal from abnormal personality* (2nd ed.). New York, NY: Springer Publishing Company.

Strayer, F. F., & Strayer, J. (1976). An ethological analysis of agonism and dominance relations among preschool children. *Child Development, 47,* 980–989. doi:10.2307/1128434

Strelau, J. (1983). *Temperament, personality, activity*. London, England: Academic Press.

Strelau, J. (1989). The regulative theory of temperament as a result of East–West influences. In G. A. Kohnstamm, J. E. Bates, & M. K. Rothbart (Eds.), *Temperament in children* (pp. 35–48). New York, NY: Wiley.

Strelau, J. (2001). The role of temperament as moderator of stress. In T. D. Wachs & G. Kohnstamm (Eds.), *Temperament in context* (pp. 153–172). Mawah, NJ: Erlbaum.

Stevenson-Hinde, J., Stillwell-Barnes, R., & Zung, M. (1980). Subjective assessment of monkeys over four successive years. *Primates, 21,* 660–682. doi:10.1007/BF02383825

Sulloway, F. J. (1996). *Born to rebel: Birth order, family dynamics, and creative lives*. New York, NY: Pantheon.

Susman, E. J., Inoff-Germaine, C., Nottelman, E. D., Loriaux, E. D., Cutler, G. B., Jr., & Chrousos, G. P. (1987). Hormones, emotional dispositions, and aggressive attributes in young adolescents. *Child Development, 58,* 1114–1134. doi:10.2307/1130551

Svartberg, K. (2005). A comparison of behavior in test and in everyday life: Evidence of three consistent boldness-related personality traits in dogs. *Applied Animal Behaviour Science, 91,* 103–128. doi:10.1016/j.applanim.2004.08.030

Svartberg, K., & Forkman, B. (2002). Personality traits in the domestic dog. *Applied Animal Behaviour Science, 79,* 133–155. doi:10.1016/S0168-1591(02)00121-1

Tafarodi, R. W. (1998). Paradoxical self-esteem and selectivity in the processing of social information. *Journal of Personality and Social Psychology, 74,* 1181–1196. doi:10.1037/0022-3514.74.5.1181

Tafarodi, R. W., & Milne, A. B. (2002). Decomposing global self-esteem. *Journal of Personality, 70,* 443–484. doi:10.1111/1467-6494.05017

Tafarodi, R. W., & Swann, W. B., Jr. (1995). Self-loving and self-competence as dimensions of global self-esteem. *Journal of Personality Assessment, 65,* 322–342. doi:10.1207/s15327752jpa6502_8

Tafarodi, R. W., & Swann, W. R., Jr. (1996). Individualism-collectivism and global self-esteem: Evidence for a cultural trade-off. *Journal of Cross-Cultural Psychology, 27,* 651–672. doi:10.1177/0022022196276001

Tafarodi, R. W., & Swann, W. B., Jr. (2001). Two-dimensional self-esteem: Theory and measurement. *Personality and Individual Differences, 31,* 653–673. doi:10.1016/S0191-8869(00)00169-0

Tafarodi, R. W., & Vu, C. (1997). Two-dimensional self-esteem and reactions to success and failure. *Personality and Social Psychology Bulletin, 23,* 626–635. doi:10.1177/0146167297236006

Teasdale, J. D., & Green, H. A. C. (2004). Ruminative self-focus and autobiographic memory. *Personality and Individual Differences, 36,* 1933–1943.

Tedeschi, J. T., & Norman, N. (1985). Social power, self-presentation, and the self. In B. R. Schlenker (Ed.), *The self in social life* (pp. 293–322). New York, NY: McGraw-Hill.

Telch, M. J., Broulliard, M., Telch, C. F., Agras, W. S., & Taylor, C. B. (1989). Role of cognitive appraisal in panic-related avoidance. *Behaviour Research and Therapy, 27*, 373–383. doi:10.1016/0005-7967(89)90007-7

Telch, M. J., Jacquin, K., Smits, J. A., & Powers, M. B. (2003). Regulatory sensitivity as a predictor of agoraphobia, status among individuals suffering from panic disorder. *Journal of Behavior Therapy and Experimental Psychiatry, 34*, 161–170. doi:10.1016/S0005-7916(03)00037-5

Tellegen, A. (1985). Structures of mood and personality and their relevance to assessing anxiety, with an emphasis on self-report. In A. H. Tuma & J. D. Maser (Eds.), *Anxiety and the anxiety disorders* (pp. 681–706). Hillsdale, NJ: Erlbaum.

Tellegen, A., Lykken, D. T., Bouchard, T. J., Wilcox, K. J., Segal, N., & Rich, S. (1988). Personality similarity in twins reared apart and together. *Journal of Personality and Social Psychology, 54*, 1031–1039. doi:10.1037/0022-3514.54.6.1031

Tesser, A. (1980). Self-esteem and family dynamics. *Journal of Personality and Social Psychology, 39*, 77–91. doi:10.1037/0022-3514.39.1.77

Tesser, A. (2000). On the confluence of self-esteem maintenance mechanisms. *Personality and Social Psychology Review, 4*, 290–299. doi:10.1207/S15327957PSPR0404_1

Tesser, A., & Campbell, J. (1982). Self-esteem maintenance and the perception of friends and strangers. *Journal of Personality, 50*, 261–279. doi:10.1111/j.1467-6494.1982.tb00750.x

Thiessen, D., & Gregg, B. (1980). Human assortative mating and genetic equilibrium: An evolutionary perspective. *Ethology and Sociobiology, 1*, 111–140. doi:10.1016/0162-3095(80)90003-5

Thomas, A., Chess, S., & Birch, H. G. (1968). *Temperament and behavior disorders in children.* New York, NY: New York University Press.

Thomas, A., Chess, S., Birch, H. G., Hertzig, M., & Korn, S. (1963). *Behavioral individuality in early childhood.* New York, NY: New York University Press.

Thomas, M. H., Horton, R. W., Lippincott, E. C., & Drabman, R. S. (1977). Desensitization of real-life aggression as a function of exposure to televised violence. *Journal of Personality and Social Psychology, 35*, 450–458. doi:10.1037/0022-3514.35.6.450

Thornton, B., & Moore, S. (1993). Physical attractiveness contrast effect: Implications for self-esteem and evaluations of the social self. *Personality and Social Psychology Bulletin, 19*, 474–480. doi:10.1177/0146167293194012

Thurstone, L. L. (1951). The dimensions of temperament. *Psychometrika, 16*, 11–20. doi:10.1007/BF02313423

Tice, D. M. (1991). Esteem protection or enhancement? Self-handicapping motives and attributions differ by trait self-esteem. *Journal of Personality and Social Psychology, 60,* 711–725.

Tiedens, L. Z. (2001). Anger and advancement versus sadness and subjugation: The effect of negative emotional expressions on social status conferral. *Journal of Personality and Social Psychology, 80,* 86–94. doi:10.1037/0022-3514.80.1.86

Tiedens, L. Z., & Fragile, A. R. (2003). Power moves: Complementarity in dominant and submissive nonverbal behavior. *Journal of Personality and Social Psychology, 84,* 558–568. doi:10.1037/0022-3514.84.3.558

Tiger, L., & Fox, R. (1971). *The imperial animal.* New York, NY: Holt, Rinehart & Winston.

Tobey, E. L., & Tunnell, G. (1981). Predicting our impressions on others: Effects of public self-consciousness and acting, a self-monitoring subscale. *Personality and Social Psychology Bulletin, 7,* 661–669. doi:10.1177/014616728174024

Tomasello, M., & Call, J. (1997). *Primate cognition.* New York, NY: Oxford University Press.

Toulmin, S. (1986). The ambiguities of self-understanding. *Journal for the Theory of Social Behavior, 16,* 41–55.

Towner, S. (2010). Concept of mind in non-human primates. *Bioscience Horizons, 3,* 96–104. doi:10.1093/biohorizons/hzq011

Tracy, J. L., & Robins, R. W. (2008). The nonverbal expression of pride: Evidence for cross- cultural recognition. *Journal of Personality and Social Psychology, 94,* 516–530. doi:10.1037/0022-3514.94.3.516

Trapnell, P. D., & Campbell, J. D. (1999). Private self-consciousness and the five-factor model of personality. *Journal of Personality and Social Psychology, 76,* 284–304. doi:10.1037/0022-3514.76.2.284

Tremblay, R. E., Nagin, D. S., Seguin, J. R., Zoccollillo, M. D., Zelazo, P. D., Boivin, M., . . . Japel, C. (2004). Physical aggression during early childhood: Trajectories and predictors. *Pediatrics, 114,* e43–e50. doi:10.1542/peds.114.1.e43

Tremblay, R. E., Pihl, R. O, Vitaro, F., & Dobkin, P. L. (1994). Predicting early onset of male antisocial behavior from preschool behavior. *Archives of General Psychiatry, 51,* 732–739.

Triandis, H. C. (1989). The self and social behavior in differing cultural contexts. *Psychological Review, 96,* 506–520. doi:10.1037/0033-295X.96.3.506

Triandis, H. C. (2001). Individualism–collectivism and personality. *Journal of Personality, 69,* 907–924. doi:10.1111/1467-6494.696169

Tryon, W. W. (1939). Evaluation of adolescent personality by adolescents. *Monographs of the Society for Research in Child Development, 4.*

Tuckerman, N., & Dunnan, N. (1995). *Amy Vanderbilt complete book of etiquette.* New York, NY: Doubleday.

Turkheimer, E., & Gottesman, I. I. (1991). Individual differences and the canalization of behavior. *Developmental Psychology, 27,* 18–22. doi:10.1037/0012-1649.27.1.18

Turner, R. G. (1978). Consistency, self-consciousness, and the predictive validity of typical and maximal measures. *Journal of Research in Personality, 12,* 117–132. doi:10.1016/0092-6566(78)90088-0

Uher, J., & Asendorpf, J. B. (2008). Personality assessment in the great apes: Comparing ecologically valid behavior measures, behavior ratings, and adjective ratings. *Journal of Research in Personality, 42,* 821–838. doi:10.1016/j.jrp.2007.10.004

Underwood, M. K., Beron, K. J., & Rosen, L. H. (2009). Continuity and change in social and physical aggression from middle childhood through early adolescence. *Aggressive Behavior, 35,* 357–375. doi:10.1002/ab.20313

Vale, J. R., & Vale, G. R. (1969). Individual differences and general laws in psychology: A reconciliation. *American Psychologist, 24,* 1093–1108. doi:10.1037/h0028920

Waddington, C. H. (1957). *The strategy of the genes.* London, England: Allen & Unwin.

Waschull, S. B., & Kernis, M. H. (1996). Level and stability of self-esteem as predictors of children's intrinsic motivation and reasons for anger. *Personality and Social Psychology Bulletin, 22,* 4–13. doi:10.1177/0146167296221001

Watson, D., & Clark, L. A. (1997). Extraversion and its positive emotional core. In R. Hogan, J. Johnson, & S. R. Briggs (Eds.), *Handbook of personality psychology* (pp. 767–793). San Diego, CA: Academic Press. doi:10.1016/B978-012134645-4/50030-5

Watson, D., Clark, L. A., & Carey, G. (1988). Positive and negative affectivity and their relation to anxiety and depressive disorders. *Journal of Abnormal Psychology, 97,* 346–353. doi:10.1037/0021-843X.97.3.346

Watson, D., Clark, L. A., & Tellegen, A. (1988). Development and validation of brief measures of positive and negative affectivity. *Journal of Personality and Social Psychology, 54,* 1063–1070. doi:10.1037/0022-3514.54.6.1063

Wellman, H. M., Cross, D., & Watson, J. (2001). Meta-analysis of theory-of-mind development: The truth about false belief. *Child Development, 72,* 655–684. doi:10.1111/1467-8624.00304

Wells, L. E., & Marwell, G. (1976). *Self-esteem: Its conceptualization and measurement.* Beverly Hills, CA: Sage.

Weisfeld, G. E., Omark, D. R., & Cronin, C. L. (1980). A longitudinal and cross-sectional study of dominance in boys. In D. R. Omark, J. Strayer, & D. G. Freedman (Eds.), *Dominance relations: An ethological view of human conflict and social interaction* (pp. 205–216). New York, NY: Garland.

Werner, N. E., & Crick, N. R. (2004). Maladaptive peer relationships and the development of relational and physical aggression during middle childhood. *Social Development, 13,* 495–514. doi:10.1111/j.1467-9507.2004.00280.x

Whiteside, S. P., & Lyman, D. R. (2001). The five factor model and impulsivity: Using a structural model of personality to understand impulsivity. *Personality and Individual Differences, 30*, 669–689. doi:10.1016/S0191-8869(00)00064-7

Wicklund, R. (1979). The influence of self on human behavior. *American Scientist, 67*, 187–193.

Widiger, T. A., & Frances, A. (1985). The *DSM-III* personality disorders: Perspectives from psychology. *Archives of General Psychiatry, 42*, 615–623.

Widiger, T. A., & Samuel, D. B. (2005). Diagnostic categories of dimensions? A question for the *Diagnostic and Statistical Manual of Mental Disorders—Fifth Edition*. *Journal of Abnormal Psychology, 114*, 494–504. doi:10.1037/0021-843X.114.4.494

Widiger, T. A., & Trull, T. J. (2007). Plate tectonics in the classification of personality disorder: shifting to a dimensional model. *American Psychologist, 62*, 71–83. doi:10.1037/0003-066X.62.2.71

Wiggins, J. S. (1979). A psychological taxonomy of trait-descriptive terms: The interpersonal domain. *Journal of Personality and Social Psychology, 37*, 395–412. doi:10.1037/0022-3514.37.3.395

Wiggins, J. S., Phillips, N., & Trapnell, P. (1989). Circular reasoning about interpersonal behavior: Evidence about some untested assumptions underlying diagnostic classification. *Journal of Personality and Social Psychology, 56*, 296–305. doi:10.1037/0022-3514.56.2.296

Wiggins, J. S., & Pincus, A. L. (1989). Conceptions of personality disorders and dimensions of personality. *Psychological Assessment, 1*, 305–316. doi:10.1037/1040-3590.1.4.305

Williams, H. W. (1935). A factor analysis of Bernes' "Social Behavior Patterns in Young Children." *Journal of Experimental Education, 4*, 142–146.

Wills, T. A. (1981). Downward comparison principles in social psychology. *Psychological Bulletin, 90*, 245–271. doi:10.1037/0033-2909.90.2.245

Windle, M., & Lerner, R. M. (1986). Reassessing the dimensions of temperamental individuality across the life-span: The Revised Dimensions of Temperament Survey. *Journal of Adolescent Research, 1*, 213–229. doi:10.1177/074355548 8612007

Wolf, W. (1943). *The expression of personality*. New York, NY: Harper.

Wood, J. V., Giordano-Beech, M., Taylor, K. L., Michela, J. L., & Gaus, V. (1994). Strategies of social comparison among people with low self-esteem: Self-protection and self- enhancement. *Journal of Personality and Social Psychology, 67*, 713–731. doi:10.1037/0022-3514.67.4.713

Wylie, R. C. (1974). *The self-concept* (rev. ed., Vol. I). Lincoln: University of Nebraska Press.

Yerkes, R. M. (1943). *Chimpanzees*. New Haven, CT: Yale University Press.

Yip, T., Klang, L., & Fuligni, A. J. (2008). Multiple social identities and reactivity to daily stress among ethnically diverse young adults. *Journal of Research in Personality, 42*, 1160–1172. doi:10.1016/j.jrp.2008.03.005

Zajonc, R. B. (1965). Social facilitation. *Science, 149,* 269–274. doi:10.1126/science.149.3681.269

Zillman, D. (1979). *Hostility and aggression.* Hillsdale, NJ: Erlbaum.

Zuckerman, M. (1971). Dimensions of sensation seeking. *Journal of Consulting and Clinical Psychology, 36,* 45–52. doi:10.1037/h0030478

Zuckerman, M. (1979). *Sensation seeking: Beyond the optimal level of arousal.* Hillsdale, NJ: Erlbaum.

Zuckerman, M. (1995). Good and bad humors: Biochemical bases of personality and its disorders. *Psychological Science, 6,* 325–332. doi:10.1111/j.1467-9280.1995.tb00521.x

Zuckerman, M. (2005). *Psychobiology of personality* (2nd ed.). New York, NY: Cambridge University Press.

Zuckerman, M. (2007). *Sensation seeking and risky behavior.* Washington, DC: American Psychological Association. doi:10.1037/11555-000

Zuckerman, M., Eysenck, S. B. G., & Eysenck, H. J. (1978). Sensation seeking in England and America: Cross-cultural, age, and sex comparisons. *Journal of Consulting and Clinical Psychology, 46,* 139–149. doi:10.1037/0022-006X.46.1.139

Zuckerman, M., Kolin, E. A., Price, L., & Zoob, I. (1964). Development of a sensation seeking scale. *Journal of Consulting Psychology, 28,* 477–482. doi:10.1037/h0040995

INDEX

Conscientiousness trait (Big Five
    classification), 83, 146, 195
Constraint, 183
Contingent self-esteem, 155
Continuity
    of abnormality, 172–176
    of identity, 164–165
Continuity–discontinuity dichotomy,
    168
Control theory, 136
Conway, L. C., III, 167
Cooperation, 69–70
Coopersmith, S., 155
Coping, 49, 180–181, 196
Counterconditioning, 172
Cronbach, L. J., 3
Culture
    elements of, 18
    and identity, 24, 163, 166–167
    and public self-consciousness, 200
    and self-esteem, 150, 157–158
    sexism in, 119
    and social identity, 159
    of social mammals, 20
    and women, 113
Curiosity
    of dogs, 18
    of humans, 19
    individual differences in, 21
    of mammals, 12
    of primates, 15, 18

Daniels, D., 34
Darwin, C. R., 11, 95, 139
Dating, 65
Death, 156
Deci, E. L., 155
Decisiveness, 111
Defensive aggression, 106
Defensive pessimists, 49, 181
Delay of gratification, 81
Deliberation, 78, 83
Delinquent behavior, 81–82
Demeanor, 137
deMonchaux, C., 173
DePaulo, B. M., 185
Dependent personality disorder, 182, 183
Depression, 54, 175–176, 180
Desynchronizers, 55
Development, 27–39, 200–201

activity in, 45–47
aggressiveness in, 101–105
dominance in, 114–117
emotionality in, 50–53
environment's role in, 29–30
eras in, 35–39
fearfulness in, 57–58
heredity's role in, 28–29
identity in, 163–165
impulsiveness in, 81–83, 201–202
inhibition in, 34–35
instrumentality in, 35
person's effect on environment in,
    30–34
self-conscious shyness in, 131–133,
    203
self-esteem in, 152–154
sensation seeking in, 91–93
shyness in, 62–65
sociability in, 75–77, 201
de Waal, F., 14, 17
*Diagnostic and Statistical Manual of
    Mental Disorders* (4th ed., text
    revision; *DSM–IV–TR*), 174,
    179, 183–184
Diamond, S., 21, 30, 84, 87
Dickens, W. T., 33
Differential Personality Questionnaire,
    183
Differentiation
    of activity, 44–45, 202
    of aggressiveness, 97–98
    defined, 7, 200
    of dominance, 112–113
    of emotionality, 49–50, 202
    of fearfulness, 55
    of handedness, 28
    in human development, 27
    of impulsiveness, 78–80
    and person's effect on environment,
        31–32
    of sensation seeking, 90
    of shyness, 61–62
    of sociability, 73–75, 202
Discipline, 79, 83, 150, 178
Disinhibition, 94
Displacement, 188–189, 196
Distractibility, 174
Dixon, J. J., 173
Dodge, K. A., 106

sex differences in, 31, 46, 115
use of fantasy in, 125
Playfulness
    in dogs, 18
    in primates, 18
    and style, 191
Playful–serious dimension (style),
        190–191, 193, 195
Pleasure, loss of, 176
Plomin, R., 30, 34, 44, 83, 87
Poggi, I., 139
Polygyny, 109
Positive Emotionality, 176, 183
Positive–negative dichotomy, 168
Posttraumatic stress disorder, 179
Posture, 185, 186. *See also* Style
Power, 147, 155. *See also* Dominance
A Prairie Home Companion (radio
        program), 141
Praise, 78, 130, 146, 153
Precise–loose dimension (style),
        191–193, 195
Prefrontal cortex, 126
Prehensile animals, 23
Preschool-age children
    activity of, 46
    aggressiveness in, 101–103
    cultural identity of, 24
    dominance in, 114–115
    emotionality of, 52
    fearfulness in, 57
    identity in, 163
    impulsiveness in, 81–82
    overview, 37–38
    self-consciousness in, 125, 126
    self-esteem of, 152–153
    sensation seeking in, 91–92
    shyness in, 63–64
    sociability of, 76
The Presentation of Self in Everyday Life
        (E. Goffman), 137
Primates. *See also specific species*
    activity levels of, 47
    fearfulness of, 56
    fear of strangers by, 62–63
    humans' similarity to, 14–16
    image recognition by, 22–24
    male and female roles in, 74
    personality in, 16–17
    stimulation seeking by, 36

temperaments shared by, 87
and theory of mind, 19
Privacy, 130, 132, 134
Private self, 168
Private self-consciousness, 123–126,
        176, 178, 180, 203
Proactive aggression, 106
Prosocial behavior, 132
Psychological privacy, 130
Psychology of Aggression (A. H. Buss), 106
Psychotherapy, 55, 61
Puberty, 128–129. *See also* Adolescents
Public self, 168
Public self-awareness, 24
Public self-consciousness
    of balding men, 149
    of narcissists, 178
    overview, 126–129
    as part of human uniqueness, 200, 203
    and self-presentation, 136
Public speaking, fear of, 59, 172, 177
Pullinen, L., 166

Questionnaires
    assessing anger and hostility, 96
    assessment of sensation seeking in, 94
    dominance items on, 110, 111
    impulsiveness items on, 83
    questions about activity on, 48
    and sociability, 77

Rachman, S., 55
Radke-Yarrow, M., 64
Ramsey, D., 139
Reaction time, 196
Reactive aggression, 106
Reactivity, 13, 48, 85
Rebelliousness, 100, 105, 114, 115
Reflection, 79, 178
Relational aggression, 71, 97, 103
Relational identity, 167
Religion, 151, 159–163
Resistance, 110
Respect, 146
Responsiveness, 71
Reticent children, 76
Reznick, J. S., 63
Rhesus monkeys, 16, 17, 47, 59
Ridicule, 132, 133
Rimoldi, H. J., 196

ABOUT THE AUTHOR

Arnold H. Buss, PhD, is professor emeritus of psychology at the University of Texas (UT) at Austin, where he has also been head of the Personality Graduate Program (1969–1986) and head of the Graduate Clinical Training Program (1990–1992). Dr. Buss received his BA from New York University in 1947 and his PhD from Indiana University in 1952. Before joining the UT Psychology Department's faculty in 1969, Dr. Buss was an instructor at the University of Iowa (1951–1952), chief psychologist at Indianapolis's Carter Hospital (1952–1957), and professor at the University of Pittsburgh (1957–1965) and Rutgers University (1965–1969). He received his diplomate in clinical psychology in 1956.

Dr. Buss is the author or coauthor of close to a dozen books on psychology and personality, including *The Psychology of Aggression* (1961), *Self-Consciousness and Social Anxiety* (1980), *Social Behavior and Personality* (1986), and *Psychological Dimensions of the Self* (2001). He has published nearly 100 professional journal articles and chapters in edited volumes on aggression, temperament, self-consciousness, and shyness.